Nineteenth-Century Major Lives and Letters

Series Editor: Marilyn Gaull

This series presents original biographical, critical, and scholarly studies of literary works and public figures in Great Britain, North America, and continental Europe during the nineteenth century. The volumes in *Nineteenth-Century Major Lives and Letters* evoke the energies, achievements, contributions, cultural traditions, and individuals who reflected and generated them during the Romantic and Victorian period. The topics: critical, textual, and historical scholarship, literary and book history, biography, cultural and comparative studies, critical theory, art, architecture, science, politics, religion, music, language, philosophy, aesthetics, law, publication, translation, domestic and public life, popular culture, and anything that influenced, impinges upon, expresses or contributes to an understanding of the authors, works, and events of the nineteenth century. The authors consist of political figures, artists, scientists, and cultural icons including William Blake, Thomas Hardy, Charles Darwin, William Wordsworth, William Butler Yeats, Samuel Taylor, and their contemporaries.

The series editor is Marilyn Gaull, PhD (Indiana University), FEA. She has taught at William and Mary, Temple University, New York University, and is Research Professor at the Editorial Institute at Boston University. She is the founder and editor of *The Wordsworth Circle* and the author *of English Romanticism: The Human Context*, and editions, essays, and reviews in journals. She lectures internationally on British Romanticism, folklore, and narrative theory, intellectual history, publishing procedures, and history of science.

PUBLISHED BY PALGRAVE:

Shelley's German Afterlives, by Susanne Schmid
Coleridge, the Bible, and Religion, by Jeffrey W. Barbeau
Romantic Literature, Race, and Colonial Encounter, by Peter J. Kitson
Byron, edited by Cheryl A. Wilson
Romantic Migrations, by Michael Wiley
The Long and Winding Road from Blake to the Beatles, by Matthew Schneider
British Periodicals and Romantic Identity, by Mark Schoenfield
Women Writers and Nineteenth-Century Medievalism, by Clare Broome Saunders
British Victorian Women's Periodicals, by Kathryn Ledbetter
Romantic Diasporas, by Toby R. Benis
Romantic Literary Families, by Scott Krawczyk
Victorian Christmas in Print, by Tara Moore
Culinary Aesthetics and Practices in Nineteenth-Century American Literature, Edited by Monika Elbert and Marie Drews
Reading Popular Culture in Victorian Print, by Alberto Gabriele
Romanticism and the Object, Edited by Larry H. Peer
Poetics en passant, by Anne Jamison
From Song to Print, by Terence Hoagwood
Gothic Romanticism, by Tom Duggett
Victorian Medicine and Social Reform, by Louise Penner
Populism, Gender, and Sympathy in the Romantic Novel, by James P. Carson
Byron and the Rhetoric of Italian Nationalism, by Arnold A. Schmidt
Poetry and Public Discourse in Nineteenth-Century America, by Shira Wolosky
The Discourses of Food in Nineteenth-Century British Fiction, by Annette Cozzi
Romanticism and Pleasure, Edited by Thomas H. Schmid and Michelle Faubert

Royal Romances, by Kristin Flieger Samuelian
Trauma, Transcendence, and Trust, by Thomas J. Brennan, S.J.

FORTHCOMING TITLES:

The Business of Literary Circles in Nineteenth-Century America, by David Dowling
Popular Medievalism in Romantic-Era Britain, by Clare A. Simmons
Beyond Romantic Ecocriticism, by B. Ashton Nichols
The Poetry of Mary Robinson, by Daniel Robinson
Romanticism and the City, by Larry H. Peer
Coleridge and the Daemonic Imagination, by Gregory Leadbetter
Romantic Dharma, by Mark Lussier
Regions of Sara Coleridge's Thought, by Peter Swaab

ROMANTICISM AND PLEASURE

Edited by

Thomas H. Schmid
and
Michelle Faubert

palgrave
macmillan

First published in 2010 by
PALGRAVE MACMILLAN®
in the United States—a division of St. Martin's Press LLC,
175 Fifth Avenue, New York, NY 10010.

Where this book is distributed in the UK, Europe and the rest of the world,
this is by Palgrave Macmillan, a division of Macmillan Publishers Limited,
registered in England, company number 785998, of Houndmills,
Basingstoke, Hampshire RG21 6XS.

Palgrave Macmillan is the global academic imprint of the above companies
and has companies and representatives throughout the world.

Palgrave® and Macmillan® are registered trademarks in the United States,
the United Kingdom, Europe and other countries.

ISBN: 978–0–230–10263–7

Library of Congress Cataloging-in-Publication Data

    Romanticism and pleasure / edited by Thomas H. Schmid and
Michelle Faubert.
      p. cm.—(Nineteenth-century major lives and letters)
      ISBN 978–0–230–10263–7 (alk. paper)
     1. English literature—19th century—History and criticism.
    2. English literature—18th century—History and criticism.
    3. Pleasure in literature. 4. Pleasure—Philosophy. 5. Romanticism—
Great Britain. I. Schmid, Thomas H. II. Faubert, Michelle.

PR457.R6446 2010
820.9'145—dc22   2010014002

A catalogue record of the book is available from the British Library.

Design by Newgen Imaging Systems (P) Ltd., Chennai, India.

First edition: December 2010

10 9 8 7 6 5 4 3 2 1

Printed in the United States of America.

For Joanie and Javi

CONTENTS

FOREWORD

It is the basic fear of... pain which makes man throw himself, without even realizing it, toward the opposite extreme, and give himself up completely to the small number of pleasures which Nature has permitted him.

It is for the same reason that he enlarges them, perfects them, complicates them, and finally worships them, as is shown by the fact that during the days of idolatry and for a long series of centuries all the pleasures were classified as secondary gods, presided over by their superior deities.

— Jean-Anthelme Brillat-Savarin,
The Physiology of Taste

Any study of Romanticism's relation to pleasure is bound to reveal the inextricability of pleasure and pain. In the midst of dejection, Coleridge finds that joy bursts forth, just as melancholy haunts Keats's "Temple of Delight." Knowledge is the all-too-bitter fruit of experience, or, as Byron declares in the voice of Manfred, "Sorrow is knowledge." Three years later, Keats warned his brother and sister-in-law that "we cannot expect to give way many hours to pleasure—Circumstances are like Clouds continually gathering and bursting—While we are laughing the seed of some trouble is put into [the] wide arable land of events—while we are laughing it sprouts, grows and suddenly bears a poison fruit which we must pluck" (*Letters* 79). Innocence, for the Romantics, in order not to constitute ignorance, must accommodate itself to lived experience, and experience inevitably involves pain. In Blake's formerly blissful "Garden of Love," priests in black gowns haunt the grounds, binding with briars the poet's joys and desires. In a fallen world, the very idea of unmitigated bliss, of pleasure estranged from pain, is sheer folly or perversity. Their pettish limits cannot be defined, Keats suggests in *Lamia*, a poem in which he attempts to envision "a maid/ More beautiful than ever twisted braid,/ ... Not one hour old, yet of sciential brain/ To unperplex bliss from its neighbour pain" (*Poems* 185–91). But Lamia is an ontological anomaly, a beautiful monster no more human than a snake stripped of its skin; humanity, Keats recognizes, cannot so easily disentangle bliss from pain. The essays that follow in this volume reveal the full range of Romantic pleasure as above all "aching pleasure," a complex delight that turns to poison while the bee-mouth sips.

Even those who advocated pleasure for its own sake, for example, those connoisseurs of good living known in the Romantic period as gastronomers or gourmands (in the modern sense of "gourmets"), recognized pain as central to the human condition. The French gastronomer Jean-Anthelme Brillat-Savarin observed in 1826 that it is the vulnerability to pain that spurs humanity to seek more refined pleasures: "Man is incontestably, among the sentient creatures who inhabit the globe, the one who endures most pain. Nature from the beginning has condemned him to misery by the nakedness of his skin, by the shape of his feet, and by that instinct for war and destruction which has always accompanied the human species wherever it has gone" (180). Other animals may have the protection of scales or fur, but the human is condemned to its "own naked, shivering nature." These are, of course, also the words of the philosopher Edmund Burke, who believed that it is taste (or a predilection for beauty) that distinguishes humans from beasts and conceals from them their own beastly appetites. "Kill me to eat," as the hapless animal begs the man about to ravage him in Plutarch's *Moralia*, "but not to please your palate!" (547–51). Yet those very pleasures of the palate are what constitute discourses of "taste," a synonym for aesthetic pleasure.

In a series of essays on "The Pleasures of the Imagination," published in *The Spectator* (1712), Joseph Addison remarked that "A man of polite imagination is let into a great many pleasures, that the vulgar are not capable of receiving. . . . He meets with a secret refreshment in a description, and often feels a greater satisfaction in the prospect of fields and meadows, than another does in the possession" (63). The imagination entails a mental gratification transcending any physical pleasures obtained through material means. One can buy property, but one cannot buy taste, which is (in theory) no commodity. It has to be earned through painstaking mental labor, eighteenth-century taste philosophers argued. Addison divided aesthetic pleasure further into "the primary pleasures of the imagination, which intirely [*sic*] proceed from such objects as are before our eyes" and "those secondary pleasures of the imagination which flow from the ideas of visible objects, when the objects are not actually before the eye, but are called up into our memories, or formed to agreeable visions of

things that are either absent or fictitious" (62). These latter imaginary
pleasures are preferable because they can be summoned up without
external stimulation and give the possessor a property in everything
he sees. *Homo aestheticus* trumps *homo economicus.*

Unlike appetite, taste was a pleasure both instinctual and guided
by certain fixed rules that philosophers sought to identify. Burke
remarked that "if Taste has no fixed principles, if the imagination
is not affected according to some invariable and certain laws...it
must be judged an useless, if not an absurd undertaking, to lay down
rules for caprice, and to set up for a legislator of whims and fancies"
(*Philosophical* 12). The project of sublimating taste, as I have argued
elsewhere, from the conceptual apparatus of appetite was a central
project of Enlightenment. The third earl of Shaftesbury held that aesthetic taste was a mental compulsion amounting to law, or "a taste
which governs men" (413). His successor, Hume, defined the standard of taste as the "joint verdict" of all ideal critics, believing that
beauties will necessarily "maintain their authority over the minds of
men" (241). Garnering the authority left over from the divine, taste
became the most vivid strand of a civilizing process intended to teach
individuals to regulate themselves and their motivating appetites from
within.

Early modern philosophers, by contrast, had little use for the pleasures of the imagination in conceptualizing the human condition.
They believed that appetites and aversions drove animal behavior and
that the body was separate from the soul. Hobbes, for one, argued
that human instinct, "when it is toward something which causes it, is
called APPETITE, or DESIRE; the later, being the generall name;
and the other, often-times restrayned to signifie the Desire of Food,
namely *Hunger* or *Thirst*" (31). The tradition dates back at least to
Plato, who imagined the body as a "lower" realm of appetites and
aversions, cordoned off from the mind. Whereas the latter was the
seat of the divine, the stomach was "like a wild animal...chained
up with man" that "must be nourished if man was to exist" (1994).
Humans have appetite in common with beasts, and aesthetic philosophers in the "Century of Taste" following Hobbes's *Leviathan*
replaced the craving center of human nature—appetitive desire—
with the more critical capacity for aesthetic pleasure. In his *Critique
of Aesthetic Judgement*, Kant separated "mere enjoyments of sense"
from the pleasures associated with taste (162). The latter could not
be reduced to pure cognition, however, insofar as they hinged on
sensuous pleasure. "Taste must," according to Kant, "be represented
in conjunction with something else, if the delight attending the mere

reflection upon an object is to admit of having further conjoined with it *a pleasure in the real existence* of the object (as that wherein all interest consists)" (154; italics in text). Humans increase their pleasures through reflection, distinguishing themselves from animals and compensating their added burden of pain.

Thought is required for taste, and the aesthetic pleasures of the imagination were to be pursued across a variety of media, *ab ovum usque ad malum* (from the egg to the apple). At a time when proliferating definitions of the human being ranged from man as a "rational" to man as a "social animal," James Boswell's (slightly tongue-in-cheek) depiction of the human being as "a cooking animal" complemented the expanding sphere of the arts. "The beasts have memory, judgment, and all the faculties and passions of our mind, in a certain degree; but no beast is a cook," Boswell commented in conversation with Burke, adding, "Man alone can dress a good dish; and every man whatever is more or less a cook, in seasoning what he himself eats." "Your definition is good," replied Burke, "and now I see the full force of the common proverb, 'there is *reason* in roasting of eggs'" (Boswell 177–8; italics in text). There have always been techniques for cooking food, and for more reasons than survival. Boiling, broiling, and roasting are all inventions stemming from the human need to avoid aversion (not only for raw eggs, but for primarily raw meat) and, moreover, to expand and complicate pleasure. Following the apple, there appears a world of difference between the "pleasure of eating," defined by Brillat-Savarin as "the actual and direct sensation of satisfying a need," and "the pleasures of the table," which together comprise "a reflective sensation which is … born from the various circumstances of place, time, things, and people who make up the surroundings of the meal" (182). Physical pleasure is shared with animals, and "it depends solely on hunger and on what is needed to satisfy it" (182). The pleasures of the table, by contrast, are independent of hunger and appetite and unique to the human race.

The traditional philosophical hierarchy of the senses, mapped directly onto the hierarchy of the arts, placed sight and hearing above taste and smell. For this reason, Aristotle maintained that the arts of perfumery and cookery (like other arts of pleasure) ought not to be considered as having anything to do with real art: "That there should be no art devoted to the production of pleasure is only natural" (437). Granting the distinction between bodily pleasures and those of the soul, he argued, the only pleasures worthy of philosophical discussion are the latter. As the mind becomes involved, it remakes the object, so to speak, in its own image, covering it with intellection.

To see a painting or hear an aria required a representative distance between the object of sensation and the subject doing the perceiving. The imagination thereby ensured that the object (of sight or hearing) would not invade the personal space of the embodied subject. Objects of smell and taste, on the other hand, physically obtrude themselves into one's physicality, requiring "chemical" rather than "objective" sensation. By the Romantic period, discourse stemming directly from the gustatory metaphor of taste had elevated the culinary arts, but considerable cultural anxiety remained regarding physical pleasure, and gastronomers covered their mock-philosophical precepts, principles, and professions with a thick coat of irony.

Poets, by contrast, were earnest in declaring their dedication to pleasure. "Poetry is ever accompanied with pleasure," Shelley wrote, "all spirits on which it falls open themselves to receive the wisdom which is mingled with its delight." Delight and wisdom, although not the same thing, are bound up dialectically together and also with pain. Shelley based his claims in part on Wordsworth, who also argued that the poet's job is to cultivate taste, hence the moral fiber of the nation, by advancing the pleasures of the imagination: "The Poet writes under one restriction only, namely, the necessity of giving immediate pleasure to a human Being possessed of that information which may be expected from him, not as a lawyer, a physician, a mariner, an astronomer, or a natural philosopher, but as a Man" (139). Poetry gives pleasure to the human being conceived holistically, rather than as a unit of specialized expertise. Pleasure in fact *pulls* man together, as the pleasures of the imagination are synthetic. In *Biographia Literaria*, Coleridge defined poetry as that "that species of composition, which is opposed to works of science, by proposing for its immediate object pleasure, not truth" (13). This was not to say that poetry does not convey truth, or wisdom mingled with delight. But it does not take truth as its principal objective separate from beauty, and consequently separate from imaginative pleasure as a mental activity.

We may go so far as to say that, for the Romantics, aesthetic pleasure was constitutive of the human. "In order to derive pleasure from the occupation of the mind, the principle of unity must always be present," according to Coleridge, a "unity in multeity" that he called "the principle of beauty...[and] equally the source of pleasure in variety, and in fact a higher term including both" ("Poesy" 262). In current academic circles, statements such as these tread close to critical taboo, or a supposedly naïve return to the aesthetic. Yet, pleasure remains at the core of aesthetic education. In his essay "On Classical

Education," William Hazlitt distinguished "useful knowledge" from "a knowledge of useful things" in a formulation that remains useful to the humanities today: "Knowledge is only useful in itself, as it exercises or gives pleasure to the mind," whereas "knowledge that is of use in a practical sense, is professional knowledge" (9). At a time of increased professionalization, he turned the conventional idea of the "useful" on its head. Sorrow may be knowledge, but knowledge is also delight. If pleasure and pain are "simple ideas, incapable of definition," as Burke described them, "simple" does not mean "simplistic" (*Philosophical* 30). Like literary texts, such ideas are conceptually irreducible, endlessly generative of the mental activity that is the only thing (from a humanities perspective) truly useful. I believe it is in this context that the present volume has been compiled and to this perspective that it is dedicated.

Denise Gigante,
Stanford University

WORKS CITED

Addison, Joseph. *The Spectator.* Vol. 6. London: J. and R. Tonson, and R. Draper, 1749. Oxford: Clarendon Press, 1965. Print.

Aristotle. *The Nicomachean Ethics.* Trans. H. Rackham. Cambridge, MA: Harvard UP, 1934. Print.

Boswell, James. *The Journal of a Tour to the Hebrides with Samuel Johnson.* Ed. Ian Mcgowan. Edinburgh: Canongate Classics, 1996. Print.

Brillat-Savarin, Jean-Anthelme. *The Physiology of Taste; Or, Meditations on Transcendental Gastronomy.* Trans. M.F.K. Fisher. Washington, D.C.: Counterpoint, 1949. Print.

Burke, Edmund. *A Philosophical Enquiry into the Origin of our Ideas of the Sublime and Beautiful.* Ed. James T. Boulton. Notre Dame, IN: U of Notre Dame P, 1958. Print.

———. *Reflections on the Revolution in France.* Ed. Adam Phillips. Oxford: Oxford UP, 1990. Print.

Coleridge, Samuel Taylor. *Biographia Literaria.* Ed. James Engell and W. Jackson Bate. Vol. 2. Princeton, NJ: Princeton UP, 1983. Print.

———. "On Poesy or Art." *Biographia Literaria, with His Aesthetical Essays.* Ed. John Shawcross. Vol. 2. Oxford: Clarendon Press, 1907. 253–63. Print.

Hazlitt, William. *The Selected Writings of William Hazlitt.* Ed. Duncan Wu. Vol. 2. London: Pickering & Chatto, 1998. Print.

Hobbes, Thomas. *The Leviathan.* Ed. Richard E. Flathman and David Johnston. New York: W.W. Norton, 1997. Print.

Hume, David. *Essays: Moral, Political, and Literary.* Ed. Eugene F. Miller. 2nd ed. Indianapolis: Liberty Fund, 1985. Print.

Kant, Immanuel. *The Critique of Aesthetic Judgement.* Trans. James Creed Meredith. Oxford: Clarendon Press, 1952. Print.

Keats, John. *Complete Poems.* Ed. Jack Stillinger. Cambridge, MA: Harvard UP, 1982. Print.

———. *The Letters of John Keats.* Ed. Hyder Edward Rollins. Vol. 2. Cambridge, MA: Harvard UP, 1958. Print.

Plato. *The Collected Dialogues of Plato, including the Letters.* Ed. Edith Hamilton and Huntington Cairns. Princeton, NJ: Princeton UP, 1961. Print.

Plutarch. *Moralia.* Trans. Harold Chreniss and William C. Helmbold. Vol. 12. Cambridge, MA: Harvard UP, 1957. Print.

Shaftesbury, Anthony Ashley Cooper, third earl. *Characteristics of Men, Manners, Opinions, Times.* Ed. Lawrence E. Klein. Cambridge: Cambridge UP, 1999. Print.

Shelley, Percy Bysshe. *Shelley's Poetry and Prose.* Ed. Donald Reiman and Neil Fraistat. New York: W.W. Norton, 2002. Print.

Wordsworth, William. *The Prose Works of William Wordsworth.* Ed. W. J. B. Owen and Jane Worthington Smyser. Vol. 1. Oxford: Clarendon Press, 1974. Print.

Acknowledgments

Romanticism and Pleasure was conceived during an informal discussion between the co-editors at the 2005 meeting of the International Conference on Romanticism, and we feel very lucky—and truly thankful—for the productive collaboration and friendship that followed. We would like to thank Larry Peer and the ICR for the collegial and stimulating meetings that fostered this book and that provided, in 2007, a forum for several panels on pleasure that enriched the conversation and brought talented scholars to our attention—as did the 2007 Canadian Society for Eighteenth-Century Studies conference in Winnipeg. Our contributors have been gratifyingly engaged in the exchange of ideas on pleasure and both timely and responsive at every stage of writing and editing; this book is the product of many minds and pens, and we extend heartfelt thanks to all. Release time for the final preparation and editing was provided by the Dean of the College of Liberal Arts at UTEP, Dr. Howard Daudistel, and Dr. Richard Sigurdson, Dean of the Faculty of Arts at the University of Manitoba; we are grateful for their generosity. We would also like to thank the Canadian Social Sciences and Humanities Research Council and the University of Manitoba for their financial support of some of the research for this volume, as well as the Affect Group in the Department of English, Film, and Theatre at the University of Manitoba for funding a lecture based on this volume. Many thanks to Lee Norton, our editorial assistant at Palgrave Macmillan U.S.A., who has offered invaluable aid with the thorny details of permissions, contracts, and manuscript preparation. Most of all, our deepest appreciation to Marilyn Gaull, the editor of the *Nineteenth-Century Lives and Letters* series, who believed in the book and provided unfailingly sound editorial suggestions and cheerful encouragement. We are proud to be part of this expertly piloted and distinguished series: thank you, Marilyn.

INTRODUCTION

Michelle Faubert and
Thomas H. Schmid

In his chapter for Northrop Frye's *Romanticism Reconsidered*, published nearly fifty years ago, Lionel Trilling stresses the centrality of pleasure to definitions of Romantic aesthetics, beginning with Wordsworth's Preface to *Lyrical Ballads*. According to Trilling, Wordsworth's aesthetic manifesto is defined not so much by the idea of "emotion recollected in tranquillity" as by the numerous statements concerning what Wordsworth calls "'the grand elementary principle of pleasure,'" which "constitutes 'the naked and native dignity of man' [and]...is the principle by which man 'knows, and feels, and lives, and moves'" (74). For Wordsworth, "pleasure [is] the defining attribute of life itself and of nature itself," and "the fallen condition of humanity...is comprised by the circumstance that man alone of natural beings does not experience the pleasure which, Wordsworth believes, moves the living world" (77). Romanticism at large, Trilling suggests, registers the celebration of an embodied pleasure native to humanity and the lamentation for its inevitable loss, its perennial "bidding adieu," in Keats's famous phrase.

Forty-one years after Trilling's essay, Alan Richardson, in "Romanticism and the Body," provides another reassessment of Romantic studies, one with significant methodological implications for the study of pleasure in the period. Richardson begins by surveying the laudable accomplishments of scholars during the 1990s, whose work, especially in gender, cultural, and postcolonial studies, has "transformed and rejuvenated the field" (1). Nevertheless, these studies "left certain leading critical tenets in place," particularly the tendency to see "canonical Romanticism...as a transcendentalizing, idealist literary movement, implicitly hostile not only to the feminine and to the racially or ethnic 'other,' but to physical nature and to the material body" (2). In contrast, much of the criticism of the early twenty-first century, Richardson emphasizes, focuses on the physical body in Romanticism, locating a concurrent materialist discourse that runs alongside the idealism, while "bring[ing] together several subfields within Romantic scholarship, including literature and medicine, literature and scientific psychology, ecocriticism, environmental and diet studies, recent developments in colonial discourse studies and feminist criticism, and cognitive and neuroscientific approaches to reading Romanticism" (1). For Richardson such work usefully returns to the affective and bodily focus typical of early twentieth-century Romantic scholarship (he cites Irving Babbitt on sensibility and Mario Praz on feeling in this context), while benefiting from and contributing to the rejuvenating theoretical innovations of recent years.

Trilling's urge to reconsider the importance of Romantic pleasure and Richardson's interest in freshly theorized Romantic discourses of the body help to establish the historical and critical axes of *Romanticism and Pleasure*. As Trilling's essay demonstrates, pleasure has long interested scholars, and that interest has tended to split precisely along the lines Richardson suggests—either emphasizing the felt experience of pleasure as a bodily sensation or analyzing its function within the idealizing discourses of philosophy, morality, and art. An analogous division can be observed within Romantic texts themselves, as both Trilling's essay makes explicit and Richardson's corroborates. For Trilling, the idea of an "elementary" and "native" pleasure in Wordsworth's Preface suggests its material, appetitive quality, something close to Freud's later idea of an instinct or "drive" (76); at the same time, Trilling recognizes that much of Wordsworth's poetry "ruled out pleasures that are 'strictly physical'" and aspired instead toward a "highly sublimated" pleasure, "a purer and more nearly transcendent state" (77). In his more general discussion, Richardson uses Wordsworth's "Tintern Abbey" to suggest the way in which a single Romantic text can both "prize those times when 'we are laid asleep/ In body, and become a living soul,'" and yet ground "such transcendent moments not in a denial of 'this corporeal frame' but in a history of embodied experiences with a particularized landscape and the 'sensations' and 'feelings' it inspires" (3). Pleasurable feelings constitute one such experience and have been analyzed from both materialist and idealist perspectives, which in recent years have been combined with the critical approaches Richardson identifies as predominant in the current field.

The essays in *Romanticism and Pleasure* reflect a similar diversity, approaching the study of pleasure with an interest in its somatic and psychological aspects and in its cultural implications and effects.

While not setting out to do so, the essays included here use many of the interdisciplinary and cultural approaches or "subfields" cited by Richardson. The essays discuss canonical and non-canonical male and female writers, along with a variety of genres and discourses, including novels, poems, essays, reviews, medical treatises, and political tracts. They also analyze pleasure within specific texts from a variety of critical perspectives, which serve to frame new questions about the importance of Romantic-period medical discourses on pleasure and psychology, the function of gender and sexuality in relation to pleasure, the uneasy pleasures of colonialist appropriation, the role of the "appetite" in constructing pleasurable experiences of novel-reading, the eco-poetics of pleasure, and the neuroscience of addictive pleasure in Romantic writers. The book responds to recent work on Romantic pleasures, such as Richard Sha's *Perverse Romanticism*, Denise Gigante's *Taste: A Literary History*, and Anya Taylor's *Bacchus in Romantic England*, and provides a more inclusive forum for a diversity of critical approaches than a typical monograph or single article can encompass.

The essays in *Romanticism and Pleasure* do not focus exclusively on what Margaret Iversen calls the "august tradition of philosophical aesthetics" represented most influentially by Kant's *Critique of Judgement* (1). Kant's influence on Romantic aesthetics has been extensively discussed, and articles such as Mark Packer's "Kant on Desire and Moral Pleasure" and Rachel Zuckert's "A New Look at Kant's Theory of Pleasure" have examined Kant's attitudes toward pleasure. Where the rich tradition of eighteenth and early nineteenth-century philosophy does enter into particular essays, as in Betsy Winakur Tontiplaphol's discussion of "Keats's Material Sublime," Joel Faflak's examination of "Romantic Psychiatry and the Addictive Pleasures of Moral Management," and Richard Sha's essay on "Byron, Polidori, and the Epistemology of Romantic Pleasure," it serves an interdisciplinary focus that sets philosophy in the context of science, medicine, politics, or the cultural uses of pleasure. In so doing, these essays follow the lead of studies such as Denise Gigante's *Taste: A Literary History*, which regards questions of the relationship of taste to cannibalism, urban experience, nausea, and "*too* intense bodily pleasure," while providing a thorough discussion of the philosophy of taste, especially in its third chapter (3; italics in text). Similarly, the essays in *Romanticism and Pleasure* examine aesthetic philosophy in relation to numerous cultural discourses, an approach that is in line with mainstream scholarship on the subject of pleasure in eighteenth- and nineteenth-century Britain.

A prominent subject for literary theorists of pleasure is, to quote Roland Barthes, "the pleasure of the text," the pleasures that are available through reading and writing.[1] Terry Eagleton's essay on "Poetry, Pleasure and Politics" in *Formations of Pleasure* (edited by Tony Bennett and Frederic Jameson) presents the most straightforward foray into this subject through a close reading of the types of pleasure that a reader of a single poem—W. B. Yeats's "Easter, 1916"— experiences as she reads; Eagleton presents this experience through a psychoanalytic lens to show how the reader's fluctuating feelings of uncertainty and eventual success and mastery determine the levels of pleasure that the text produces in her. Eagleton's essay illustrates that even the most direct delineation of readerly pleasure is tied up with the push and pull of servitude and mastery, and that power relations intervene in the experience of pleasure. Jameson's essay in the same book, "Pleasure: A Political Issue," further troubles the subject of the relationship of pleasure to the political by questioning "who has the *authority*—and in the name of what?" to make social distinctions between legitimate and illegitimate pleasures (3; italics in text). While Eagleton shows that the immediate experience of pleasure inspires polarized reactions in the reader, who seeks mastery in order to gain pleasure, Jameson shows that readers go beyond their own experiences of pleasure to judge the legitimacy of others' pleasures.

In relation specifically to the Romantic period, Chloe Chard's *Transports: Travel, Pleasure, and Imaginative Geography, 1600–1830* takes up the issues in Eagleton's and Jameson's essays by positing the reliance of travel pleasure on travel writing itself. Her analysis foregrounds the "pleasure of the text" that Eagleton discusses, and, in keeping with Jameson's concerns, examines the way in which travelers from the era judged the success, or, indeed, *legitimacy*, of one another's pleasure based on the language they used to represent their experiences. According to Chard, it was an unacknowledged rule that the travel writer must use hyperbolic language in order to "establish any claim that he is able to grasp the foreign as a domain that, by definition, must differ from the familiar. Only hyperbole...can affirm that the traveler has succeeded in discerning the drama and excitement that proclaim this difference" (5). Travel writing that fails to convey the requisite excess of pleasure was deemed inadequate by contemporary readers. Far from considering pleasure as unmediated, Chard shows that, beginning in the eighteenth century, English culture was engaged actively in discriminating pleasures according to their intensity and denying the very existence of pleasure in untrained perceivers.

Other critics have shown that discriminating pleasures was bound up with disciplinary distinctions between human perceptions and sensations that are considered acceptable and those that are embarrassing and better left unarticulated. In *Taste: A Literary History*, Denise Gigante explains that "various 'committees of taste' established in early nineteenth century Britain elevated food to the status of the fine arts, adopting the same juridical language and concern with philosophical principles that defined the eighteenth-century discourse of aesthetics" (1). Gigante notes that, although the aesthetic and gastronomic realms were essentially devoted to bodily perceptions, "mental discriminations" were closely related to them (2); she also demonstrates that the body and consciousness were related in eighteenth-century thought, especially in John Locke's philosophy, which made identity a "complex social construct of selfhood dependent on how human beings process experience through the senses. Once the flesh was involved in the formation of selfhood, identity could not be explained away on Cartesian principles as a disembodied thinking spirit" (3 and 4). Gigante thus reveals a continuum between the body and higher consciousness in eighteenth-century thought.

In contrast, Carolyn Korsmeyer maintains in "Taste and Pleasures," her essay from the *Romantic Gastronomies* series in *Romantic Circles* edited by Gigante, that Romantic-era philosophers posited an absolute break between body and mind:

> the vast majority of philosophers writing about aesthetic taste dismiss or even disparage the literal sense of taste, its objects, and its pleasures, developing the concept of the aesthetic in explicit contrast to bodily taste sensation....As Lord Kames put it..., "The fine arts are contrived to give pleasure to the eye and the ear, disregarding the inferior senses." (paragraph 4)

In this period of theorizing about sensual pleasure, some senses were classified as higher than others. Yet, as Gigante points out in the introductory essay to the series, the "gastronomers" who were dedicated to the development of the sensation of taste promoted the "fine art of food" and showed that even the pleasures of the supposedly lower senses could act "as a path out of the everyday into the more elevated pleasures of the imagination" (paragraph 1). Taste, like the sense of touch and sexual pleasure, gained philosophical purchase in Romantic-era culture through the classification of its experiences.

Focusing on the pleasures of drinking rather than eating, Anya Taylor's *Bacchus in Romantic England* illuminates the range in

Romantic responses to alcohol and concludes that the period's writers were "remarkable" for "their representations of drinking, whether they explored the fragmentation of self, the defeats of the will, the pressure of hedonistic anxiety...or the vivacity of poetic fervour" (221). Taylor stresses that "Although [the Romantics]...expressed their anger at the social cost to groups and the human debasement for individuals [from drinking], they nevertheless also exulted in wildness and release. Their rich and complex investigation into both pleasure and pain has not been regained in later representations of drinking" (221–2). In a more recent study of the experiences of the "lower" senses, "The Loves of Plants and Animals: Romantic Science and the Pleasures of Nature," Ashton Nichols asserts that the focus on pleasure in poetry by Wordsworth, Coleridge, Shelley, and Keats illustrates the connection between the human and non-human realms. According to Nichols, these poets incorporate ideas from works by writers such as Georges-Louis Leclerc (Comte de Buffon) and Erasmus Darwin that investigate human community with the natural world through the pleasures of the senses. With a focus on gender politics, Jillian Heydt-Stevenson makes a similar claim regarding Romantic-era writers' use of "low" pleasures in their work. In "'Pleasure is now, and ought to be, your business': Stealing Sexuality in Jane Austen's Juvenilia,"[2] Heydt-Stevenson investigates Jane Austen's protest against and resistance to limitations upon women's pleasures through representations of excess in her early writing—in which "her heroines' fighting and drinking and lovemaking and thieving...offer a language for deciphering the robust, lusty female energy that social rules encrypt or entomb" (paragraph 5)—as well as through narrative form, in which the indulgence in sensual pleasures that were denied women in the Georgian era take the form of fantasy and exaggeration (paragraph 3), an argument that echoes Chard's focus on hyperbole as representative of the pleasures of travel. Instead of denying the "low" pleasures of the body, Austen highlights them as natural and necessary to women's freedom.[3]

In contrast, Richard Sha reveals that the sensual pleasure Heydt-Stevenson claims was off-limits to Georgian-era women was, in fact, promoted by governing bodies, medical and otherwise, whose chief concern was not to abolish, but to normalize sensual pleasure. In "Medicalizing the Romantic Libido: Sexual Pleasure, Luxury, and the Public Sphere," Sha claims,

> Medical literature helped to efface [the] gap between the ideal proper experience of sexual pleasure and the somatic experience of that

pleasure in part by pathologizing those bodies that did not understand the true meaning of pleasure, and in part by attempting to give form (embodiment, moderation) and directionality (heterosexuality, marriage) to sexual pleasure and sensation. (31)

Sha reveals that, far from negating the existence of and indulgence in bodily pleasures, medical literature from the Romantic era encouraged such practice as a means of regulating society, a finding he discusses more expansively in *Perverse Romanticism*. Sha thus suggests that the experience of pleasure is not entirely "singular," as Korsmeyer claims (paragraph 27), nor a matter of individual taste and expression of self-identity, as Gigante suggests (*Taste* 1), but rather a culturally learned and disciplined response. In this sense, the critical study of pleasure perhaps contributes to the externalization and regularization of pleasures by objectifying them as the focus of inquiry. Even the process of critical illumination may negate pleasure, Jameson suggests, for "pleasure...can never be fixed directly by the naked eye—let along [*sic*] pursued as an end, or conceptualized—but only experienced laterally, or after the fact, as something like the by-product of something else" (1).

Several closely related studies linking Romantic pleasure with consumerism suggest that eradicating certain pleasures might lead to positive social advances. In *Romanticism and the Painful Pleasures of Modern Life*, Andrea Henderson asserts that the getting and spending, investing and speculating, and producing and developing that characterized the "modern life" of the Industrial Revolution was represented by sadomasochistic imagery that reveals the deep ambivalence people felt about the direction in which British culture was heading. For instance, Henderson claims, "contemporaries feared...[that] sexuality lent its energy to speculation even as speculation promoted new forms of perverse sexuality" (41), thus rendering the practice a vicious kind of pleasure for which modern man had to develop a taste if he was to survive in the world of business. Another study that reveals the downside of Romantic pleasure is *Luxury and Pleasure in Eighteenth-Century Britain*, by Maxine Berg, who delineates the vast quantities and types of luxury products that the middle classes bought in their effort to replicate the lifestyle of aristocrats; this history explores "the cultural discourse and invention of the new goods, their manufacture and marketing, and who consumed them and how" (5). It is, in short, the prehistory of a present-day consumer society that is busily engaged in destroying the natural environment with the detritus from more than two hundred years of producing and consuming luxury, of creating new and increasingly destructive pleasures. Nor do the canonical Romantic poets escape from these histories of crass consumerism: Ayumi Mizukoshi's *Keats, Hunt and the Aesthetics of Pleasure* illustrates the influence of the "bourgeois aesthetics of pleasure" (9) on Keats's early poetry in a demonstration of how another kind of "low" pleasure—this time with reference to class, instead of the body—is indistinguishable from the higher sort. Henderson, Berg, and Mizukoshi demonstrate that class divisions were bound up with perceptions of luxury and ideas about how pleasure could be produced.

Significantly, such critical judgments take a retrospective view of pleasure, luxury, and consumerism that reflects, perhaps unfairly, present perceptions and prejudices. Even luxury, which tends to be synonymous with decadence and wastefulness in the present era of increased ecological awareness, was viewed as virtuous leading up to the Romantic period. As Roy Porter attests in his introductory essay to his *Pleasure in the Eighteenth Century* (co-edited with Marie Mulvey Roberts), the Enlightenment promulgated the notion that "the pursuit of pleasure would advance the general good" (17), which indicates that the Christian judgment of pleasure as sinful—that is, as submission to the temptations of the flesh—was at least partially replaced by an opposing ethical construction of reason as the new god and of the senses as necessary for the acquisition of knowledge. This was also the period, Porter notes, that celebrated self-determination and individualism (and which gave birth to the much-vaunted Romantic self); thus, personal sensations, unique likes and dislikes—what Gigante and Korsmeyer identify as the "singularity" of pleasure—took on a new importance. Porter concludes that the "ideology" of pleasure that emerged by the end of the eighteenth century "promoted civilised hedonism within the values of rational self-interest in a capitalist system" (18). The pursuit of pleasure was not necessarily perceived as decadent by the time of the Romantic period but could be seen as a bold expression of modernity and an inalienable personal right.

Porter's essay on the social and political utility of individual pleasure in the eighteenth century emphasizes the fundamental division of pleasure studies into explorations of material, bodily concerns, on the one hand, and transcendent or cultural ideals, on the other. The individual essays within Porter and Roberts's book cover a range of subjects on both sides of this division, including consumerism, food, the pleasures of society, conduct, altruism and charity, opera, the sublime, and, in a final essay on the Romantic period by Susan Manning, the contrast between Burns's poetry of "delight" (197) and Wordsworth's sober poetic construction of a "*joy* removed from sensual impulse, a pure and irreducible absolute in human experience and memory" (204; italics in text).[4] If Manning's discussion takes up the same dichotomy between sensual pleasure and transcendent joy that Trilling articulated for Romantic aesthetics, it also concludes Porter and Roberts's series of chapters on the cultural uses of pleasure in the earlier eighteenth century. In a sense, *Romanticism and Pleasure* takes up where Manning's essay leaves off. In the twelve years since the publication of *Pleasure in the Eighteenth Century* there has been no omnibus treatment of pleasure in Romanticism, specifically; yet, as the survey of the critical literature suggests, the dichotomy—or, more properly, the fluid relationship—between sensual and aesthetic/cultural aspects of pleasure remains critically productive for scholars of the period. The purpose of this book is to examine that relationship from a variety of new directions.

Richard Sha and Betsy Tontiplaphol initiate this examination by addressing, in different ways, the question of aesthetic pleasure in Byron and Keats, respectively. Sha's essay confronts the philosophical challenge of discriminating the physical and moral effects of pleasure in the period. Invoking the tradition of Locke and Kant, Sha questions how pleasure can lead to knowledge for Romantic-era writers, how excess of pleasure can lead to pain, and on what basis pleasure can lead to moral behavior. Synthesizing a combination of texts by John William Polidori and Lord Byron, Sha argues that these works "form a key if unacknowledged part of a genealogy of thinking about what Freud would later call the 'beyond' of pleasure: the recognition of the inadequacy of the term 'pleasure' to encapsulate the complexities of human motivation." The reason for that complexity involves the question of excess. For Polidori, excess bodily pleasure led, in keeping with the standard medical thought of the period, to poor health and disease, while "real" pleasure resulted only from the mind's contemplation of pleasure as something beyond the physical; for Byron, pleasurable excess leads to the productive self-awareness and contemplation of pleasure that Polidori lauds. In a reading of sections of *Childe Harold's Pilgrimage*, Sha claims that exhaustion—an excess of pleasure so great it leads finally to anaesthesia—allows Byron's protagonist to achieve the distance from pleasure necessary to assess its effects properly.

In "Pleasure in an Age of Talkers," Betsy Tontiplaphol reads the wealth of sensuous "fullness" in Keats's poetry in relation both to the conventional category of the Burkean sublime and to the tendency toward abstraction in the period's conversational ideals, as criticized by William Hazlitt in *The Spirit of the Age*. Tontiplaphol thus recasts the sensuous/aesthetic dichotomy in terms of spatial constriction, or what she calls the "material sublime," the "corner-stone of Keatsian pleasure." Analyzing Keats's poetics in relation to a range of cultural discourses, including the discourse of imperial expansion, Tontiplaphol illustrates that in *Lamia*, especially, Keats ponders the reliance of pleasure upon "spatial limitation" rather than upon the spatial grandiosity of the traditional sublime, and that the poem "embraces...materio-sensory engorgement as the purest, if most difficult to sustain, experience of pleasure." Keats's poetics of material richness in compact spaces resists the abstraction that Hazlitt associated with the wrong kind of conversation and proposes an alternative aesthetic to what Tontiplaphol sees as the dominant association of pleasure with the large open spaces of the sublime.

The relationship of pleasure to body and mind also preoccupies several essays that explore Romantic psychology, medicine, and disease. In "John Ferriar's Psychology, James Hogg's *Justified Sinner*, and the Gay Science of Horror Writing," Michelle Faubert traces John Ferriar's psychological explanation for the pleasurable experience of haunting in his *Essay Towards the Theory of Apparitions* and its influence on James Hogg's later literary depiction of the Brocken Spectre in *Confessions of a Justified Sinner*. Ferriar, both a medical man and avid participant in Romantic-era literary circles, analyzes the entertainment value—the pleasure—of ghost stories, which he says can cause readers irrationally, albeit pleasurably, to hallucinate, to "see" ghosts. In advancing this argument, Ferriar suggests, according to Faubert, that

> hallucinations are fun, that pleasure is a worthy end of its own, and that literature should endeavor to reach this goal in two connected ways: through the exploration of psychological subject matter and the production of unreason in the reader, manifest as hallucinations produced by the stories he tells. Put simply, Ferriar presents his psychological treatise on "spectral delusions" (14) as entertainment.

Faubert discusses numerous thematic and stylistic connections between Ferriar's text and Hogg's, culminating in the figure of the Brocken Spectre, to which both writers point as an example of pleasurable "unreason" in viewers/readers. In Faubert's reading, Hogg's novel perfectly "replicates Ferriar's valorization of the irrational over the scientific, or the mysterious and entertaining over the merely informative" and shows how horror, psychology, and pleasure could be linked across disciplines within the period.

For Joel Faflak in "'Was It for This?': Romantic Psychiatry and the Addictive Pleasures of Moral Management," the historical emergence of psychiatry in the Romantic period is linked with a social mandate to "addict" the bourgeois subject to moral management, whose reward for the successful subject is to experience pleasure, to feel good. Faflak analyzes Wordsworth's revisions to both *The Prelude* and *The Recluse* as indications of a "conserving impulse of feeling that speaks directly to the issue of moral management." The revisions to both texts illustrate the pleasures of the self's victory over trauma, enacted through a healthy return to nature that keeps incipient madness at bay and demonstrates the greater social good that comes from "the production of the morally useful man." Faflak gives a fresh historical explanation for the socially sanctioned pleasures of solipsism, the therapeutic action of self-analysis and cure for a greater good.

While Faflak's essay deals with the pleasures of self-generated mental health, Clark Lawlor's focuses on the "paradoxical pleasures" of "fashionable disease" in both British and American Romanticism. Lawlor suggests that the understanding of consumption as a medical condition, as a key component in the larger discourses of literary sensibility and melancholy, and as aesthetically linked with love and beauty all sponsor a notion of consumptive disease as pleasurable "from at least two perspectives: that of the individual sufferer, who might accrue 'cultural capital' from its poetic or beautiful qualities, and that of the beholder of the sufferer, who might be uplifted, inspired spiritually or even sexually attracted . . . by the vision or works of the consumptive." Lawlor reads the conflicted poetic representations of famous literary consumptives such as the British Mary Tighe and the American Davidson sisters, Lucretia and Margaret Davidson, as "authenticated in their poetic mission" by the illness itself, which confers paradoxical pleasure on both authors and readers. If each of these female writers, all of whom died young from pulmonary tuberculosis, was acutely aware of the painful reality of the disease, each was able in turn to create an "authentic" poetic self that both pleased contemporary audiences and became mythologized by posterity. For Lawlor, each writer ultimately learned to "manipulate" the poetic representation of her wasting illness for pleasurable aesthetic ends, in spite of the pains of the disease itself.

From a postcolonial perspective, Jeffrey Cass's chapter on "The Uneasy Pleasures of Colonialist Space in *Mansfield Park*" examines the ways in which Austen's heroine, Fanny Price, takes pleasure in the "proper" use and manipulation of space, a pleasure that is uneasily dependent upon the "colonialist paradigm" that Mansfield upholds. Building on Edward Said's reading of the relationship between aesthetic enjoyment and imperialism in *Mansfield Park* and Moira Ferguson's observation that Fanny Price represents, in Cass's summary, "a kinder, gentler version of colonialism" that "recognizes the problematic nature of colonialist hegemony, even as it reluctantly continues to support it," Cass concludes that "the colonialist pleasure arising from occupying space still lurks" within the novel to the end, transforming, through the character of Fanny, "the human comedy in *Mansfield Park* into brooding, watchful waiting." For Cass, Austen asserts the pleasures of colonialism while simultaneously discomfiting readers on account of those pleasures.

The uneasy pleasures of reading figure centrally in Samantha Webb's essay on "Exhausted Appetites." Following the trajectory of scholars such as Denise Gigante, James Raven, and Janice Radway, Webb questions the traditional critical association of Romantic-period novels with unhealthy literary consumption, claiming instead that Romanticism was not so much "hostile to consumer models of literary reception" as to "the passivity and lack of agency inculcated by a certain type of consuming reader." Webb also contextualizes literary consumption through radical tracts on working-class literacy, scarcity, and frugality, which responded to the food crisis and the need of the poor to eat. In this context, books became as necessary to life as food, and the consumption of both represented not unhealthy excess but sanative nourishment: a healthy pleasure. Webb suggests that radical writers in the period thus "appropriated figures of consumption rather than rejecting them or reacting against them," theorizing the pleasures of reading as politically activist and socially necessary, rather than as unhealthily passive and indulgent.

The complexities of pleasure in the period figure finally in two essays that return to the prominent issue of the response to nature in Romanticism, one from the standpoint of the neuroscience of addiction and the other from the perspective of eco-criticism. Thomas Schmid's chapter on "'Diminished Impressibility'" in Coleridge deploys recent neuroscientific research on the effects of addictive drugs on the experience of pleasure in a reading of dysphoria in "Dejection: An Ode." For Schmid, the Ode records the suppression of hedonic affect as a predictable result of Coleridge's addiction to opium, a substance that acts, according to researchers such as George Koob, to "hijack" the brain's normal neurochemical response to pleasurable stimulus. "Particularly," Schmid argues, "Coleridge recognizes in the Ode his own inability to respond in a non-addictive way to nature, to take the kind of pleasure in the contemplation of nature that typified his own pre-addicted responses, as well as those of non-addicts such as Wordsworth." The neuroscientific evidence shows clearly that, with the onset of addiction, "ordinary" pleasures fail to be experienced as pleasure, and Coleridge, in Schmid's reading, gives an early account of that loss in the Ode. From a different perspective, Kevin Hutchings examines the loss of nature's pleasures not as a result of addiction's limbic suppression, but as the consequence of ideological suppression and moral stricture. In an eco-critical reading of Blake's "Garden of Love," Hutchings critiques the scholarly assessment of Blake as rejecting the material and sensual in favor of the spiritual and imaginative, claiming instead that "sensual pleasure is a key theme in *Songs of Innocence and of Experience* (1794)" and that the poem "Garden of Love," particularly, "encapsulates [Blake's] iconoclastic critique of the dualistic theology that functions to negate both the material world and the flesh by advocating, in the name of piety and chastity, an ascetic renunciation of both." In Hutchings's reading, the speaker of the poem seeks the pleasures of nature in the garden and actively resists the "imposed social order" that "prohibits" nature's sensual delights. The poem in this reading thus presents a broad critique of the very dualism between material pleasures and spiritual renunciation that acts to "demonize" both "sensual expression and the physical world in which such expression occurs." In this regard, Hutchings's interpretation articulates once more the potential of Romantic conceptions of pleasure to question the line separating spirit and body, imagination and sensual enjoyment, material reality and moral absolutes.

Such questioning runs throughout Romantic discourses of pleasure. "Oh Pleasure!" Byron famously quipped in *Don Juan*, "you're indeed a pleasant thing,/ Although one must be damned for you, no doubt" (1.119). On the one hand, Byron's tautological construction (pleasure as pleasant) suggests pleasure's self-sufficiency, its pure existence as a "thing" to be experienced bodily, without reflection; on the other, the assertion of probable damnation suggests the obvious and traditional moral judgment of pleasure as something for which one must eventually pay in absolute, spiritual terms. Byron's concise pair of lines thus asserts both the internal sensations and cultural influences that form all experiences of pleasure. Romantic literature and culture appear less to choose between those two aspects than to question, complicate, and critique their literary, political, and ontological ramifications. This book is dedicated to a renewed critical engagement with that spirit of Romantic questioning and Romantic pleasure.

NOTES

1. Similarly wide-ranging, *Pleasure and Change: The Aesthetics of Canon*, by Frank Kermode (with responses by Geoffrey Hartmann, John Guillory, and Carey Perloff) investigates the value of pleasure in discussions of canon formation. As Robert Alter notes in his introduction, "The principal topic of debate in the exchanges [about the literary canon]...is pleasure" (6).
2. Like Nichols's and Korsmeyer's essays, as well as Gigante's introduction, Heydt-Stevenson's essay is published in the online journal *Romantic Circles*. The popularity of the topic of Romantic pleasures in this online source suggests the need for more work in the field.
3. On the same topic of "low" bodily pleasures, but with reference to the present period, Wendy Steiner discusses the sadomasochistic subjects of Robert Mapplethorpe's photographs in *The Scandal of Pleasure: Art in an Age of Fundamentalism*. Here, Steiner contends that art cannot be held up to judgment, moral or otherwise, because it is open to individual interpretation.
4. A similar comparison of the divergent senses of pleasure in Burns and Wordsworth is advanced by Anya Taylor in *Bacchus and Romantic England*. "The convivial, passionate Burns was the type of the Romantic artist," Taylor claims, "in part because he was a drunk" (37); in contrast, "Wordsworth tacks and veers through difficult waters of poetic enthusiasm and the problem of artificially heightening it. Artificially inducing such states by wine is a moral problem, arising from a belief that pleasure and inspiration should be 'natural'" (38).

WORKS CITED

Berg, Maxine. *Luxury and Pleasure in Eighteenth-Century Britain*. Oxford: Oxford UP, 2005. Print.

Byron, Lord. *Don Juan*. Ed. T. J. Steffan, E. Steffan, and W. W. Pratt. London: Penguin, 1986. Print.

Chard, Chloe. Introduction. *Transports: Travel, Pleasure, and Imaginative Geography,1600–1830*. Ed. Chloe Chard and Helen Langdon. New Haven, CT: Yale UP, 1996. 1–29. Print.

Eagleton, Terry. "Poetry, Pleasure and Politics." *Formations of Pleasure*. Ed. Tony Bennett and Frederic Jameson. London: Routledge & Kegan Paul, 1983. 59–65. Print.

Gigante, Denise. "Romantic Gastronomy: An Introduction." Ed. and Intro. Denise Gigante. 2007. 16 paragraphs. *Romantic Circles Praxis Series*. College Park: U of Maryland P, 2007. Web. Nov. 28, 2008.

———. *Taste: A Literary History*. New Haven, CT: Yale UP: 2005. Print.

Henderson, Andrea K. *Romanticism and the Painful Pleasures of Modern Life*. Cambridge: Cambridge UP, 2008. Print.

Heydt-Stevenson, Jillian. "'Pleasure Is Now, and Ought to Be, Your Business': Stealing Sexuality in Jane Austen's Juvenilia." *Historicizing Romantic Sexuality*. Ed. and Intro. Richard Sha. 2006. 44 paragraphs. *Romantic Circles Praxis Series*. College Park: U of Maryland P, 2006. Web. Nov. 28, 2008.

Iversen, Margaret. *Beyond Pleasure: Freud, Lacan, Barthes*. University Park: Pennsylvania State UP, 2007. Print.

Jameson, Frederic. "Pleasure: A Political Issue." *Formations of Pleasure*. Ed. Tony Bennett and Frederic Jameson. London: Routledge & Kegan Paul, 1983. 1–13. Print.

Kermode, Frank. Introduction. *Pleasure and Change: The Aesthetics of Canon*. Oxford: Oxford UP, 2004. 3–14. Print.

Korsmeyer, Carolyn. "Tastes and Pleasures." *Romantic Gastronomies*. Ed. and Intro. Denise Gigante. 2007. 30 paragraphs. *Romantic Circles Praxis Series*. College Park: U of Maryland P, 2007. Web. November 28, 2008.

Manning, Susan. "Burns and Wordsworth: Art and 'The Pleasure Which There Is in Life Itself.'" *Pleasure in the Eighteenth Century*. Ed. Roy Porter and Marie Mulvey Roberts. New York: New York UP, 1996. 182–206. Print.

Mizukoshi, Ayumi. *Keats, Hunt and the Aesthetics of Pleasure*. New York: Palgrave, 2001. Print.

Nichols, Ashton. "The Loves of Plants and Animals: Romantic Science and the Pleasures of Nature." *Romanticism & Ecology*. Ed. and Intro. James McCusick. 2001. 27 paragraphs. *Romantic Circles Praxis Series*. College Park: U of Maryland P, 2001. Web. Nov. 28, 2008.

Packer, Mark. "Kant on Desire and Moral Pleasure." *Journal of the History of Ideas* 50.3 (1989): 429–42. Print.

Porter, Roy. "Enlightenment and Pleasure." *Pleasure in the Eighteenth Century*. Ed. Roy Porter and Marie Mulvey Roberts. New York: New York UP, 1997. 1–18. Print.

Richardson, Alan. "Romanticism and the Body." Blackwell *Literature Compass Online* 1.1 (2004). 15 Dec. 2005. Web. Jan. 3, 2009.

Sha, Richard C. *Perverse Romanticism: Aesthetics and Sexuality in Britain, 1750–1830*. Baltimore: Johns Hopkins UP, 2008. Print.

———. "Medicalizing the Romantic Libido: Sexual Pleasure, Luxury, and the Public Sphere." *Nineteenth-Century Contexts* 27.1 (2005): 31–52. Print.

Steiner, Wendy. *The Scandal of Pleasure: Art in an Age of Fundamentalism.* Chicago: U of Chicago P, 1995. Print.

Taylor, Anya. *Bacchus in Romantic England: Writers and Drink, 1780–1830.* Basingstoke and New York: Palgrave, 1999. Print.

Trilling, Lionel. "The Fate of Pleasure: Wordsworth to Dostoevsky." *Romanticism Reconsidered: Selected Papers from the English Institute.* Ed. Northrop Frye. New York: Columbia UP, 1963. 73–106. Print.

Zuckert, Rachel. "A New Look at Kant's Theory of Pleasure." *The Journal of Aesthetics and Art Criticism* 60.3 (2002): 239–52. Print.

CHAPTER ONE

BYRON, POLIDORI, AND THE
EPISTEMOLOGY OF ROMANTIC PLEASURE

Richard C. Sha

Pleasure in Romanticism provided the very basis of moral theory. Locke not only insisted that all action is directed towards pleasure and the avoidance of pain (Foot 83), but he also linked pleasure with good, and pain with evil.[1] Jeremy Bentham believed so strongly in the motivating force of pleasure that he went so far as to invent a means of calculating it, his infamous felicific calculus. Immanuel Kant linked pleasure with self-interest and mere empirical knowledge, and this meant not only that pleasure was potentially selfish, but also that, unless it could be universally shared, it was not knowledge. Pleasure could be a form of knowledge only when it was apprehended in terms of purposiveness (Kant 68). The pleasurable sensation of beauty could become knowledge only if one thought of its sensuousness as if it were designed, without assuming any actual designer. By linking form with purposiveness, the inescapably subjective feelings of pleasure could be transformed into necessary and shareable knowledge. Kant thus made pleasure central to his moral theory, stipulating that feeling good could often be at odds with moral knowledge.

Yet the moral weight accorded pleasure in both Locke and Kant is problematic. In Thomas Pfau's words, how can "something as ostensibly private and inward as a feeling...be imbued with so much social energy" (4)? How might something so insistently inside the individual body be externalized and made public? Leo Bersani has called "pleasure" a "scandalously vague word," one that cannot "stop refer-ring to that which is alien to it" (59). Such vagueness was inten-sified in Romanticism by questions about whether pleasure was a bodily or mental experience (or both), and whether pleasure could become an object of empirical knowledge when one had to antici-pate its consequences before experiencing it in order to appreciate it properly. While Locke firmly connects pleasure with the sensate body, Kant insists that, although pleasure begins as a bodily entity, it becomes an object of knowledge only when universally shared and not merely experienced empirically. He thus replaces corporeal embodiment with aesthetic embodiment, thereby making pleasure resistant to materialism. Similarly, since Epicureanism dictated that one's bodily experience of pleasure had to be mastered through the pain of self-discipline, how might one distinguish between pleasure and pain? Building upon the work of Elaine Scarry, Ronald Schliefer notes that pleasure is experienced but not remembered through the physiological responses that often accompany pain, suggesting that such pleasure resists the very corporealization that would grant it tangibility and immediate meaning. This gap between pleasures and bodies helps explain why the attempt to embody pleasure slides so easily into the embodiment of pain.

To address the complex Romantic epistemology of pleasure and pain, I here juxtapose Byron's remarks on pleasure in *Childe Harold's Pilgrimage* (1812–18) with those of his physician, John William Polidori, who published *An Essay on the Source of Positive Pleasure* in 1818. Although Byron did not particularly care for Polidori or think highly of his medical judgment, both Polidori and the Byron of *Childe Harold* agree that life is a vale of suffering and that pleasure, at best, can offer a mere temporary respite from that pain. Polidori sub-mits that "Pain pursues us from our birth to the grave. We come into the world weeping, and pass from the bed of sickness to our tomb" (5). Both Polidori and Byron also agree that pleasure could work to lessen pain only if it were based upon a healthy mind/body interac-tion. They therefore build upon the Epicurean distinction between kinetic pleasures, derived from some satisfaction of bodily want, and catastematic pleasures, which are more intellectual than physical, more durable, worthier, and include a sense of well-being devoid of desire (Lockridge 439–40).

Nonetheless, since catastemic mastery of desire could be experi-enced as pain, pleasure and pain became hopelessly entangled with one another, a knot Polidori and Byron struggle to untie. This entan-glement not only threatened to undermine prevailing moral systems, but it also compromised the teachings of medicine itself. Doctors attempted to align health, pleasure, and moral good, and, in so doing, mandated that disease be associated with pain and moral evil. In spite of their attempts to weld noble pleasures to the mind, and thereby to separate mental pleasure from bodily pain, both Polidori and Byron recognize that "all 'pleasure,' if it is to appear for the consciousness whose formal and social authority it underwrites, demands the materiality of 'sensation' " (Pfau 37).[2] And yet, as Schliefer explains, pleasure lacks the materiality of sensation (130). A further problem with sensation was that it always has the potential to make pleasure degrading rather than uplifting.

My larger aim here is to think about how Romantic writers sought to distance pleasure from the body because excessive bodily pleasure could only lead to pain. This distancing had the unintended effect of widening the gap between sensation and feeling. For doctors, such a gap meant that they might lose whatever authority they had over the psyche: the only recourse to the mind for physicians was through the body. To close this gap, however, Romantic writers on pleasure cited previous definitions of it, as if earlier attempts to capture the sensation of pleasure could substitute for current ones. While the citation of pleasure stands in for the experience of it, the gap between experience and language becomes less visible due to the resistance of pleasure to embodiment.[3] Pleasure is fittingly embodied in language because it cannot be embodied in bodies: even if pleasure is described in terms of orgasm, orgasm is itself figured in terms of disembodiment (i.e., *petit mort*). Although Burke famously defined pain and pleasure as "simple ideas, incapable of definition" (30), he undercut their simplicity when he insisted that lust was merely a negative pleasure: not an experience but the far more tenuous experience of not having an experience. "The absence of this so great an enjoyment scarce amounts to an uneasiness; and, except at particular times, I do not think it affects us at all" (36), Burke comments. Because writers on pleasure distance pleasure from bodily sensation, they have little recourse but to return to previous definitions of pleasure, thereby grounding it not in bodily experience but in philosophical language. By locating pleasure in language, writers are able to defer the experience of pleasure even at the moment of its articulation.

Polidori

Polidori's training as a physician culminated in his dissertation on painful dreams leading to sleepwalking (Viets 554), demonstrating his early interest in the psyche's dominion over the body. Given that medicine demanded that the psyche be treated as part of the material body, because an immaterial psyche was immune to a physician's reach, Polidori struggled with the mind/body problem. In his *Essay Upon the Sources of Positive Pleasure* (1818), J. W. Polidori, MD, Byron's traveling physician in 1816, sought to pin down "the nature and causes" of positive pleasure. Polidori tried to distinguish between positive pleasures, relative pleasures, and animal pleasures. Through these categories, he attempted to clarify the relation between moral and immoral pleasures:

> Pleasures of the body can be converted to positive pleasures by the imagination vesting them in certain colors, yet in the gratification of the senses or appetites, there is no simple positive feeling like pleasure. When we see men sacrificing health, reputation, and fortune, to voluptuousness and low debauchery, we might expect that this was done for the acquirement of some object worthy of attainment by a being, who thinks himself the mirror wherein a God may perceive his own image. A Man of animal pleasure has a body like a leaking vessel, always filling yet never full. (10–11)

In much the same way that Burke attempts to minimize the power of erotic pleasure by emptying it of positive force, Polidori attempts to persuade readers that, although lust may feel like real pleasure, pleasure is not real until the imagination actively superimposes its ideal over it. Empirically felt pleasures, thus, are not positive, but can be made positive—"converted"—through the clothing of the imagination.

The problem with Polidori's schema is this: if what is empirically felt is not real pleasure, how does one know what real pleasure is? In his *Diary*, he recounts seeing a "theatrical amusement" that "only seems fitted to excite the pleasurable sensation of yawning" (60), along with the "lookers-on acting pleasure" (60). A number of problems arise: yawning is hardly typically considered a pleasure, and how does one know whether the symptoms of pleasure are feigned or genuine? To return to the category of a positive pleasure, I note that when Polidori wants to distinguish between moral and immoral pleasures, categories proliferate and break down. Thus, bodily pleasure is not a positive pleasure, but only a physical sensation. The assertion that "in the gratification of the senses or appetites, there is no simple positive feeling like pleasure" makes sensual stimulation merely the ontological ground of pleasure, while locating pleasure itself elsewhere. What distinguishes feeling from pleasure? And how does one learn to recognize the difference? To exacerbate matters, although imaginative pleasure can convert bodily feeling into a positive pleasure, the imagination itself hovers between ontology and epistemology in that its own status as real is in question, and thus its ability to deliver the ideal is under considerable stress. The imagination can become the active organ that discriminates between sensation and moral pleasure only if human beings can be convinced that what seems like bodily pleasure is not itself positive or moral. But perhaps the ontological status of the imagination is more of an issue for poets than it is for physicians. When medical writers demonize the imagination and link it to both masturbation and impotence, they take for granted its existence as well as its effects.

As if he had not already made things complicated enough, Polidori further argues that one must first know whence pleasure arises before one seeks it by name (2–3). That is, the origins of pleasure precede the definition of it. Epistemology precedes ontology on at least two levels. First, one must know where to seek pleasure before experience can yield any knowledge of it. Second, causality precedes sensation. Polidori asks, "what would we say of a chemist, who in forming a certain salt, should attempt it, not by mixing the ingredients analysis had shown him to be its component parts, but by mixing everything in his laboratory till blundering chance threw salt into his hands[?]" (2). Empiricism here is neither knowledge nor a means to knowledge; it is rather a form of happenstance. Given the enormous stakes of pleasure, Polidori criticizes what he sees as similarly random attempts to define it: "this is…the conduct pursued by almost all, in search of pleasure—not knowing and generally not enquiring, whence it arises. They seek what they know of but by name, and then complain of their stars and of providence when they do not find it" (3). For Polidori, the metaphysical principles of causality and origin take precedence over sensation, especially since sensation does not acquire cognitive value until one can think about the consequences of that sensation. Sensation, therefore, can only result in unreliable knowledge because the moment of pleasure is isolated from the consequences of that pleasure, and in any case the consequences cannot be known in the moment.

Polidori attempts thus to "destroy the illusion of positive active pleasure" (54). Doing so makes clear that bodily "pleasures" are pleasures in name only. But his turn to causality as a weapon against false pleasure is even shrewder: since those who seek pleasure mistake "the power of stupefying" for pleasure, the doctor distances corporeal effects from any cause. Polidori comments, "another effect which causes many to take to this gratification in search of pleasure, is the power of stupefying, which, as it approaches that state just before sleep, allows phantasmic forms to dance, undisturbed by reason, before our heavy eyes. But even under all these effects, the great gratification is the taking away from pain" (12). By distinguishing between "gratification" and pleasure, and by further linking such "gratification" with the alleviation of pain, not pleasure, the doctor grants the imagination and mind power over pleasure because only they can link effect with the right cause. Here, Bersani's observation that the vagueness of pleasure mandates that it "refer to that which is alien to it" (59) allows readers to notice that the sensation of pleasure has become equated with both stupefaction, a form of anesthetic, and pain. Since for him real pleasure depends completely upon the imagination's intervention, human beings cannot "be shut out by the doors of a dungeon, or lost under the immense vault of heaven" (54). Happiness is thus within the control of one's mind. Yet, as in the case of Milton's Satan, this control has its price. For Satan, who falsely believes that "the mind is its own place, and in itself/ Can make a Heav'n of Hell, a Hell of Heav'n" (*Paradise Lost* I:254–5), this happiness could merely be a form of delusion. Polidori further suggests that, although pleasure is corporealized most fully in its excess—excess that becomes legible upon the body in the form of, for instance, impotence—such pleasure was never really pleasure to begin with. The very moment that pleasure is written on the body in the form of excess, Polidori cancels it out as pleasure.

When Polidori examines why incest is not pleasurable, he makes clear the limits of what the imagination can do to transcend actual sensation. He argues, "How seldom is it, that we hear of first cousins [becoming lovers]; how much more anomalous of brothers and sisters falling in love with one another: and does this not arise from seeing too closely, so that the imagination, in trying to act, finds its way clogged by all those petty obstacles of frailties and weaknesses, which are exposed by intimacy[?]" (33). Here, Polidori anticipates the Westermarck hypothesis: intimacy in the sense of being raised together prevents the imagination from seeing a sibling as a desirable sexual object.[4] Incest thus indicates the outer limit of the imagination's powers to idealize: it cannot overcome the familiarity of habitual sensation. The unforeseen difficulty with this line of argument is that it dooms marriage generally, an implicit claim that is at odds with the general medical advice that marriage is good for one's health. Once a married couple lives intimately, sexual desire will, by these lights, inevitably die. For my purposes here, Polidori's attention to incest suggests that sensation is at odds with imagination; moreover, when mind and body collide, sensation will win.

BYRON

Polidori did not just theorize pleasure. In fact, given his remarks about the "man of animal pleasure," one suspects he might have had to deliver these words just two years earlier to Byron himself. As a third wheel, Polidori unwittingly prevented Claire Claremont and Byron from consummating their relationship as often as they would have liked while at the Villa Diodati (Marchand, *Byron* 2:627). In exasperation, Claremont writes, "Pray if you can send M. Polidori either to write another dictionary or to the lady he loves. I hope this last may be his pillow & then he will sleep; for I cannot come at this hour of the night & be seen by him; it is so extremely suspicious" (627). More prophylactic than physician, though even in this office he was too late to prevent conception of Allegra, Polidori had to settle initially for interrupting Byron's pleasures rather than educating him about them.[5] Polidori further helps us to unpack what Byron may have meant when he insisted that the protagonist of *Childe Harold* was a "child of imagination" (McGann 2:4). In light of Polidori's essay, since the imagination elevates the baser bodily pleasures into mental moral pleasures, Byron's yoking together of Harold and the imagination explains why Harold almost never feels pleasure, and why melancholy and irony insistently bracket pleasure so that it might become the basis for contemplation. Polidori's idealized stance toward the imagination glosses Harold's attempts to convert pleasure from mere bodily sensation to imaginative cognition. Such attempts, however, risk failure because cognition tends to cancel out sensation.

Polidori was far from the only physician educating Byron about pleasure. Early in his youth, Byron learned of the bodily consequences of too much pleasure. In February 1808, because of his "too frequent connection," the adolescent Byron thought of himself as akin to a "leaky vessel" (Marchand, *BLJ* 1:160). Too much intercourse not only led him to "apprehend a complete Bankruptcy of Constitution" (Marchand, *BLJ* 1:160), but also to seek medical help from a physician named Pearson.[6] The poet of libertine pleasure thus was profoundly aware that pleasure had bodily consequences, and these consequences might in fact make any pleasure from bodily sensation merely temporary. Excess pleasure, indeed, led inexorably to pain.

Like his doctor, Byron warns that one must be careful when choosing one's pleasures. Bullfighting, for example, is dangerous because it confuses pleasure and pain. Byron wryly observes, "Nurtur'd in blood betimes, his heart delights/ In vengeance, gloating on another's pain" (McGann 1.80). His commas advertise the use of chiasmus, a rhetorical structure that highlights how easily pleasure and pain can change places. The 6/4 split in syllable count in the first line is deformed in the second to a 3/7 split. When crossed, the lines are either a syllable short or a syllable too long. The poet thereby implies that the crossing of pain and pleasure deforms the subject. Byron is also aware of how despots impose their pleasures upon others, and in the process further the transformation of pleasure into pain. Commenting on gladiatorial combat in Ancient Rome, Byron insists, "Such were the bloody Circus' genial laws,/ And the imperial pleasure.—Wherefore not?" (McGann 4:139). Of course, there is nothing genial at all about blood. Byron underscores this fact by highlighting rotting "maws/ of worms" (ibid.).

As Byron recognizes, the problem with any neat moral correlations between pleasure with good and pain with evil is that one does not know that too much pleasure leads to pain until after the fact. And even when he knows this, Byron still "hope[s] to live and reestablish Medmenham Abbey, or some similar temple of Venus, of which I shall be a Pontifex Maximus" (Marchand, *BLJ* 1:160–1). Why would the poet choose excess pleasure/pain along with its consequences? Such a choice undercuts the moralizing strain of Byron's travelogue. Indeed, the poet opens *Childe Harold* by insisting that his protagonist is an example of how "early perversion of mind and morals leads to satiety of past pleasures and disappointments in new ones, and that even the beauties of nature, and stimulus of travel...are lost on a soul so constituted, or rather misdirected" (McGann 2:6). If Byron seeks to make Harold an exemplar of the consequences of perversion, he nonetheless recognizes that excess pleasure makes his protagonist immune to pleasure and thereby capable of being skeptical of it. More crucially, Byron understands that in order for pleasure to be a form of freedom, one must deliberately choose it despite its consequences. On the one hand, if one chooses pleasure for the sake of pleasure, one becomes merely addicted to pleasure and it loses whatever ethical value it had. On the other hand, if one avoids pleasure to avoid consequences, one is letting consequences determine one's pleasures. To the extent that excess pleasure leads to pain and that one can know this beyond of pleasure, pleasure has the potential to invite the contemplation of the freedom to choose what might be bad for us. Doctors of course do not see unhealthy choices as free choices since these choices are by definition pathological, but Byron, as a poet, is not limited by medical strictures.

To get from pleasure to freedom, however, one must rethink why certain pleasures are associated with vice and others with virtue. To be sure, Byron at times seems merely conventional in his moral judgments. When he connects vice to the crumbling walls of Spain—"Vice clings to the tott'ring walls" (McGann 1.46)—Byron indulges in a kind of expected poetic justice. In spite of these gestures towards moral convention, Byron acknowledges that vice is experienced as pleasurable, and such a claim dooms any moral system that relies upon pleasure as that which leads mankind to the good. Addressing vice, the poet remarks, "how soft are thy voluptuous ways!" (McGann 1.65). Unlike Polidori, who would reject any connection of vice and pleasure by pointing out that the sensations of the body are merely sensations and not pleasure, the poet connects vice and pleasure. Harold functions not simply as a warning against the consequences of perversion. When Byron makes one of Harold's first European stops at William Beckford's home in exile at Cintra, he not only invites parallels to his own exile after the separation from his wife, but he also leans toward a celebration of the perverse rather than a condemnation of it. Granted, commentators have acknowledged the homophobia of Byron's remarks (Crompton 122–6), and, although the poet stresses the isolation of Beckford's home—it is "as if a thing unblest by Man" (McGann 1.23)—his conclusion places fault not at the door of any particular vice, but rather at the door of pleasure in general. Byron notes, "Vain are the pleasaunces on earth supplied,/ Swept into wrecks anon by Time's ungentle tide!" (McGann 1.23). This concluding couplet is blithely indifferent to any specific act. Byron's vaporous platitude about pleasure, nonetheless, masks his return to an Ancient Greek view of sex where what matters is less the morality of any particular sexual act than whether or not the actor is indulging in either passivity or excess. His substitution of the archaic word "pleasaunces" for "pleasure" hints at this return to the morals of an antiquated past.

Byron's very linking of the imagination with love may owe something to Polidori. Regarding the role of imagination in love, Polidori asserts that "Constancy depends more upon the imagination of the lover than on the merits of the beloved" ("Pleasure" 33). By equating the imagination with constancy, Polidori can establish love as a mental and therefore moral pleasure. However, by locating constancy in the mind of the perceiver rather than in the object of love, he makes the lover's conduct virtually irrelevant to the case. In a similar vein, Byron argues that love is an imaginative mental construct:

> Oh Love! No habitant of earth thou art–
> An unseen seraph, we believe in thee,

A faith whose martyrs are the broken heart,
But never hath seen, nor e'er shall see
The naked eye, thy form, as it should be;
The mind hath made thee. (McGann 4:121)

The mind and imagination create love: "The mind hath made thee." In contrast to Polidori, who yokes together love and the imagination to elevate them both, Byron connects love to the imagination to dematerialize it, and to make his readers skeptical of its existence. Pointedly insisting that love is a product of belief and yet denying any empirical proof for that belief, the poet warns that, instead of any ocular proof of love, all he can offer is the look of martyrdom, the symptom of a broken heart. Byron turns to the figure of address, apostrophe, to ironize both love and the imagination: the absence of a referent to "thee" shows the artifice of the trope. In the process, of course, he portrays himself as the victim of his and his wife's (Annabella's) recent separation: the broken heart to which he gestures is presumably his. His heart is torn across multiple stanzas: five of them later, he is still wallowing "with heart-aches ever new" (4:126).

If Polidori underscored the medical consequences of too much bodily pleasure, and sought to make real the pleasures of contemplation, Byron in *Childe Harold* paints his protagonist as pleasure's victim, and implies that one can truly contemplate pleasure only when one is removed from it. Where Polidori emphasizes the unhealthy corporeal consequences of bodily pleasure, Byron wants to think about how an excess of pleasure both individualizes the subject and grants him or her power to think about pleasure.[7] After all, pleasure cannot be an object of study if it is inseparable from the subject contemplating it. This separation further points to the subtle ways in which Byron reorients his audience's attitudes toward pleasure. Far from being necessarily unhealthy, excess pleasure has the power to enable self-consciousness about pleasure because the excess can grant immunity to pleasure in the present, which explains the poet's interest in exhaustion (Lockridge 441): exhaustion paradoxically enables some control over sensation.

Melancholy helps Byron to anesthetize pleasure generally and negate bodily sensation. Indeed, this anesthetized space is essential to the very contemplation of it. Harold is "with pleasure drugg'd [and] he almost long'd for woe" (McGann 1.6). Like Polidori, who sees pleasure as both cure and poison, Byron sees it as a drug, and one that suspends the will. Hence the poet throughout *Childe Harold* describes not so much the feeling of pleasure but the absence of feeling it: "And feeling still with thee in my crush'd feeling's dearth" (McGann 3.6). This dearth is what gives the poet the ironic distance he needs to contemplate pleasure rather than feel it. Moreover, Byron consistently aligns pleasure with the youthful past, thus insisting upon temporal distance from the experience of pleasure as a means to facilitate consciousness about it. "Youth and pleasure meet" (McGann 3:22), for example, on the morning of the Battle of Waterloo, only to be undone by war's devastation. Byron's bracketing of even youthful pleasure as irony immunizes him from the seductions of pleasure. "Others rapt in pleasure seem" (McGann 7), Byron comments. Only in this way can pleasure be connected to freedom; again, doing things because they are pleasurable allows one to be determined by pleasures rather than determine them.

The ironic distance between pleasure and the sensate body is perhaps most felt in Byron's Wordsworthian canto. Byron begins stanza 178, Canto 4, with the following series of observations:

> There is a pleasure in the pathless woods,
> There is a rapture on the lonely shore,
> There is society, where none intrudes,
> By the deep Sea, and music in its roar...

In this remarkable passage, which anticipates Matthew Arnold's apostrophe to the sea in "Dover Beach," Byron's cognitive recognition of the existence of pleasure and of rapture is pointedly undercut by his refusal to feel it. Moreover, the rather bland anaphora—"There is," "There is"—insists that such feelings are not here but there. The phrase also superimposes a kind of clinical gaze that negates these feelings, at least for the speaker. Wordsworth might feel such compensation, but Byron emphatically does not. Nor is this necessarily a bad thing, because "rapture" deprives its victims of agency.

The speaker's insistence here upon the gaps between feeling and cognition helps explain Byron's foundational redefinition of art away from Romantic expressiveness and toward concealment. In his final alexandrine, Byron writes that he "feel[s]/ What I can ne'er express, yet can not all conceal" (4.178). Feeling is divorced from expression and yet the sensations of feeling resist concealment; "not conceal" points to the gaps between sensation and cognition even as the negation shows how expression is necessarily distorted. Since one cannot claim expression, the best one can do is to claim a failure to conceal. The emotional content thus will out, but it is not clear what control, if any, the poet has over it. Pleasure, in addition, is often feigned to "conceal the pique" (McGann 2:97), making it more unknowable. This passage on art as concealment further invites readers to assess the extent to which sensation and cognition are reconcilable. Noel Jackson, for instance, turns to science to suggest that Romantic sensation was a form of cognition.[8] Insofar as they represent sensation at some distance from cognition, neither the Byron of *Childe Harold* nor Polidori quite bears this out.

Adding to his skepticism that pleasure can be an object of knowledge, Byron insists upon a gap between interiority and exteriority, one exacerbated by his protests of a gap between Childe Harold's thoughts and his own. And yet, even within Harold, the gap between inner and outer threatens to swallow him whole. Byron describes Harold's contemplation of the battles fought on the banks of the Rhine as follows:

> Thus Harold inly said, and pass'd along,
> Yet not insensibly to all which here
> Awoke the jocund birds to early song
> In glens which might have made even exile dear:
> Though on his brow were graven lines austere,
> And tranquil sternness which had ta'en place
> Of feelings fierier far but less severe.
> Joy was not always absent from his face,
> But o'er it in such scenes would steal with transient trace.
>   (McGann 3:52)

Instead of describing joy and pleasure as that which unify inner and outer, Byron clearly frames these stanzas as being about Harold's consciousness, and his consciousness is pointedly aloof from the landscape. Although Harold is "not insensible" to the external world, or even the song of the "jocund birds," the fact that Byron can describe the possibility of feeling only through negation, coupled with the conditional form of the verb—"might have"—demands readerly skepticism about any such unity. Even the presence of joy is framed from the vantage of absence: "joy was not always absent from his face." More tellingly, the "graven lines" on Harold's face refuse to reveal anything. These lines provide merely the "transient trace" of joy, and such a trace is rendered even less legible by their palimpsestic referent: the "tranquil sternness which had ta'en the place/ Of feelings fierier far but less severe." This sternness is a metonymy for the "fierier feelings," which are themselves caught between the fiery and severe, while "fierier" specifies only a relation to something else, not the something else. By making metonymy and adjectival modifiers the figures for thinking about pleasure, Byron points to the fact that it is really some kind of shell game: a promise of originary unity that is endlessly deferred.

Byron's emphasis on the elongated temporality of pleasure undermines it still further as an object of knowledge. He warns, "Oh! Let him seize/ Pure pleasure while he can;..." (2:50). His semicolon arrests such pleasure even as it delineates the experience of it. Byron similarly comments, "To feign the pleasure or conceal the pique:/ Smiles form the channel of a future tear" (2:97). Smiles hide future tears, and pleasure is undercut by an imagined future. The poet here recalls Polidori's claim that "Pleasure, in a positive sense, is only excited by allowing the mere imagination to act, and vest the past with the shades it had not, the present with hues it has not, and the future with colors it will never have" ("Pleasure" 18–9). Because pleasure is imbued with both past and future feelings, and is thus changed by those feelings, time consistently alters the meanings of pleasure, making it an insecure foundation of morality. Because it is imbedded in past, present, and future, pleasurable sensation is also immune to causality. Without a clear sense of time, how can one know cause from effect? Such a confused temporality makes pleasure particularly ill suited as a foundation for morality.

At times, Byron suggests that, far from uniting signifier and signified, pleasure is like the Lacanian real, something that always exceeds signification. To the extent that the very term cannot be pinned down, it resists knowledge. He comments,

> There is a fire
> And motion of the soul which will not dwell
> In its own narrow being, but aspire
> Beyond the fitting medium of desire;
> And, but once kindled, quenchless evermore,
> Preys upon high adventure, nor can tire
> Of aught but rest; a fever at the core,
> Fatal to him who bears, to all who ever bore. (3:42)

Not only does Byron associate pleasure with combustion, but he also insists that it will "aspire/ Beyond the fitting medium of desire." His enjambment here gestures toward the beyond he tries to name, and even his fastidious syllable counts fail to house this being. When he appropriates the medical term "fever" to describe pleasure, Byron connects it with the symptom of disease.[9] Because "fevers" were the symptom and not the cause of disease, the poet's diagnosis is severely limited. Physicians were very conscious of how suspect a patient's claimed symptoms could be since symptoms were subjectively felt. What the body feels is at some distance from the cause of that feeling.

Both Byron's and Polidori's skeptical awareness of the gaps between pleasure and sensation, writ large in the gaps between pleasure, knowledge, and morality, thus manifests itself in their endlessly recursive accounts of pleasure. These accounts recognize the inescapable links to a "beyond" of pleasure long before Freud associated it with the death drive. Any alleged immediacy of sensation is complicated by the need to represent sensation as it was described by others. In this "re-presentation," pleasure moves from an open signifier to a recoverable object that can be presented as if it existed.[10] In his attempts to define pleasure, Polidori rehearses what Zeno, Plato, Hutcheson, and Berkeley have said about pleasure. Where Zeno defined pleasure as a "nullity" ("Pleasure" 6), Hutcheson divided pleasure into simple and complex, the latter being "those which arise upon some previous idea, or assemblage, or comparison of ideas, forgetting that the cause from which the feeling arises cannot change the nature of the feeling, except in intensity or duration" ("Pleasure" 8). Berkeley further divided pleasure into the categories of reason, imagination, and sense ("Pleasure" 9). In the same way that Hutcheson forgets that cause has only limited impact on the feeling, Berkeley's categories show only the "varieties of causes, not perceiving that the feeling is the same" ("Pleasure" 9). And yet if Polidori chides his predecessors with generating false categories based on their desire to specify causes, causes that cannot change the nature of the feeling, he replaces causes with origins in the body or mind to distinguish between positive pleasure and mere sensation. He thus redeploys their divisions in service of his own categories.

Because Byron insists in *Childe Harold* upon connecting the experience of pleasure with the past through antiquated language, his accounts of it are almost always recursive. For instance, when in his original Preface to the first Canto of *Childe Harold* Byron takes Edmund Burke to task for idealizing chivalry, he undermines the power of pleasure to deliver immediate sensation. Pleasure once again fails to gesture toward a kind of language that achieves full embodiment. In the Preface, the poet remarks that "Burke need not have regretted that days [of chivalry] are over" (2). He thereby pulls the rug out from under Burke, who mistakenly imbued chivalry with nostalgic pleasure and in so doing sought to restore custom and class hierarchy to pride of place in British society. Byron reminds his readers that chivalry hardly prevented all kinds of bad behavior, and he turns to Edward III's rape of the Countess of Salisbury to indicate the mixed legacy of chivalry. If on the one hand the Order of the Garter was the highest chivalric honor, on the other hand it was created perhaps to cleanse Edward's conscience about the rape. After her rape, the Countess allegedly dropped her garter at a ball, and King Edward restored it to her. Byron's point is that the Order of the Garter is a metonymy for the restored garter, which itself is a metonymy for the Countess's unviolated sexuality. When he adds Sir Joseph Banks to the genealogy of chivalry, Byron hints at this scientist's assignations with Tahitian girls. Rumors of Banks's conduct swirled about London upon his return (Holmes 42). By pointing out that the good old days were hardly as pleasurable as Burke thinks, by distancing chivalry from "moral" pleasures, and by insisting that one's pleasure can be another's pain, Byron obliquely comments on how pleasure has become weaponized in class warfare. Once again, pleasure is difficult to know for its own sake. Chivalry, then, idealizes aristocratic pleasure and legitimates the aristocracy's right to rule. Byron's intervention, however, is far too late now that the Bourbon kings have been restored to the thrones of Europe.

A second example of recursiveness occurs when Byron alludes to Horace's Ode 1.9 about Mount Soracte in stanzas 74–7 of Canto 4.[11] Horace wrote,

> You see Soracte standing there white and deep
> With snow, the woods in trouble, hardly able
> To sustain their burden and the rivers
> Halted by sharp grip of ice.[12]

Where Horace invokes the mountain covered in snow to represent the pains of old age that will make the speaker now revel in the pleasures of youth, Byron invokes Horace to remind himself of "classic raptures" and "recollections rake," alluding to the many loves, both male and female, of the Horatian odes. Horace ends this ode by recounting how the "delightful laughter" of a young girl who is hiding from her lover gives her position away so that he can snatch a token from her finger:

> Now is the time for the lovely laugh from the secluded corner
> Giving away the girl who hides there,
> And a token is snatched from an arm
> Or feebly resisting finger. (West 41)

What interests me here is that Byron's invocation of Horace's description of pleasure is already at the source ironized by a nostalgic futurity that instills the addressee's (Thaliarchus's) current experience with the Horatian speaker's regret, a regret that is not possible in the now of the pledge but that can be anticipated only if the snow-covered Soracte is interpreted as a symbol of old age. Pleasure thus is mired in an anachronistic temporality that resists the integration of feeling and meaning. Horace violates time, investing present pleasure (in summer) with a (winter) future regret that has not been experienced by Thaliarchus; only by doing violence to time can he imbue pleasure with the significance he wants it to have. While the name "Thaliarchus" comes from the Greek past, and means "master of the revels," the speaker's regret makes it clear that the addressee is only seemingly in control of a past pleasure.[13] West suggests that Thaliarchus is in fact a slave, given that he is asked to pour the wine and to keep the fire stoked (42), and his status as slave renders any mastery absurd. Finally, Horace's description of pleasure returns to Theocritus's and Alcaeus's accounts of it (Catlow 76), and thus a Roman poet in Hellenistic Rome (West 43) seeks to triumph over a Greek past whose past triumph over pleasure is already undercut by Horace's desire to reanimate a dead past with a Greek name, one in a language that is being superseded by Latin.

Byron takes an already complex moment and enjambs it over three stanzas. When Byron insists that the Soracte is "not now in snow" (McGann 4:75), he highlights Horace's violations of time, his movement from winter to summer. Furthermore, he layers Horace's account of pleasure with the fact that he was force-fed Horace: "the drill'd dull lesson, forced down word by word/ In my repugnant youth, with pleasure to record/ Aught that recals the daily drug which turn'd/ My sickening memory" (McGann 4:74–5). Pleasure thus is embedded within Byron's painful education, and if he had previously connected pleasure and youth, he now severs even that connection. Hence, if pleasure was thought to be an authentic experience one had in the past, one recognizes that, when looking at the past, even youthful pleasure is inseparable from pain. Faced squarely and without nostalgia, youth is now "repugnant." Moreover, since pleasure lacks physiological embodiment, and since memory too cannot quite corporealize pleasure, Byron turns to the alimentary canal and to consonance ("daily," "drug," "turn'd") to embody pain. His remembrance of Horace's account of pleasure is tainted with pain, so much so that he "with pleasure...record[s]" that forced feeding. Byron imagines that his mind could have "relish[ed] what it might have sought,/ If free to choose" (McGann 4:76). Yet he "cannot now restore/ Its health; but what it then detested, still abhor" (McGann 4:76). Although Byron frames "relish" as being contingent upon freedom and by extension abhorrence upon being forced to do something, his rhymes ("restore"/"abhor") insist that nothing escapes the determining force of contingency. The trick, then, is to take pleasure in the causes one allows oneself to be determined by.

In the same way that Horace ends his Ode with metonymies like "token" and "finger," parts for the whole that erase the fullness of pleasure, Byron relegates whatever pleasure he had to preterition. Byron's echo between "abhor" and "Horace" solidifies that preterition, and in truncating Horace, the poet reminds readers of Horace's metonymic coy finger. Against medical accounts of pleasure that insist that regulation of the mind and body can heal the mind, Byron maintains that such damage is irreparable. Whether or not this damage is ultimately unhealthy is another question entirely, especially if the gap between sensation and reflection is necessary to have some control over it.

Byron then takes leave of Horace on Soracte's ridge, noting that "it is a curse/ To understand, not feel thy lyric flow" and "to comprehend, but never love thy verse" (McGann 4:77). Horace invoked this ridge to separate his speaker from any immediate feeling of pleasure so that he might reflect on what it means. More poignantly, the speaker tells Thaliarchus to enjoy the love of a girl because, as time passes and he undergoes puberty, he will no longer be attractive to men (West 43–4). Horace reminds Byron that cognition is at a distance from feeling, that feeling is removed from desire, and that these ironies offer the only possibility of learning from one's experiences of pleasures. And yet such irony always tinges pleasure with pain; because the pleasure will be lost, it is freighted with nostalgia. Despite his insistence that Soracte's ridge is not now covered with snow, thus removing tension between winter and summer, Byron's use of medial caesuras twice separate thought and feeling here ("understand"/"feel" and "comprehend"/"love"). His commas stand in for the mountain ridge; they mark an impasse between present feeling and future thought. The recursivity of pleasure thus captures its ambiguous and curiously disembodied status threatening to become materialized in terms of pain. The body in question—is it Thaliarchus's or Byron's?—potentially straddles pre-pubescence and post-pubescence, which intensifies the question regarding how bodies experience pleasure as meaningful. Ancient Greek notions of sex mandated that, once bearded, a boy's body could no longer be attractive to men (West 43). Given that the very name Thaliarchus occurs once on a fifth-century Athenian vase as a *kalos* name—the name of a beautiful boy (West 43)—such a shift in age would have been especially costly to his identity.

Byron literally leaves Horace dangling on a ridge: "Awakening without wounding the touch'd heart,/ Yet fare thee well—upon Soracte's ridge we part" (McGann 4:77). The gerund form of the first two verbs lets Horace hang in perpetuity. Byron's "fare thee well" recalls the poem he wrote to Lady Byron the day after their separation agreement was signed (McGann 3:494) and thus allows Horace and Thaliarchus to substitute for the previously legal object of his erotic pleasure. Unlike the girl in Horace's poem whose finger feebly resists, Byron had hoped "fare thee well" would move Lady Byron toward reconciliation. This ability for one erotic object to be replaced by another, even one of another sex, further makes pleasure difficult to materialize. That pleasure circulates so easily from love to hatred renders it more intangible, as does the fact that pleasure easily slides outside the law. Does Byron wish to leave Horace hanging, or Lady Byron? Is Byron the master of his pleasures, or is he like the Thaliarchian slave? Byron thus turns to the foundational couplet of the Spenserian stanza (heart/part) and breaks it apart, insisting upon a gap in the heart that can never be foreclosed. Horace thus now names the abyss of pleasure.

To the extent that Romantic thinkers like Byron and Polidori identified pleasure as one of humanity's primary motivators, they were right to consider how pleasure might in fact lead to moral good. Indeed, Hume shut the door to the Enlightenment when he claimed that reason was powerless to motivate, that it was "utterly impotent" (509). Reason's impotence was pleasure's gain. Romantic faith in pleasure's ability to motivate did not, however, prevent the neat dotted lines connecting pleasure and moral good from becoming hopelessly confused. Pleasure could not be unambiguously equated with knowledge. Nor could pleasure be purely good, since there were gaps between interiority and exteriority, between individual and society, between pleasure as sensation and pleasure as something known, and between the immediate sensation of pleasure and the contemplation that ensues from it (or in Byron's case, the contemplation that ensues from the excess experience of pleasure). Because pleasure was so difficult to corporealize, it tended to shade imperceptibly into pain because pain has clearer physiological markers. Finally, pleasure was bound up with an anachronistic temporality in which sensation and meaning resist simultaneous integration. Byron and Polidori, then, form a key if unacknowledged part of a genealogy of thinking about what Freud would later call the "beyond" of pleasure: the recognition of the inadequacy of the term "pleasure" to encapsulate the complexities of human motivation. As such, pleasure allegorizes language itself as human beings strive to harness its illusory corporeality to suture the gaps between language and meaning.

NOTES

1. Foot shows the long legacy of Locke's theory to modern moral theories, and she labels this "psychological hedonism" (83).
2. Pfau invokes "mood" as a way of thinking about the intersubjectivity of feeling and pleasure. While I agree that mood has the potential to accomplish this intersubjectivity, this essay will advocate a much more skeptical treatment of Romantic emotion.
3. Schliefer makes the important point that since pleasure lacks embodiment, pleasure is akin to the semiotics of meaning (130).
4. Alan Richardson demonstrates how Coleridge anticipates Westermarck (553–60).
5. According to Fiona MacCarthy, Allegra was conceived in the days before Byron left England (273).
6. For an extended examination of the parallels between Pearson and Byron, see chapter 6 of my *Perverse Romanticism: Aesthetics and Sexuality in Britain, 1750–1832.*
7. I recall here Andrew Elfenbein's argument that genius in Romanticism becomes defined in terms of pushing against notions of gender and sexuality.
8. Jackson, *Science and Sensation in Romantic Poetry.*
9. For a survey of the medical literature on fevers, see Leonard G. Wilson.
10. I am here indebted to Ruth Mack, Chapter 4. On quotation and the epistemology of Romantic emotion, see Adela Pinch, 164–92.
11. I am grateful to Steven J. Willett for his attempts to educate me about Horace and for his careful reading of this essay, which prevented numerous errors. Any remaining faults are mine, not his. West submits that there are no violations of time in this Horace ode, since we are being given general laws, not particular descriptions (42). My attention to the misfit between pleasure and linear time, however, leads me to emphasize the temporal ruptures.
12. I have derived these translations through a combination of Rudd and West.
13. Lawrence Catlow discusses the significance of the name on pages 76–7. The Greek name might also serve as a metonymy for Greek Epicurean philosophy, which colors Horace's odes and further calls attention to violations of time.

WORKS CITED

Bersani, Leo. *The Freudian Body. Psychoanalysis and Art.* New York: Columbia UP, 1986. Print.

Burke, Edmund. *A Philosophical Inquiry into the Origins of Our Ideas of the Sublime and Beautiful.* New York: PP Collier, 1969. Print.

Catlow, Lawrence. "Fact, Imagination, and Memory in Horace: 'Odes' 1.9." *Greece and Rome.* 23. 1 (April 1976): 74–81. Print.

Crompton, Louis. *Byron and Greek Love.* London: Faber and Faber, 1985. Print.

Elfenbein, Andrew. *Romantic Genius.* New York: Columbia UP, 1999. Print.

Foot, Philippa. "Locke, Hume, and Modern Moral Theory: A Legacy of Seventeenth- and Eighteenth-Century Philosophies of Mind." *The Languages of Psyche.* Ed. George S. Rousseau. Berkeley: U of California P, 1990. 81–104. Print.

Holmes, Richard. *The Age of Wonder: How the Romantic Generation Discovered the Beauty and Terror of Science.* London: HarperPress, 2008. Print.

Hume, David. *A Treatise of Human Nature.* London: Penguin Books, 1984. Print.

Jackson, Noel. *Science and Sensation in Romantic Poetry.* Cambridge: Cambridge UP, 2008. Print.

Kant, Immanuel. *Critique of Judgment.* Trans. Werner S. Pluhar. Indianapolis: Hackett Publishing, 1987. Print.

Lockridge, Laurence. *The Ethics of Romanticism.* Cambridge: Cambridge UP, 1989. Print.

MacCarthy, Fiona. *Byron: Life and Legend.* New York: Farrar, Straus and Giroux, 2002. Print.

Mack, Ruth. *Literary Historicity: Literature and Historical Experience in Eighteenth-Century Fiction.* Stanford, CA: Stanford UP, 2009. Print.

Marchand, Leslie. *Byron: A Biography.* 3 vols. New York: Alfred Knopf, 1957. Print.

———, ed. *Byron's Letters and Journals.* 11 vols. Cambridge, MA: Harvard UP, 1973–81. Print.

McGann, Jerome J., Byron, Lord. *Childe Harold's Pilgrimage. Lord Byron: The Complete Poetical Works.* 7 vols. Oxford: Oxford UP, 1980–93. Vol. 2. Print.

Milton, John. *Complete Poems and Major Prose.* Ed. Merritt Y. Hughes. Indianapolis: Bobbs-Merrill, 1957. Print.

Pfau, Thomas. *Romantic Moods: Paranoia, Trauma, and Melancholy, 1790–1840.* Baltimore: Johns Hopkins UP, 2005. Print.

Pinch, Adela. *Strange Fits of Passion: Epistemologies of Emotion, Hume to Austen.* Stanford, CA: Stanford UP, 1996. Print.

Polidori, John William. *The Diary of Dr. John William Polidori 1816.* Ed. William Michael Rossetti. London: Elkin Mathews, 1911. Print.

———. *An Essay on the Source of Positive Pleasure.* London: Longman, 1818. Print.

Richardson, Alan. "Rethinking Romantic Incest: Human Universals, Literary Representation, and the Biology of Mind." *New Literary History* 31.3 (2000): 553–72. Print.

Rudd, Niall, ed. and trans. *Horace: Odes and Epodes.* Cambridge, MA: Harvard UP, 2004. Print.

Schliefer, Ronald. *Intangible Materialism: The Body, Scientific Knowledge, and the Power of Language.* Minneapolis: U of Minnesota P, 2009. Print.

Sha, Richard C. *Perverse Romanticism: Aesthetics and Sexuality in Britain, 1750–1832.* Baltimore: Johns Hopkins UP, 2009. Print.

Viets, Henry R. "John William Polidori, MD and Lord Byron—A Brief Interlude in 1816." *The New England Journal of Medicine* 264.11 (1961): 553–7. Print.

West, David. *Horace Odes I: Carpe Diem.* Oxford: Clarendon P, 1995. Print.

Wilson, Leonard G. "Fevers." *Companion Encyclopedia of the History of Medicine.* Ed. W. F. Bynum and Roy Porter. Vol. 1. London: Routledge, 1993. 382–411. Print.

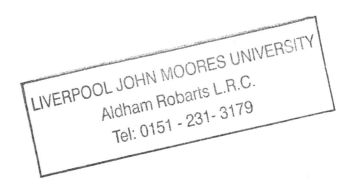

CHAPTER TWO

PLEASURE IN AN AGE OF TALKERS: KEATS'S MATERIAL SUBLIME

Betsy Winakur Tontiplaphol

In *The Spirit of the Age*, William Hazlitt characterizes the historical moment that others subsequently christened "Romantic" as "an age of talkers." He distinguishes talkers from "doers," asserting that in this "world...growing old," there ostensibly is not much for would-be activists to accomplish: "We are so far advanced in the Arts and Sciences, that we live in retrospect and doat on past achievements.... What niche remains unoccupied? What path untried?" (38). For Hazlitt the unfazed radical, word unmoored from deed was surely disappointing, but for Hazlitt the portraitist, an age of talkers must also have seemed disorienting, bizarre. After all, talk is neither corporeal nor pictorial; even as he crafts vibrant prose sketches of influential Romantic-era writers, Hazlitt calls upon his training as a painter, and those skills are more closely associated with the hand and eye—in other words, with sensation and active muscles—than with the intellect. For instance, Jeremy Bentham, who "devoted his life to the pursuit of abstract and general truths" (9), is *drawn* in Hazlitt's essay as a person of Milton-esque "appearance": "the same silvery tone, a few disheveled hairs, a peevish, yet puritanical expression" (11). Hazlitt relies on verbal signifiers, but his medium somehow seems closer to drawing; if the sketch successfully evokes a foul-tempered elder, it does so with color ("silvery tone"), texture ("disheveled hairs"), and line (the facial creases that produce a "puritanical expression").

But what of pleasure in an age of talkers? What place does sensual gratification have in a culture whose leaders prize abstraction and whose literary artists cherish, like Wordsworth, "the simplest elements of nature and of the human mind, the mere abstract conditions inseparable from our being, and [try] to compound a new system of poetry from them" (111)? Pleasure is not a prominent theme in *The Spirit of the Age*, but the essay on Bentham that opens the collection (and finds Hazlitt so memorably exercising his painter's scrutiny) targets the Utilitarian conflation of pleasure with "good." "Every pleasure, says Mr. Bentham, is equally a good, and is to be taken into the account as such in a moral estimate," writes Hazlitt. "But it is not so," he continues; "[p]leasure is that which is so in itself: good is that which approves itself as such on reflection, or the idea of that which is a source of satisfaction" (13–14). Goodness is gutless and therefore undrawable. Hazlitt intimates that *real* pleasure— that which is "sweet in the mouth" (14), soft to the touch, or lovely to the eye—is a threatened category in an age of talkers, and, although his primary concern in the Bentham piece is the infeasibility of Utilitarian government ("[V]irtue, to be sincere and practical, cannot be divested entirely of the blindness and impetuosity of passion!" (16)), Hazlitt also frets about the limitations of intellection generally. He observes that Bentham expresses "great contempt for out-of-door prospects, for green fields and trees, and is for referring everything to Utility. There is a little narrowness in this; for if all the sources of satisfaction are taken away, what is to become of utility itself?" (22). Civil society should regulate our animal appetites, not eradicate them. In a world devoid of pleasure, Hazlitt wonders, what is the useful *for*?

In conversations dedicated to pleasure in Romantic literature, John Keats—poet of fragrant bodices, crushed grapes, slippery kisses, and embalmed darkness—is a more likely subject than Hazlitt, but critics frequently acknowledge Keats's debts to the older writer, whose lectures he attended in London and whose essays he read in Leigh Hunt's liberal journals. Keats admired Hazlitt's sustained radicalism, shared his dislike of egoistic display, and praised his "depth of Taste" (*Letters* 79), but there is also something of Hazlitt in Keats's oft-cited preference for "a Life of Sensations rather than of Thoughts" (*Letters* 68). Most notably, Keats and Hazlitt associate pleasure with cozy spaces, with environments distinguished by smallness instead of grandeur. Consider, for example, the following passage, in which Hazlitt hints that Bentham defines pleasure not only too abstractly but also, quite literally, too broadly:

> Could our imagination take wing (with our speculative faculties) to the other side of the globe or to the ends of the universe, could our

eyes behold whatever our reason teaches us to be possible, could our
hands reach as far as our thoughts and wishes, we might busy ourselves
to advantage with the Hottentots, or hold intimate converse with the
inhabitants of the Moon; but being as we are, our feelings evaporate in
so large a space—we must draw the circle of our affections and duties
somewhat closer—the heart hovers and fixes nearer home. (15)

In Hazlitt's view, breadth is the enemy of pleasure, or gratified "feelings," and Keats echoes that sentiment in poem after poem celebrating
the Spenserian bower in its various guises: the glade in "Calidore,"
the garden in "Ode to a Nightingale," the island in "An Imitation of
Spenser," the bedchamber in *The Eve of St. Agnes*. However, rather
than abandon largeness altogether, Keats repeatedly describes its involution. His spaces, always drawn close in accordance with Hazlitt's
"circle," generally hold "globe"-scaled stores of sense-gratifying stimuli and thereby foster a brand of pleasure not only more material
than Bentham's "good" but also more intense than Hazlitt's "satisfaction," or what he called in a key essay "gusto." Keats's spaces valo-
rize something closer to Hazlitt's "gusto," but, as I will show, Keats
distinguishes his ideal of pleasure with even subtler distinctions.

In his essay "On Gusto," Hazlitt glosses his titular subject as the
"power or passion defining any object" (597), and although that
description suggests a quality akin to intensity, Hazlitt's gusto is fundamentally neat, an ally of "precis[ion]" (597) and "appropriate character" (598). Hazlitt writes that "gusto consists in giving...truth of
character from the truth of feeling...in the highest degree of which
the subject is capable" (597). Gusto is not largeness involuted, magnificence compressed; rather, it is a decorous union of size and sensation,
a pleasure that maximizes capability without straining it. Titian's ren-
derings of human flesh, for instance, are "like flesh, and like nothing
else" (598). Shakespeare wants gusto in his failure to make the most
of his faculties—"He never insists on anything as much as he might"
(599)—while Milton, a poet "of great gusto," pushes his creativity
to (but not beyond) its limits, a quality that Hazlitt depicts with calculated, arithmetic language: "He repeats each blow twice, grapples
with and exhausts his subject" (599). Even when Hazlitt's meditation
seems to laud disproportion, it subtly honors decorum. The "gusto
of Michelangelo," he explains, "consists in expressing energy of will
without proportionate sensibility," while Correggio's consists "in
expressing exquisite sensibility without energy of will." The ostensibly imbalanced quality of each artist's work is, however, appropriate
to his chosen "style": Michelangelo's is "hard and masculine," "the

reverse of Correggio's, which is effeminate" (598). Their gusto, as in the cases of Titian and Milton, derives, perhaps counterintuitively, from aptness and an almost mathematical sense of suitability.

A "delicate subject" (599), Hazlitt's gusto is a tailored relish; but Keats's preference, however indebted to the larger body of Hazlitt's incisive and often sensory criticism, leans toward less neoclassical ratios—toward, in fact, a *tension* between container and contained that originates in the strange involution described above. That indecorous relationship is the cornerstone of Keatsian pleasure, an experience most concisely described as material sublimity and best illustrated in *Lamia*, the opening act of the volume that eventually made Keats's name. To assert as much may seem strange, given *Lamia*'s classical setting and Drydenian cadences. In his tellingly titled "The Decorum of *Lamia*," O. B. Hardison, Jr., rejects other critics' sense of the poem's neoclassical quality: "the couplet in *Lamia* is distinctly secondary to the verse sentence or paragraph, and...where Keats typically describes by qualitative adjective, Dryden describes through action" (34). However, he still champions the poem as an extraordinary exercise in decorum, which he defines "in terms of the adaptation of the part...to the whole" (37): "In his early work, at every point, [Keats] sacrifices larger unity for the sake of local and spectacular effect. Gradually, this tendency is brought under control, until, in the *Odes* and *Lamia*, the poetry has the kind of ultimate decorum which we most commonly associate with Horace and Virgil" (33). Like readers both before and after him, Hardison acknowledges that Keats relies heavily upon "sense-appeal" and "accretion" (35)—what Jeffrey Robinson has recently described as the "paratactic syntax" of fancy (13)—but he ultimately finds the poem roomy enough to accommodate such profusion decently, without distension. I have observed, in contrast, that the poem not only relies on images of astonishing fullness, but that it also finds Keats pondering pleasure's *own* reliance upon spatial limitation. Pleasure in an age of talkers (be they Benthamite philosophers, Wordsworthian poets, or Apollonian sophists) is threatened by sensation-dismissing abstractionism and the revaluation of spatial proportion that necessarily accompanies the veneration of the intellect. As Hazlitt puts it, abstract thinkers are diminished bodies that inhabit stunningly "large" spaces, but an age of talkers can generate, even in its ostensible opponents (in, that is, critics like Hazlitt), a suspicion of the inverse: massive materiality packed indecorously inside an intimately delimited "circle." Hazlitt prefers pulses to proofs, so long as the measured movement of the latter characterizes the rhythm of the former. There is always room for another *idea*; although the term "gusto" may conjure images of bulging blood vessels, Hazlitt's gusto manifests in an unstrained pleasure that speaks to the insidious influence of his contemporaries' abstract vision. In *Lamia*, Keats embraces materio-sensory engorgement as the purest, if most difficult to sustain, experience of pleasure.

To distinguish Keats as a poet of distension is, at least initially, to question the attitudes toward space and materiality that prevailed in the decades preceding and constituting the Romantic era. As Rachel Crawford observes in *Poetry, Enclosure, and the Vernacular Landscape, 1700–1830*, an expansionist ideology dominates the best-known political, philosophical, and aesthetic treatises of the eighteenth century and, as a result, eighteenth-century studies in our own time. In the period bookended by the Act of Union with Scotland (1707) and the French Revolution, England saw a dramatic increase in everything, Crawford notes, from export revenues and military expenditures to the scale of farms and civic buildings:

> Containment is not the first thing to come to mind when reading histories of Great Britain's eighteenth century.... During this entire century trade, liberty, and empire apotheosized the increasing reach of Britain's arm and fabricated an image of a small nation defined on all sides by the sea which formed a vital core of centrifugal power, a vigorous heart pumping lifeblood outward into the extremities of a Britannizable world. Even during times of foreign threat that produced sentiments of strident isolationism, expansion remained the key discourse. (3–4)

Indeed, students and scholars of late eighteenth- and early nineteenth-century British literature internalize a narrative that foregrounds not only big ideas—revolution, sublimity, and epic ambition, to name only a few—but also grand spaces: soaring skies, vast oceans, deep chasms, towering mountains, and, of course, imperial landscapes. Romantic artists prefer getting high to getting close; when Wordsworth and Coleridge occupy scanty plots and lime-tree bowers, it seems that they do so only briefly and/or for a lack of more expansive alternatives. In "Frost at Midnight," for instance, Coleridge's speaker feels "vex[ed]" (9) and smothered by the quiet intimacy of his "cottage" (4), and, for the infant "cradled by [his] side," he wishes a life defined by infinite space, not domestic comfort:

> But *thou*, my babe, shalt wander like a breeze
> By lakes and sandy shores, beneath the crags
> Of ancient mountain, and beneath the clouds

Which image in their bulk both lakes and shores
And mountain crags. (59–63)

If there is something disconcerting about Coleridge's prophecy—the terrain that he envisions is neither child-scaled nor "babe"-proofed— there is also something quintessentially Romantic about its sprawling vastness, about the way in which the sky reproduces, *ad infinitum*, the landscape's most dramatic features.

Crawford goes on, however, to explain that England's expansionist discourse was countered at the end of the eighteenth century by a significant, if more quietly conducted, revaluation of enclosure. "Contained, vernacular spaces such as town and kitchen gardens, which did not assist in the conceptualization of England's national agenda, were part of a more muted conversation conducted among a thriftier audience," Crawford asserts, adding that such "spaces form a bedrock that was jolted to the surface by a seismic shift in public perception that took place during the final quarter of the century" (4–5). Despite its affiliation with military prowess and economic strength, living large became, in some contexts, associated with waste and insecurity, while "contained spaces geared toward productivity, usually...of smaller dimension, took hold of the English imagination." According to Crawford, more intimate venues "began to receive the attention of the architects of space: building designers, gardeners and agriculturalists, even poets" (5). The sublime, in other words, began to give way to the picturesque, and coincident with this new regard for circumscription and detail (as opposed to large-scale drama) was the rediscovery of short lyric, "which reemerged after a century of neglect in dizzying numbers as a vernacular form in magazines, correspondence, and parlor games" (ibid.). Their epic projects forestalled, the major figures of British Romanticism made their names primarily with ballads, sonnets, and other brief poems, many of which integrated sublime themes with images of rural intimacy. In a way, Crawford contends, the picturesque is "an aesthetic category that in actuality extends and democratizes the judgment of the sublime by making it available to an ordinary audience of limited means and circumscribed prospects" (67). The former designation, in other words, signifies an enclosed, condensed version of the latter's pleasures: a portable Snowdon, a bite-sized Xanadu, *un petit* Mont Blanc.

My use of the term "pleasures," a word that connotes sensorily registered delight, both fails to convey and is at odds with the intellectual foundations of sublime experience, however. In that it strives to evoke not only the painter's eye but also a sense of its subject's proximity, picturesque art derives from an awareness of bodies, particularly their capacity to appreciate (in the word's dual senses of "recognize" and "enjoy") what Nicola Trott identifies as material "variety or novelty" (75). The sublime, in contrast, engages the mind; although nineteenth-century tourists came to associate sublimity with certain large-scale real-world sites, the British Romantics themselves, Trott observes, foreground the intellectual responses that those sites engender—"grandeur of thought or conception, together with vehemence or intensity of passion" (78)—at the expense of their expansive, craggy materiality. Sensual pleasure is not part of the equation. As Burke describes it in his *Philosophical Enquiry*, sublime experience not only hinges on the observer's sense of fear but systematically transmutes visible, tactile objects into concepts. As Trott explains, "[I]t is the 'idea' of the thing—or the 'idea of terror' attached to it—which produces the sublimity. So, although the *Enquiry* does indeed find certain objects 'sublime,' it is strictly speaking only the *ideas* of those objects that have this quality" (82; emphasis in original). To regard the picturesque as boxed sublimity is, then, to intellectualize an inherently sensory concept. Indeed, despite Crawford's emphasis on the "productivity" of contained gardens, her analysis privileges the abstract qualities associated with the small spaces that came to the fore around the time of the English Regency. As a result of its affiliation with insight (both creative and religious), the sublime was "[a]n aesthetic imbued with utilitarian and moral objectives," while picturesque plots, Crawford writes, came to represent similar values on a smaller scale: "[T]he intervention of utility in the aesthetics of space made possible the democratization of sublimity and associated it with domestic ideals of hearth, home, and industry" (68, 69).

   If certain poets and landscape artists worked to associate picturesque spaces with sublime ideology, did others work toward the converse, a sublime *materiality* bound by picturesque constraints? In a verse epistle, Keats posits a "material sublime" and thereby distinguishes himself from his poetic forebears and contemporaries:

> O that our dreamings all of sleep or wake
> Would all their colours from the sunset take:
> From something of material sublime,
> Rather than shadow our own Soul's daytime
> In the dark void of Night. (67–71)

W. Jackson Bate asserts that Keats's lines purposely echo "Tintern Abbey" (308), but Wordsworth's "sense sublime," though ostensibly inspired by expansive sensory experience, both begins and ends as intellection:

> And I have felt
> A presence that disturbs me with the joy
> Of *elevated thoughts*, a sense sublime
> Of something far more deeply interfused,
> Whose dwelling is the light of setting suns,
> And the round ocean, and the living air,
> And the blue sky, and *in the mind of man*—.
>   (94–100, emphasis added)

Although the term "pleasure" appears five times in "Tintern Abbey," Wordsworth consistently modifies it—"unremembered pleasure" (31), "the sense/ Of present pleasure" (62–3), "former pleasures" (118), and "sober pleasure" (139)—in ways that abstract or etherealize the experience that the word traditionally denotes. The only exception comes, of course, in his reference to the "coarser pleasures of [his] boyish days" (73), those "charm"-less (81) gratifications that thankfully give way to the "still, sad music of humanity" (91). Keats's verse epistle, in contrast, describes a different delight, a more material (if, by Wordsworthian standards, coarser) pleasure. The poet's night-time visions prove plenty cerebral—a little *too* Soul-full, even—and he longs for dreams drenched in the sun's rich color, not steeped in "elevated thoughts" that only metaphorically represent the sun's height and grandeur. "[T]o philosophize," Keats continues, "I dare not yet!—Oh never will the prize,/ High reason, and the lore of good and ill/ Be my award" (73–6). After declining the role of "philosophizer," that uneasy union of deep thinker and rapacious talker, he praises material reality: "Things cannot to the will/ Be settled, but they tease us out of thought" (76–7). Keats's use of the word "sublime" stems from its affective links to excess and extremity, but his wish is for *sensory* surfeit, not the grand immateriality of night's "dark void."

By the early months of 1818, Keats had rejected Wordsworthian "joy," but he proved no less critical of Hunt's tendency to cloy. He summarily dismisses both poets in a February letter—"I will have no more of Wordsworth or Hunt in particular" (*Letters* 96)—and despite the fact that his literary reputation would remain, in certain respects, tied to Hunt's, Keats's notion of pleasure diverged quickly and profoundly from that of his early mentor. Hunt's poetry, unlike Wordsworth's, is undeniably material, and Tory critics vilified the bourgeois sensibility on display in poems like *The Story of Rimini*, in which Hunt revels in object-dominated settings, including, among others, Francesca's well-appointed room at Giovanni's palace:

> The very books and all transported there,
> The leafy tapestry, and the crimson chair,
> The lute, the glass that told the shedding hours,
> The little urn of silver for the flowers,
> The frame for broidering, with a piece half done. (Hunt III, 153–7)

Keats's early sonnet on *Rimini* characterizes Hunt's poem as a textual "bower" (12), but what he must have realized soon after is that Hunt shares with Wordsworth a taste for unboundedness, which, as Hazlitt suggests, is necessarily abstracting in its relative diminution of the sensory human body. A bower is defined, at least in part, by enclosure, without which its pleasures—be they visual, aural, olfactory, or tactile—would dissipate, rendered less intense (even, perhaps, undetectable) by distance and dilution. Certainly, upon careful inspection, there is something strange about Francesca's chamber: it is a mere simulacrum of comfortable domesticity, a space "[f]urnished, like magic, from her own at home" (Hunt III, 152). In other words, Francesca's personal effects have, to her "surprise" (Hunt III, 149), been transported from her quarters at her father's residence, *dis*embowered, as it were, from a structure that had once afforded genuine delight and real security. In their striking transportability, Francesca's things seem, for practical purposes, to occupy a space too large to be homey, too vast to foster what Hazlitt might call pleasurable "feelings." On what "side of the globe," she may wonder, will she find herself next? More conceptual Wordsworthian "dwelling" than real Spenserian bower, the reconstructed bedchamber cannot repress the "pang" (III, 167) that strikes when Francesca remembers the husband who "had never shared her heart" (III, 170), and, ultimately, Hunt's descriptions in *The Story of Rimini* fall short—or, I might say, go long—of material sublimity. The materiality is present, but the picturesque delimitation is not. Without the constraints imposed by the latter, the former can approach muchness but not too-muchness, plenty but not excess. The procession with which *Rimini* commences is emblematic of the poem's aesthetic. The seemingly interminable parade is marked by distance and diffuseness, not compression and distillation. When, following innumerable trumpeters, heralds, pursuivants, squires, knights, and horses, the royals themselves appear, Hunt promises a "finish of fine sight" (I, 265) but realizes no such terminus. The arrival of what spectators assume is Giovanni's conveyance is likened to "the coming of a shape of light" (I, 266) and accompanied by "reeling air" that "[s]weeps with a giddy whirl around the fair" (I, 279–80). And if such imagery did not in itself evoke an airy, even infinite, spaciousness, the fact that the princely rider turns out to be Paolo, *not* Giovanni, is enough to render the lengthy account more open-ended than "finish"-ed.

When he denounces Wordsworth and Hunt, Keats charges both poets with egotism, or outsized regard for self:

> It may be said that we ought to read our Contemporaries—that Wordsworth &c. should have their due from us. But, for the sake of a few fine imaginative or domestic passages, are we to be bullied into a certain Philosophy engendered in the whims of an Egotist.... I don't mean to deny Wordsworth's grandeur and Hunt's merit, but I mean to say we need not be teazed with grandeur and merit. (*Letters* 96–7).

When Wordsworth and Hunt calculate self-worth, Keats intimates, they recall the unbounded magnificence of their verse worlds— "round ocean[s]," "shape[s] of light"—and, as a result, reckon themselves literary divinities, creators on the scale of their creations. To reject Wordsworth's and Hunt's pretensions is, then, to call into question the relationship between divinity and pleasure, and in *Lamia*, Keats turns the tables on his "Contemporaries," narrating no mortal pursuit of conventional sublimity but rather a demigoddess's quest for *material* sublimity. Godhead is perhaps best defined as the absence of limits; to be divine is to possess immortality, omnipotence, and others' unconditional devotion, and, as *Lamia* opens, Keats introduces a supernatural universe striking in its lack of restriction, both physical and philosophical. The nymph "to whom *all* hoofèd Satyrs knelt" (I, 14; emphasis added) is, quite simply, to everybody's taste. Moreover, by rendering her invisible, Lamia has, for practical purposes, positioned the nymph less "somewhere" (I, 13) or "nowhere" (I, 31) than everywhere, as the luxurious gifts that litter the shores, springs, meads, vales, and woods of Crete attest. Possessed of an abstract "sweet"-ness (I, 31), a palpable sensuality, and, presumably, a certain *je ne sais quoi* that makes her worth the trouble, the nymph promises a sublime range of pleasures. In exchange for Lamia's assistance—indeed, in this spacious world, even loyalty is only as restrictive as it is convenient—Hermes casually offers "whatever bliss thou canst devise" (I, 85).

However, a world of limitless bliss is not without its perils. In the same introductory lines that ostensibly celebrate the time "before the faery broods/ Drove Nymph and Satyr from the prosperous woods" (1–2), Keats questions the pleasure of limitlessness—and, as a result, the value of limitless pleasure. Lamia explains that the "woe" brought about by an endless parade of would-be lovers has rendered the nymph's "immortality" "[p]ale" (I, 104–5) and Hermes himself is "ever-smitten" (I, 7), a figure dedicated to the pursuit of erotic pleasure rather than the experience thereof. Unlike the stationary figures on Keats's Grecian urn, Hermes can move at will, but his unfettered agency seems almost to cripple his capacity to recognize, let alone feel, sensory delight. "Real are the dreams of Gods," Keats writes, "and smoothly pass their pleasures in a long immortal dream" (I, 127–8); these famous lines would describe an enviable state of existence if not for the elegiac connotations of "pass," a term that, in combination with "smoothly," suggests that divinity inhibits the absorption of joy, "whatever" the "bliss." As Neil Fraistat puts it, Hermes is "always desiring and always fulfilling desire, never and ever satiated" (103), and the union of nymph with god is characterized as sacrifice, not consummation. When, like a flower to a bee, the nymph "[gives] up her honey" (I, 143), the pair simply disappears.

As Hermes and his object fade from the poem, Keats ironically asserts that they do not grow "pale, as mortal lovers do" (I, 145). The divine couple, free but clear (as in "transparent"), never rematerializes, while Lamia, constrained in nearly every sense, debuts and remains the very antithesis of pallor. She is, in other words, colorful in the most literal sense of that term: tint-saturated, color-*full*. From the outset, Lamia describes her body as a "wreathèd tomb" (I, 38), and when Hermes stumbles upon her "cirque-couchant" (I, 46), she strikes a compact silhouette that nonetheless "palpitat[es]" (I, 45) with sense-seducing shades, with a barely contained aesthetic energy. "She was a gordian shape of dazzling hue," Keats writes,

> Vermilion-spotted, golden, green, and blue;
> Striped like a zebra, freckled like a pard,
> Eyed like a peacock, and all crimson barr'd;
> And full of silver moons, that, as she breathed,
> Dissolved, or brighter shone, or interwreathed
> Their lustres with gloomier tapestries—
> So rainbow-sided, touch'd with miseries,

> She seem'd at once, some penanced lady elf,
> Some demon's mistress, or the demon's self. (I, 47–56)

If Hermes's nymph—of limitless interest and, essentially, bound-less body—signifies enormous pleasure, she does so proportionately, decorously. The spaces with which the poet associates the nymph seem scaled to accommodate the delight that Hermes anticipates, and despite the presence of "a world of love…at her feet" (I, 21), Keats's descriptions of the poem's first romance remain unhurried and uncluttered. The initial setting, in sum, evokes the airy sublimity of the quintessential Wordsworthian vista, and when clever Lamia recounts her "splendid dream" of "Fair Hermes," she flatteringly portrays the god as a beam of light, "severing the clouds, as morning breaks" (I, 68–9, 77). In contrast, Lamia herself emerges as a literal tangle of tones and textures, a figure who lacks not only Hermes's wide-open prospects—no "Phoebean dart" (I, 78), she lies on the ground—but also a neoclassical disposition toward balance. Lamia's "gordian shape," like the nymph's "loveliness" (I, 108), hints at an affiliation with a broad spectrum of pleasurable experiences (includ-ing the titillation of the exotic and the heft of the costly), but Keats's language simultaneously suggests something like engorgement or distension. The sensory delights represented in and on Lamia's body threaten almost to destroy it; she "seem'd" so much "at once" (I, 55) that the very integrity of her person—the "fit"-ness of her form "for life" (I, 39)—is *almost* compromised. Lamia's body is not balanced, proportionate, or decorous; in her inability to evoke the "living air" of the open Wordsworthian prospect or the "reeling air" of the rau-cous Huntian procession, Lamia embodies the congestion intrinsic to Keats's material sublime. Her "very breath," Fraistat observes, possesses magical "potency" (104). In Keats's exceptional heroine appears the involution of Coleridge's "Frost at Midnight" vision: no babe toddling through enormity, Lamia is enormity compressed into a babe-sized package.

However, although Lamia longs to abandon her "serpent pris-on-house" (I, 203), the reality for which she pines is, strangely, as limiting and delimited as the one she presently inhabits. In lieu of godhead, Lamia requests constraint. When offered "whatever bliss [she] canst devise," Lamia opts for narrowness and striking specific-ity: "'O the bliss!/ Give me my woman's form, and place me where he is'" (I, 119–20). "He," of course, is Lycius, and the "where" is the outskirts of Corinth. Still, despite the banal particularity—a mortal body, a dirty city—of the boon that she requests, Lamia refuses to sacrifice her signature excess. Denise Gigante observes that in the wake of physiologist John Hunter's theory regarding the "possibility of a supervenient vital principle" (433), this excess would have defined her as a monster. "The aesthetic definition of monstrosity changed significantly during this period," Gigante explains, "from an Enlightenment concept of defect or deformity to a Romantic notion of monstrosity as too much life…. Such monstrosity does not remain at the level of theory but becomes the motivation for a new kind of monster in the literature of the Romantic period, one whose life force is too big for the matter containing it" (434). The disproportion that Gigante describes in that last clause might sound like material sublimity, but Keats associates small spaces (especially those dense with sensory energy, kinetic or potential) with pleasure, *not* with danger or atrocity. When Lamia first addresses Lycius, she identifies herself as a creature of "many senses" (I, 284) and "a hundred thirsts" (I, 285), and, though she seems cruel indeed when she taunts her beloved with his presumed inability to satisfy her sensory desires, Keats's readers understand that her words are meant as bait, that Lamia has chosen the smallness that Lycius represents. This is no chance encounter, and Lycius's mortal limitations seem to enhance, rather than encumber, the couple's experience of pleasure. Earth-bound Lycius seems an unlikely erotic hero, but his initial encounter with Lamia is characterized by none of the lukewarm "bland"-ness (I, 141) that distinguishes the union of Hermes and his nymph. Rather, Lycius experiences a jolt of pleasure far larger—that is, richer, broader, and more enduring— than his body and, therefore, more *potent* than anything associated with immortality. Lamia's words are "so delicious," "[i]t seem'd he had loved them a whole summer long" (I, 249–50), and her beauty, Keats notes, seems bottomless, unending: "And soon his eyes had drunk her beauty up,/ Leaving no drop in the bewildering cup,/ And still the cup was full" (I, 251–3). Were Lycius a god and therefore blessed with an existence defined by infinity and perpetuity, the pleasure afforded by Lamia's magnificence would have recalled the proverbial raindrop in the ocean, not the tsunami imaged here.

For Gigante, when Lamia "overruns 'the bewildering cup' of her beautiful form in an abundance that Lycius can never fully consume, she becomes a devouring presence who inverts the rules of aesthetic contemplation" (444). Yet while Lamia's union with Lycius inverts decorum, her wish is not so much to consume her lover as to be consumed by him—by, that is, the narrowness and restriction that he embodies. Her desire, in other words, is to secure herself within Lycius's delimited world, to "unperplex bliss from its neighbor pain" by "[d]efin[ing] their pettish limits" and "[e]strang[ing] their points of contact" (I, 192–4). To that end, Lamia engineers a love nest that boasts a remarkable solidity in addition to the protective invisibility with which she had once provided Hermes's nymph. The space is impossible to see—even "the most curious/ Were foil'd, who watched to trace [the mute Persian servants] to their house" (I, 392–3)— despite its dramatic materiality:

> While yet he spake they had arrived before
> A pillar'd porch, with lofty portal door,
> Where hung a silver lamp, whose phosphor glow
> Reflected in the slabbèd steps below,
> Mild as a star in water; for so new
> And so unsullied was the marble hue,
> So through the crystal polish, liquid fine,
> Ran the dark veins, that none but feet divine
> Could e'er have touch'd there. Sounds Aeolian
> Breathed from the hinges, as the ample span
> Of the wide doors disclosed a place unknown
> Some time to any, but those two alone. (I, 378–97)

The rich stuff that constitutes the enclosure—precious metals, expensive stones, fine finishes—goes a long way toward fulfilling the promise of sensory pleasure inscribed in and on Lamia's spectacular body. Her body itself makes up the difference. Notwithstanding the staid classicism of its architecture—the "calm'd twilight of [its] Platonic shades" (I, 236)—the place pulsates with a scarcely controlled erotic energy, with a dynamic sensuality best signified by the "couch" made "sweet" with "use" (II, 18, 23). Sensory distension seems inevitable, but Lamia's charms maintain the integrity of the nest, the "complete"-ness (II, 12) of the arrangement, in spite of Love's "jealous" "buzz" above "the lintel of their chamber door" (II, 12–14).

In fact, Lycius, not Lamia, initiates the devouring, the cannibalistic consumption that culminates in the narrative's dramatic finale. When the sharp sounds of distant Corinth's trumpets make Lycius "start" (II, 28), they simultaneously puncture the bubble of pleasure that Lamia has so carefully inflated, and Keats's account of the events that follow seems to rely more heavily on simple laws of physics than complex theories of biological organization. When Lycius twitches, Lamia's "purple-linèd palace of sweet sin" (II, 31) sustains something like a tear; the magic bubble does not pop, but it does begin to leak. The pressure exerted by its pleasure-filled interior against its own pierced walls sets in motion a process of equilibration, a drive toward balance that, though decorous, is dangerous:

> Lycius started—the sounds fled,
> But left a thought, a buzzing in his head.
> For the first time, since first he harbour'd in
> That purple-linèd palace of sweet sin,
> His spirit pass'd beyond its golden bourn
> Into the noisy world almost forsworn. (II, 28–33)

The buzz, previously confined to "the lintel of their chamber door," has infiltrated the citadel, and Keats's language—Lycius's "spirit pass'd"—not only echoes the Part I adage regarding "the dreams of Gods" but also mimics the hiss of seepage, the sound of leaching pleasure. Lamia, who sees that her lover has "mused beyond her" (II, 38), understands that "a moment's thought is passion's passing bell" (II, 39). Yet, when she tearfully describes herself as "house-less" (II, 45)—that is, unsheltered, uncontained—Lycius is quick to characterize his love as protective:

> "My silver planet, both of eve and morn!
> Why will you plead yourself so sad forlorn,
> While I am striving how to fill my heart
> With deeper crimson and a double smart?
> How to entangle, trammel up, and snare
> Your soul in mine, and labyrinth you there,
> Like the hid scent in an unbudded rose?" (II, 48–54)

Unfortunately, as Lycius's initial celestial metaphor suggests, grandeur, not intimacy, now dominates his desires, and his turn toward the sublimity of galactic space precedes a return to cool intellection: "My thoughts! shall I unveil them?" (II, 56). Rather than luxuriate in the dense pleasure that Lamia affords, philosophizer Lycius opts for the prospect of an abstract joy: a sense of pride invigorated by others' articulations of envy. Despite having stated an intention to "laby-rinth" his love, his choice requires that he exhibit her:

> Listen then.
> What mortal hath a prize, that other men
> May be confounded and abash'd withal,
> But lets it sometimes pace abroad majestical,
> And triumph, as in thee I should rejoice
> Amid the hoarse alarms of Corinth's voice.

> Let my foes choke, and my friends shout afar,
> While through the thronglèd streets your bridal car
> Wheels round its dazzling spokes. (II, 56–64)

Lycius's "passion" has "cruel grown" (II, 75), and rather than encircle Lamia in arms and walls that strain to hold her splendor, he chooses to expose her to hungry Corinthian eyes. "[S]ubdued" (II, 82), Lamia consents to the public wedding but makes one final attempt to patch and reinflate the pleasure dome that Lycius pricked. In a last-ditch effort to defuse her lover's damaging philosophic mind and to protect herself from the wideness of Corinth, Lamia makes another run at material sublimity, strategically selecting wedding decorations that downscale the "glowing banquet-room" of "wide-archèd grace" (II, 121) into a full-foliaged leafy "glade" (II, 125). "In pale contented sort of discontent," Keats writes, she stuffs the space, "mission[ing] her viewless servants to enrich/ The fretted splendour of each nook and niche" (II, 135–7). Lamia's makeshift bower boasts dense walls—

> Between the tree-stems, marbled plain at first,
> Came jasper panels; then anon, there burst
> Forth creeping imagery of slighter trees,
> And with the larger wove in small intricacies (II, 138–41)

—but the sense-treating things that fill the hall's newly intimate interior actually materialize in multiples:

> Of wealthy lustre was the banquet-room,
> Filled with pervading brilliance and perfume:
> Before each lucid panel fuming stood
> A censer fed with myrrh and spiced wood,
> Each by a sacred tripod held aloft,
> Whose slender feet wide-swerved upon the soft
> Wool-woofèd carpets; fifty wreaths of smoke
> From fifty censers their light voyage took
> To the high roof, still mimicked as they rose
> Along the mirrored walls by twin-clouds odorous.
> Twelve spherèd tables, by silk seats enspherèd,
> High as the level of a man's breast reared
> On libbard's paws, upheld the heavy gold
> Of cups and goblets, and the store thrice told
> Of Ceres' horn, and, in huge vessels, wine
> Come from the gloomy tun with merry shine.

> Thus loaded with a feast the tables stood,
> Each shrining in the midst the image of a God. (II, 173–90)

Less pious gesture than metonymic representation of Lamia's larger preoccupation, the presence of the carved deities is significant. Engulfed in a sea of sensual delights that includes perfumes, textiles, and wines, the idols "in the midst" seem reduced to mere accessories, and as a result, the limitlessness that characterizes godhead seems curiously if impossibly hemmed in. Despite Keats's "shrining," the tables are not altars but are, rather, heaped feast boards, and the pleasures that they proffer are the real object of worship. The party seems consciously bacchanalian, but there Lamia's theology enacts an interesting reversal: as Bacchus approaches "meridian height" (II, 213), the earth-bound revelers, rather than experience airy transcendence, increasingly resemble the colorful, multi-"eyed" serpent whom Hermes discovered "cirque-couchant" in the grass at the beginning of the romance: "Flush'd were their cheeks, and bright eyes double bright" (II, 214).

Keats's cornucopian vision derives its strength from a proportional mismatch, a decorum-defying amalgam of material plenty and spatial constraint. Alexander Pope's portrayals of sensory wealth in *The Rape of the Lock* afford enlightening comparison: although Belinda's boudoir table holds a vast array of cosmetics and accessories— "Unnumber'd treasures ope at once, and here/ The various off'rings of the world appear" (I, 129–30)—it never bows beneath its load; Belinda's toilet remains impeccably, incomprehensibly organized, neither untidy nor prohibitively small. Pope notes that every "silver Vase" stands "in mystic order" (I, 122), while "glitt'ring spoil[s]" (I, 132) reside in discrete, roomy boxes or lie in easy harmony on the table's spacious, uncluttered surface:

> This casket *India*'s glowing gems unlocks
> And all *Arabia* breathes from yonder box.
> The Tortoise here and Elephant unite,
> Transform'd to Combs, the speckled, and the white.
> Here files of Pins extend their shining rows,
> Puffs, Powders, Patches, Bibles, Billet-doux. (I, 133–8)

Pope's party scene is characterized by similarly ordered luxury—"For lo! the board with cups and spoons is crown'd,/ The berries cackle, and the mill turns round:/ On shining Altars of *Japan* they raise/ The silver lamp; the fiery spirits blaze" (III, 105–8)—but the material splendor of Keats's wedding banquet is, like Lamia herself, barely containable, an opulent jumble that, in generating a labyrinth of piles and puddles in the banquet hall, fashions a rich cocoon for bride, groom, and guests. Initially, visitors "themselves in order placed/ Around the silken couches" (II, 196–7), but, as "God Bacchus" ascends (III, 213), Popeian "mystic order" gives way to bloated chaos. "Louder come the strains/ Of powerful instruments," and, as the poet's syntax becomes as involuted as his setting, those "instruments" seem less certainly musical; consequently, the term "strains" seems succinctly to evoke a now familiar, if still indecorous, tension between container and contained. The colon and subsequent catalogue in the following passage may indicate that Keats's term "instruments" designates Lamia's "powerful" tools of seduction, those potent pleasures that flush cheeks, brighten eyes, and generally swell the feast space:

> Louder they talk, and louder come the strains
> Of powerful instruments:—the gorgeous dyes,
> The space, the splendour of the draperies,
> That roof of awful richness, nectarous cheer,
> Beautiful slaves, and Lamia's self, appear. (II, 204–8)

Thanks to the "instruments," pleasure suffuses the banquet, and vessels of every conceivable sort brim, as the following passage suggests, with every conceivable delight:

> Garlands of *every* green, and *every* scent
> From vales deflowered, or forest-trees branch-rent,
> In baskets of bright osiered gold were brought
> High as the handles heaped, to suit the thought
> Of *every* guest—that each, as he did please,
> Might fancy-fit his brows, silk-pillowed at his ease.
>   (II, 215–20; emphasis added)

There is nothing neoclassic, Wordsworthian, or even Huntian about this arresting imagery. When Keats combines profuse materio-sensory pleasure with space more intimately scaled and more explicitly circumscribed than his verse epistle's gaping black sky, the result is a hybrid category that unites elements of the picturesque and the sublime, an aesthetic of distension that marries the physicality and constraint connoted by the former term to the magnitude affiliated with the latter.

Keats's most famous critique of Newtonian science appears in *Lamia* and characterizes "cold philosophy" as a knife, a blade that can "clip an

Angel's wings" and rip—that is, "[u]nweave"—the rainbow's "woof" (II, 230, 234, 237). Old Apollonius, Lycius's sophist "instructor" (I, 376) and the poem's anti-Lamia, possesses "sharp eyes" (I, 364) that, at the narrative's conclusion, slit Lamia's second delight-full bubble. This time, though, rather than leak slowly, the stretched space leaches dramatically. The "stately music no more breathes," Keats writes, and the "myrtle sicken'd in a thousand wreaths./ By faint degrees, voice, lute, and pleasure ceased" (II, 263–5). Within moments, an outsized nothingness has permeated the hall—"A deadly silence step by step increased/ Until it seem'd a horrid presence there" (II, 266–7)—and, in a matter of lines, "all was blight" (II, 275). Lamia, Keats's original incarnation of material sublimity, has likewise been drained of sensory energy: "no longer fair," she simply sits, for the first time, "a deadly white" (II, 276). When, at last, "the sophist's eye,/ Like a sharp spear went through her utterly,/ Keen, cruel, perceant, stinging" (II, 299–301), Lamia evaporates and the result is a deadly vacuum, a life-sucking void. "With a frightful scream she vanishèd," Keats writes, and "Lycius' arms were empty of delight,/ As were his limbs of life, from that same night" (II, 306–8). The sudden disappearance associated earlier in the poem with the joys of pale divinity is recast as the death it really is, and following the equilibration of interior and exterior pressures—the tragic reversal not of fortune but of involution—the couch, once "sweet" with "use," becomes Lycius's bier.

I use the word "tragic" advisedly here, since *Lamia* is often read as generically unstable, as combining elements of both tragedy and comedy. For Stuart Sperry, *Lamia* "is permeated by a sense of comic fatality" (292), and elements of comedy certainly inhere in an aesthetic defined by mismatch, in a narrative driven by its heroine's indecorous desire to cultivate gargantuan sensations in tiny pastures. Readers through the decades have observed that the narrators of *Lamia*, *Isabella*, and *The Eve of St. Agnes* (the three romances from which Keats's watershed 1820 volume derives its title) share a dark sense of humor; to suggest that Lamia's story is a series of bulges, tears, and attempted repairs is, perhaps, to highlight potentially comic elements. In other contexts, however, disproportion—its tension-infused possibility, its remarkable unsustainability—can evoke tragedy. Hazlitt's "age of talkers" critique introduces his sketch of Coleridge, a writer whose career, Hazlitt suggests, was sadly, even tragically, stymied by a sense of imbalance:

> Mr. Coleridge is too rich in intellectual wealth, to need to task himself to any drudgery: he has only to draw the sliders of his imagination, and a thousand objects expand before him, startling him with their

brilliancy.... What is it he could add to the stock, compared to the countless stores that lie about him, that he should stoop to pick up a name, or polish an idle fancy? (40)

By Hazlitt's account, Coleridge seems Lamian, a figure of "rich"-ness, "brilliancy," and coiled potential. Unlike Lamia, however, Coleridge finds himself consumed by his own excess, intimidated, perhaps, by the dimensional disparity between his divine "wealth" and his mortal person. The result, Hazlitt asserts, was impotence: "Persons of the greatest capacity are often those, who for this reason do the least; for surveying themselves from the highest point of view, amidst the infinite variety of the universe, their own share in it seems trifling, and scarce worth a thought" (*Spirit* 40). Despite a similarly intimidating "capacity," Lamia resists such impotence, and to describe her tale as a quest, however romantic in its improbability, to retain integrity—to preserve, that is, both corporeal and psychic wholeness—is to align the poem more closely with the prototypical trajectory of tragedy than with the themes and structures of comedy. "It was a misfortune to any man of talent to be born in the latter end of the last century" (*Spirit* 40), Hazlitt writes; and if Coleridge was a casualty of an expansive era, Keats, like Lamia, seemed determined not to be. By exchanging "the infinite variety of the universe" for *material* sublimity, Keats redefined Romantic pleasure. *Lamia*, as he describes it, is *touching* in its distension, a poem that "must take hold of people in some way—give them either pleasant or unpleasant sensation." If Hazlitt glossed the spirit of the age, Keats tapped its veins; but both diagnosed the same disease, best described, I think, by Keats himself: in an epoch of epic talkers, people "want...sensation of some sort" (*Letters* 402). Hazlitt recognized a cultural deficiency—that is, a "want" of genuine pleasure—but only Keats, in poems such as *Lamia*, addressed readers' concomitant desire for a "purple-linéd palace" to call, however briefly, home.

WORKS CITED

Bate, W. Jackson. *John Keats*. Cambridge: Harvard UP, 1963. Print.

Coleridge, Samuel Taylor. "Frost at Midnight" (1798). *Romanticism: An Anthology*. 2nd ed. Ed. Duncan Wu. Oxford: Blackwell, 1998. 462–5. Print.

Crawford, Rachel. *Poetry, Enclosure, and the Vernacular Landscape, 1700–1830*. Cambridge: Cambridge UP, 2002. Print.

Fraistat, Neil. *The Poem and the Book: Interpreting Collections of Romantic Poetry*. Chapel Hill: U of North Carolina P, 1985. Print.

Gigante, Denise. "The Monster in the Rainbow: Keats and the Science of Life." *PMLA* 117.3 (2002): 443–8. Print.

Hardison, Jr., O. B. "The Decorum of *Lamia*." *Modern Language Quarterly* 19 (1958): 33–42. Print.

Hazlitt, William. "On Gusto." *Romanticism: An Anthology*. 2nd ed. Ed. Duncan Wu. Oxford: Blackwell, 1998. 597–9. Print.

———. *The Spirit of the Age: Or Contemporary Portraits*. Garden City, NY: Dolphin Books, n.d. Print.

Hunt, Leigh. *The Poetical Works of Leigh Hunt*. Ed. H.S. Milford. 1923. New York: AMS Press, 1978. Print.

Keats, John. *John Keats: The Complete Poems*. 3rd ed. Ed. John Barnard. London: Penguin, 1988. Print.

———. *The Letters of John Keats*. 3rd ed. rev. Ed. Maurice Buxton Forman. London: Oxford UP, 1948. Print.

Pope, Alexander. "The Rape of the Lock: An Heroi-Comical Poem in Five Cantos." *The Poetry and Prose of Alexander Pope*. Ed. Aubrey Williams. Boston: Houghton Mifflin, 1969. 78–100. Print.

Robinson, Jeffrey C. *Unfettering Poetry: The Fancy in British Romanticism*. New York: Palgrave Macmillan, 2006. Print.

Sperry, Stuart. *Keats the Poet*. Princeton, NJ: Princeton UP, 1973. Print.

Trott, Nicola. "The Picturesque, the Beautiful, and the Sublime." *A Companion to Romanticism*. Ed. Duncan Wu. Oxford: Blackwell, 1998. 72–90. Print.

Wordsworth, William. "Lines Written a Few Miles above Tintern Abbey, on Revisiting the Banks of the Wye During a Tour, 13 July 1798." *Romanticism: An Anthology*. 2nd ed. Ed. Duncan Wu. Oxford: Blackwell, 1998. 265–9. Print.

CHAPTER THREE

"WAS IT FOR THIS?": ROMANTIC PSYCHIATRY AND THE ADDICTIVE PLEASURES OF MORAL MANAGEMENT

Joel Faflak

In 1990, Andrew Scull noted the still-prevalent tendency of psychiatric history to stay on the "firm and neutral ground of value-free natural science" ("Psychiatry and Its Historians" 239).[1] More often than not, Scull argued, this scholarship traced psychiatry's moral and ethical path toward curing souls in the name of public good and scientific fact, a progressive development that was in bad faith if one felt that this narrative of well-being was not always well-intentioned.[2] Just because psychiatry emerges in the late eighteenth century with the singular intention of curing madness does not mean that it missed the opportunity to capitalize upon its own invention in other ways. Scull thus points to a tension between psychiatric history and psychiatric historiography, between the apparent facts of psychiatry's invention and the cultural articulation of this reality. My aim in this essay, following the work of scholars like Michelle Faubert who have traced the relationship between psychiatry and literature in poet-psychologists of the early British Romantic period, is to examine psychiatric invention and reinvention in William Wordsworth's early writings for *The Prelude* and *The Recluse*. These texts address the incipient madness of individuals isolated from social consolation as if to grant their depressed states autonomous cognitive and affective dignity. This profound sympathy reflects psychiatry's early utopianism: to speak the otherwise silenced voices of madness.[3] Yet Wordsworth seems equally intent in these texts to mobilize a desire for—and thus to institutionalize the pleasures of—what became known as moral well-being or "management."[4]

The specter of reclusive alienation that haunts this project's idealism manifests an even darker possibility: the social compulsion to make the desire for well-being addictive. Scull notes that the "benevolent face of moral treatment" had a "latent power...for enforcing conformity" ("Psychiatry and Social Control" 154). I want to read this latency as the Janus face of British Romanticism: the dangerous political cathexis that binds the promise of personal and social fulfillment and transformation with the control of an increasingly unwieldy public. As much as it confronts and gives expression to madness, psychiatry in the Romantic period also puts madness to work by linking mental governance to social utility. Put another way, Romantic psychiatry reflects the communal idealism of subjects empowered by their ability to confront the psyche, even at its darkest point—madness as, in Ross Woodman's description, "man's inability to inhabit himself" (2). But psychiatry also makes these same subjects self-reflectively useful citizens, so that the habitation is rather beside the point. The point is not to cure but to stage the spectacle of madness, the cultural *work* of confronting wayward thoughts and feelings, in order to internalize this labor in the name of church or state. This political efficiency worked by addicting individuals to that paramount ideal of democratic capitalism: the right to be happy.[5] But this right produces its own compulsions, turning the enlightened self-examination of feeling into the nearly evangelical imperative to feel *well* and to feel *good*, to not worry and to *be* or *get* happy. Marking the uncanny relationship between happiness and torture, Slavoj Žižek argues that happiness has become our "supreme duty": we are now required to seek and to enjoy pleasure (44).[6] We can see this duty already at work in the texts Wordsworth penned in the traumatic aftereffects of the early 1790s, not least of which because these writings, especially as Wordsworth revised them, came to have a broad-ranging, culturally therapeutic value for later nineteenth-century culture and beyond (one thinks of Mill's *Autobiography* as the model here). In these writings one can trace an emergent psychiatric consciousness, more specifically a concerted effort to orchestrate how this consciousness will manifest itself.

*   *   *

Before turning to Wordsworth in the latter half of this paper, I want first to sketch some of the historio-cultural parameters within which his writings emerge. Increasingly we have come to speak of a Romantic psychiatry that defines the discipline's earliest formation in the late eighteenth and early nineteenth centuries.[7] Apart from the historical, clinical, and professional data that might peg the first psychiatry as Romantic, the label seems right when thinking of Romanticism as what Tilottama Rajan calls a process of "restless self-examination" (25). It seems especially apt when one considers that it was precisely this restlessness that the moral or psychological management of early psychiatry sought to tranquilize, as if the period's psychological vitality was also its pathology. The German medical doctor Johann Christian Reil coined the term "*Psychiaterie*" in 1808, only three years after the British poet and philosopher Samuel Taylor Coleridge coined the word "psycho-analytical" (*Collected Notebooks* 2:2670). That the terms appeared together, nearly a century ahead of Freud, is a synchronistic phenomenon that has yet to receive full attention. Reil's psychiatry was not only medical, empirical, and scientific, but philosophical, metaphysical, and mystical, a heterogeneous and poly-math approach to the psyche often found in Coleridge's work.[8] That Reil's view is not strictly or only scientific seems as arcane now as the bizarre scene of Mesmer's Parisian salon. Modern clinical fields had not yet marked their professional and taxonomic boundaries, how-ever, and while early psychiatry's disciplinary soul arguably required an institutional body, speculative energies sustained this forming anatomy along the way.

A key aspect of this formation is the tension between psychi-atry and psychoanalysis in Romanticism. Whereas psychoanalysis proper emerges with Freud, psychiatry emerges through the socio-historical phenomena of asylum reforms or medical treatises of the late eighteenth and early nineteenth centuries. Yet psychoanalysis does not go missing during that time; the crisis-ridden and hys-terically symptomatic bodies of Gothic literature or forensic fic-tion, which emerge in William Godwin's *Caleb Williams* (1794) and James Hogg's *Memoirs and Confessions of a Justified Sinner* (1823), attest to its presence. Working outside a Freudian appa-ratus, these works *imagine* as well as *analyze* the body's psycho-somatic life. Moreover, they often respect this life's unassimilable and inarticulate nature without demanding that it speak thoughts it otherwise cannot speak and thus conform to a social or symbolic logic alien to it.[9] This Romantic psychoanalysis works in the spirit of Mesmerism, which demonstrates not only that the body has a mind of its own, but more disturbingly that the mind has a body of *its* own, a kind of parapsychological or prosthetic psychic anatomy beyond reason. Mesmer's salon produced unruly psychosomatic responses, a transfer between minds and bodies, not unlike Freud's later attempt to understand transference itself, which evaded the gaze except for its psychosomatic effects and so resisted empirical validation. The object of both excessive curiosity and dangerous politics, Mesmerism evoked the excitement of revolutionary discovery on one hand and the threat of communal frenzy on the other.[10] This crisis of individual bodies within the body politic haunted the rise of dynamic psychiatry throughout the nineteenth century, and came home to roost in Freud's office when, confronting the troubling affects and effects of hypnosis, he moved on to the supposedly more rational talking cure.

The idea of Mesmerism as both productive cause and estranging effect evokes a Romantic psychology torn between a desire to explore the psyche's "dangerous fluidity" (Henderson 9) on its own terms and a desire to externalize the psyche for public access to its social and behavioral actions. The former does not presume to make the darkness of the unconscious visible and so challenges enlightenment; the latter marks and protects the mind's boundaries by diagnosing and curing psychopathology. In short, psychiatry, unlike psychoanalysis, makes psychology useful, the catchword for which was "moral management" in the Romantic period. Moreover, moral management represents precisely the threat that psychoanalysis might have posed. Moral management emerged in the late eighteenth century to signify the shift away from the physical restraint and coercion of inmates at mad asylums toward the psychologically therapeutic treatment of mentally disordered patients. This shift was transnational and cosmopolitan, reflecting a post-Revolutionary Europe galvanized by the spirit of the humane and egalitarian treatment of all individuals. In 1789, Vincenzo Chiarugi was appointed to oversee reform at Bonifacio Hospital in Florence; in 1792, William Tuke opened the Retreat in York for the "moral therapy" of the insane; in the same year, Benjamin Rush led a campaign at Pennsylvania Hospital for the humane treatment of mental patients; and in the following year the French physician Philippe Pinel, upon becoming the supervisor of the Bicêtre asylum, famously unshackled its inmates. Physical restraint did not go out the window in all of these cases. But "in ending the agitations," Roy Porter notes, "the ultimate aim was to calm the mind, and thus render it receptive to the blandishments of sweet reason." Patients "had to be motivated through the manipulation of their passions—their hopes and fears, their sensitivity to pleasure and pain, their desire for esteem and revulsion from shame" (*Social History* 18–19).

What strikes me here is the suggestion that one can or must be "manipulated" to see moral management as pleasurable. Certainly the alleviation of mental anguish and suffering is a noble goal, and one appreciates the post-Enlightenment spirit of advance and altruism that animates this effort. Yet the startling increase in medical preoccupation with madness at the end of the eighteenth century, quite apart from a progressive desire to rehabilitate rather than restrain souls, suggests in turn a social anxiety about the *threat* of madness quite apart from its reality, a fear that the psyche's "dangerous fluidity" might lead to other breakdowns. Madness was very much preying upon the public mind with George III's first bout of madness in 1788, which precipitated the first Regency Crisis and, through successive bouts, eventually the Regency of 1811. The king's madness writ the body politic's nervous condition large at a time when in post-Revolutionary England sociopolitical and economic anxieties were running high. Indeed, from the publication of George Cheyne's *The English Malady* (1733) to Thomas Trotter's *A View of the Nervous Temperament* (1807), one witnesses the emergence of a national—and nationalist—sobriety. Trotter warns against the dissipating effects of a "nervous malady" (a term he borrows from Cheyne) resulting from a society "enervated by luxury and refinement." Trotter writes: "the temperate man is observed to bear sickness with more patience and resignation, than those accustomed to indulgence" (137). Moderation restores bodily vitality to the body politic by managing its habits, which, Trotter claims, "if not restrained soon, must inevitably sap our physical strength of constitution; make us an easy conquest to our invaders; and ultimately convert us into a nation of slaves and ideots [*sic*]" (xi).

But *View* reflects a modernity at once unable and unwilling to overcome its own indulgences, a rationalized world increasingly dependent on its own habits, both good and bad, as survival techniques, a common sense that feeds on its own excessive desire for common or *habitual* sense. Liberating madness at the end of the eighteenth century, ironically, put madness and its specters into rather prominent circulation, creating a different unrestrained desire to seek out and contain madness, the evidence of which comes in the various treatises on not only the observation and definition, but also the treatment of madness, such as John Haslam's 1798 *Observations on Insanity*.[11] The productive face of this traffic in morally managing the

mentally ill—again, quite apart from the reality of madness itself—
was to make well-being contagious. Jeremy Bentham's dictum of the
greatest happiness for the greatest number signaled a more general
post-Enlightenment spirit of individuals' natural right to a better
existence. Adam Smith's earlier Scottish Enlightenment notion of the
sympathetic and unhindered exchange of feeling between citizens
evoked this sense of a necessary felicity, especially when attending to
the suffering of others.

Such notions underpinned the democratic principles that emerged
around 1789, of course. These notions were equally the moral talking
points for Smith's faith in the "invisible hand" of a free-market political economy, which governed the ideals of human interaction defined
by the Scottish Enlightenment and its ideals of a rational, progressive
society. This faith gained ascendancy in the nineteenth century with
politically and economically ideological force. The emergent modernity of a civil society sustained by a productive balance between
commerce and state eventually gave rise in the early decades of the
nineteenth century to a proto-Victorian public sphere increasingly
consumed by a utilitarian desire for a material success and domestic
stability that would secure the myth of progress driving the Industrial
Revolution and the continued building of Empire. As psychological
study and practice became increasingly specialized throughout the
nineteenth century, works such as John Barlow's *On Man's Power
over Himself to Prevent or Control Insanity* (1843), Henry Holland's
Chapters on Mental Physiology (1852), and William Carpenter's
Principles of Mental Physiology (1874) stressed mental hygiene and
the governance of wayward mental processes. Increasingly the idea of
madness as a hereditary disorder took hold all the more compellingly
to urge a social prophylaxis or training in how to avoid the degenera-
tive signs of insanity. Sally Shuttleworth notes "the Victorian preoccupation with the exercise of self-control" (49) in the name of social
and cultural advance.

There are many reasons why British culture needed the myth of
progress to sustain and justify the optimism of its national and international development. As Nigel Leask notes, by 1816 "Britain had
just emerged from the Congress of Vienna laden with the spoils of
a second empire," and needed to get its "crisis-ridden and enervated
national culture" back to national health (213). Such imperial ambition also produced fears about how to manage growth, however. In
the second edition of *An Essay on the Principle of Population*, Thomas
Malthus argues that the "germs of existence contained in this spot
of earth, with ample food, and ample room to expand in, would fill

millions of worlds." Nature curtails social perfectibility because it is too profligate. Luckily, "Necessity, that imperious all pervading law of nature," produces the "great restrictive law" of starvation, death, misery, and vice to insure that the earth can sustain its own growth (15–17). But the idea of an "imperious" nature evokes other specters. In his opium writings, Thomas De Quincey also worries about how "this spot of earth" (England) might "fill millions of worlds" (the globe) when the world's workshop has an instinct for growth that threatens to consume rather than fuel England's expansion.[12] If Malthus treats the world as a dehumanized mass prone to its own biological necessities, De Quincey evokes a protean *polis* beyond the Empire's sobrieties. That is to say, anxieties about global control projected a domestic nervousness that came with the 1790s' rise of a subversive political culture and its subsequent curtailment long into the nineteenth century, evident in the Treason Trials, Gagging Acts, the various suspensions of habeas corpus, Peterloo, the Seditious Meetings, and Six Acts.

John Barrell argues that the period's political imagination, galvanized by the events of 1793–96, fed off the law's protean nature, which evolved through forensics and case precedent and was thus susceptible to ideological manipulation, to create an obsession with and anxiety about the Romantic imagination and its cognates. At this point, Barrell notes,

> aesthetics was anxious to pass the concept [of imagination] over to psychiatry; for when the imagination slipped the lead of the will or judgment, often when "heated" by the overwhelming power of the passions, it became "disordered," and produced elaborate structures of ideas associated on accidental rather than on substantial grounds. (7)

Barrell further notes that the "relation between insanity and the imagination had been a subject of a famous dispute in the late 1750s," but we can see that in Regency psychiatry this relation becomes especially fraught. In *An Essay on the Prevention and Cure of Insanity* (1814), George Nesse Hill fears for the ability of the emerging psychiatric profession not only to diagnose and treat, but also to detect madness, for "even physicians daily habituated to view madness find it occasionally difficult to be clear and satisfactory in their decision." This fact was worrisome when doctors had to testify in criminal and civil trials, especially in the case of a "pretender" to madness "who is endeavouring to mask crime and evade punishment" (393, 392). In such cases, psychiatry itself, already anxious about how to cure a nervous body politic, becomes equally anxious about how to morally manage itself. How to read the Janus face of madness in an increasingly complex and unwieldy public sphere, especially when the line between madness and its potentiality was fine indeed? After all, madness also signified a fierce individuality that was one of the hallmarks of Romantic psychological fulfillment, not to mention political and social entitlement.

If it was "the utopian dream of the founding fathers of Victorian asylumdom that they possessed the untrammelled ability to impose their values and norms on the mad," as Scull argues, they also had the "insidious and worrying capacity to suppress non-conformity in the name of mental health." This suppression meant that "the powers of psychiatry [became] far more modest and circumscribed, and with respect to its larger ambition, fortunately or unfortunately, the profession failed most abjectly." However, both in spite of and because of this failure, "moral management proved highly efficacious as a repressive instrument for controlling large numbers of people" ("Psychiatry and Social Control" 155–6). To put Scull's argument differently: psychiatry succeeded precisely *because* it failed to contain, if not cure, madness. What it produced instead was the *desire* for moral management: psychiatry came to exemplify the habit of wanting to be a better person. On this count, Scull suggests, the Victorians were very creative indeed. But we can find this psychiatric opportunism earlier. Indeed, the word "management" itself invokes the post-Enlightenment notion, via Smith, Malthus, and others, of society as a quantification of individuals, bodies, and feelings within a managed and thus manageable political economy. This effort became very much a project of discovering, naming, interpreting, and thus "economizing" or managing psychological motives, a fact which brings me back to Wordsworth. 1798, of course, was also the year of the publication of *Lyrical Ballads*, to which Wordsworth quickly appended a Preface, as if to rationalize the volume's various degrees of morbid affect. This effort at moral management suggests Wordsworth's own confrontation with psychic waywardness in *The Prelude*, upon which he was working at the time. I turn first to *The Prelude* and then to *The Recluse*, the composition and publishing history of which is now well known. Wordsworth's revisionary practice for both efforts reveals a certain conserving impulse of feeling that speaks directly to the issue of moral management. The larger epic or "public" project that was to be the terminable and definitive shape of *The Recluse*, at least as Wordsworth outlines it in the Preface to his 1814 *The Excursion*, gets displaced by the rather interminable personal psychoanalysis that was only meant to be its prelude. This ongoing battle with wayward thoughts and feelings can be traced to the genesis of *The Recluse* itself.

*   *   *

The earliest, two-part version of *The Prelude*, written October 1798 to February 1799, begins:

> Was it for this
> That one, the fairest of all rivers, loved
> To blend his murmurs with my nurse's song,
> And from his alder shades and rocky falls,
> And from his fords and shallows, sent a voice
> That flowed along my dreams? (1–6)

The opening is traumatic for its sudden emergence, but also because it appears to stage the aftershocks of some unknown trauma. One becomes immediately aware, as in moments of psychic trauma generally, that return is pointless, if not impossible, for one never knows if the event ever happened. The text thus manufactures its own symptom in order to demonstrate its ability to diagnose and alleviate this symptom, so that the poem becomes as much about establishing the terms of its own analytical framework as it is about analyzing the feelings this framework exists to express. All later versions of the poem bury this question at line 269 of Book One, where "this" is preceded by the added Glad Preamble. In this new opening, Wordsworth marks within the solitary pleasures of his imagination a psychic otherness that troubles its otherwise transformational energies. He describes this irritation as the "tempest" or "redundant energy" within the "corresponding mild creative breeze" that is the mind's meeting with Nature (46, 43). Within this new psychological context, "this," which previously had no antecedent, now clearly refers to the poet's "vain perplexity" (266) and "hollow thought" (259)—the poet's inability to sustain his "philosophic Song/ Of Truth that cherishes our daily life;/ With meditations passionate, from deep/ Recesses in man's heart" (229–32). This project, *The Recluse*, was to be the culmination of Wordsworth's passionate dialogue with Coleridge, to whom he addresses *The Prelude* as both silent screen and analysand, as if to work through some previous trauma that will make his future endeavors possible. This return to the past proved to be rather more dilatory, of course. In 1804–05,

Wordsworth expanded the poem to five and eventually thirteen books, a process of ongoing revision that ends only with the post-humous 1850 publication of the poem in its current fourteen-book form.

In all versions after 1798–99, "this" becomes a symptom that, put in the form of a question, becomes attached to a possibly traumatic origin in which the hiding places of power close before man can access their lesson. But the swerve offers its own abundant recompense by transposing the missed encounters of various spots of time into a pos-sible analysis and cure that forms the matrix of the Wordsworthian vision: man's habitual return to nature's nurturing presence. What is earlier eruptive, disruptive, or restless gets rooted in an analytical schema that, like Dorothy planting happy flowers in the recesses of William's otherwise craggy and intransigent ego, subdues and thus manages the unconscious. On one hand, this transforming relation-ship is rooted in an eighteenth-century Common Sense empiricism that sees the world and man's place in it clearly, beyond skepticism and speculation. On the other hand, Wordsworth expresses this transformation through the finer, visionary tone of nature's panthe-istic future, which binds man to nature as part of a community born of love and holy sacrifice.

At some level, what "this" is thus becomes a moot point. What matters is how the briefer text becomes a prelude to a longer case his-tory that explains Wordsworth's preparedness to undertake his task of greater philosophical good and thus to make him what, by the end of the eighteenth century, would be called the "morally useful" man. The phrase "was it for this?" is a psychological beginning *in medias res*, the framing of a philosophical question that determines the course of the text's longer analysis. One can recall that the end of the text, by which time Wordsworth has ostensibly worked through its opening sense of "redundancy," is where it begins: with the poet ready to write *The Recluse*. This gives the poem's narrative trajectory from symp-tom to crisis and resolution a rather more recursive and interminable shape. One might argue, however, that the absence of *The Recluse*, of which *The Prelude* is the most telling symptom, is something differ-ent from failure. For "this," like the symptom itself, demands further inquiry. One of the earliest forms of *The Recluse* is MSS. B & D of *The Ruined Cottage*, behind which lies the now-missing MS. A, which told what Helen Darbishire called the "short bare narrative of unre-lieved distress" (*Poetical Works* 5:365) that was Margaret's life. The germinal forms of *this* narrative are the short fragments "The Baker's Cart" and "Incipient Madness," in which one encounters something approximating the primal scene of Wordsworth's larger philosophical effort.[13]

In the former, the speaker comes upon a destitute woman, her name left blank in the manuscript, standing in front of her cottage. She notes that the baker's cart passes her by, which signifies that she and her children are victims of the social attrition of the period. She is left with "a mind/ Which being long neglected and denied/ The common food of hope was now become/ Sick and extravagant" (18–21). In "Incipient Madness," the speaker visits a ruined cottage empty except for a "broken pane [of glass] which glitter'd in the moon/ And seemed akin to life"—what he calls a "speck" (6-7, 13). His obsession with the pane plays out through succeeding visits to the cottage, which degenerates even further into nature. Even a "linnet" who "sang a pleasant melancholy song" eventually "vanish'd," and, as the speaker says, he "alone/ Remained" along with "the winds of heaven," with which his "heart claimed fellowship and with the beams/ Of dawn and of the setting sun that seemed/ To live and linger on the mouldering walls" (48–9). As the last vestige of social order, the broken glass signifies the speaker's nearly psychotic break from culture and reality into a world of utter solitude, a break he shares with Margaret. Wordsworth then fleshed out these fragments into the bare anatomy of Margaret's life. At one time happily married and prosperous, Margaret descends into despair. Her husband eventually abandons her and their family as all fall victim to the effects of poverty, famine, war, and death. Triangulating the natural, the national, and the international, Wordsworth thus uses the story to evoke the sociopolitical ambivalences of post-Revolutionary England. The story does not stop there, however. In MSS. B and D Wordsworth incorporates Margaret's story into the larger frame of a speaker who comes upon a pedlar/poet lying on a bench outside the ruined cottage. The pedlar appears to be the speaker of the earlier fragments, who now tells the story of his encounter with Margaret to the speaker of *The Ruined Cottage*. Their analysis between men seems to rationalize Margaret's madness back to nature—the pedlar points to the spear grass growing beside the cottage as the remaining talisman of her life—and at the end of the poem they repair to an inn to contemplate what they have learned.

This psychotherapy subdues and chastens the missed encounters with madness in the earliest versions of the text. Yet halfway through the narrative, the speaker and pedlar seem more than preoccupied with talking about Margaret. At the end of Part One the speaker, fascinated by the pedlar's "active countenance" and "eye/ So busy, that the things of which he spake/ Seemed present" (210–2), asks him to resume his story. The pedlar replies:

> "It were a wantonness that would demand
> Severe reproof, if we were men whose hearts
> Could hold vain dalliance with the misery
> Even of the dead, contented thence to draw
> A momentary pleasure never marked
> By reason, barren of all future good." (221–6)

There can be no pleasure in melancholy or " 'mournful thoughts,' " he warns.

> "…Tis a common tale,
> By moving accidents uncharactered,
> A tale of silent suffering, hardly clothed
> In bodily form, and to the grosser sense
> But ill adapted, scarcely palpable
> To him who does not think." (231–6)

However, immediately he adds: "But at your bidding/ I will proceed" (236–7). The pedlar seems to allow the speaker to persuade him to go on. Something about the pleasure of melancholy arrests both men. The otherwise palpable fear of a loss of "reason" or "thought" is here turned rhetorical, part of a melodrama of suffering in which they are playing willing victims as well as involuntary interlopers. The pedlar is more than happy to leave the "common tale" as a skeletal form, happy to have Margaret out of the way, for this allows them to flesh things out in other ways.[14] In this subtle interplay between communication and coercion, the speaker and pedlar seem to invent answers precisely because they know there can no definitive answers, no access to the truth. In short: the pedlar and speaker have—rather happily, it appears—become addicted to their own desire for moral management. It was this version of *The Ruined Cottage* that got absorbed into the opening book of *The Excursion*, which many considered an aesthetic failure. But with George III permanently out of commission and the realm in the hands of an utterly dissipated and profligate Regent, Wordsworth's text seems to respond that much more urgently to the time's *need* for moral management.

    This need recalls the idea of a nervous English body that must habituate its own pleasurable desire for containment and self-control in return for pleasurable personal and social payoffs.[15] In *Elements of Medicine* (first published in Latin as *Elementa Medicinae* in 1780),

John Brown explains bodily health in terms of the balanced excitability of the body's nervous tissue and its proper sensitivity to the environment. Prone to internal and external stimulation, the human body Brown envisions was more nervously situated between the physical and the social, a relationship explored elsewhere in the eighteenth century via the concepts of sentiment, sensibility, and sympathy, which concerned themselves with how bodily constitutions related "sensibly" to one another. Such concerns are reflected in Brown's treatment of opium as a preternatural remedy for numerous physical or nervous complaints, from hysteria and hangovers to insomnia, indigestion, typhus, venereal disease, cancer, rheumatism, and cholera. Brown's prescription pointed toward a larger debate about opium's medicinal utility versus its recreational habituation. For in the latter case, opium both produced and signified altered states of mind and body beyond society's control, which is why drug intoxication was increasingly demonized through an emergent temperance movement and calls for health and social reform among the working class.[16] Trotter's *An Essay, Medical, Philosophical, and Chemical, on Drunkenness*, cautioning against Brown's optimism, warned against the use of stimulants. Drug habituation in England's industrial centers, as De Quincey notes, was of special concern: "happiness might now be bought for a penny, and carried in the waistcoat pocket: portable ecstacies might be had corked up in a pint bottle: and peace of mind could be sent down in gallons by the mail coach" (89). Unlike William Marsden's version of an unprincipled and unbridled East in *History of Sumatra*, where opium was too expensive, De Quincey argues that English affluence has made opium too accessible. But his tone is also ironically celebratory. On one hand, workers cannot handle such "luxuries"; on the other, workers stoned on Saturday night were otherwise productive during the week, a necessary evil for larger economic payoff. Moreover, opium diverted them from political congregation. In short, an opiated subject signified a body politic prone to other forms of social habituation.

*   *   *

In *Observations on Madness and Melancholy*, John Haslam asks English psychiatrists to adopt a less formidable and intrepid method of "moral management" than that of Philippe Pinel. Whereas Pinel used the "thunder in [his] voice" or "lightning in [his] eye" to impose his character on his patients, Haslam wanted to "discover the character of the patient," "to obtain the confidence, and conciliate the esteem of insane persons," thus "procuring from them respect and obedience." The statement is rather ironic, given Haslam's rather limited sympathy for his most famous patient, James Tilley Matthews, in *Illustrations of Madness.*[17] In a further irony, Haslam nationalizes his approach as what he calls the *"English secret* for the moral management of the insane" (293–5). Haslam's model reflects the influence of Smithean sympathy, but also its subtle coercion of feeling. David Marshall argues that Smith "can't believe...that fellow-feeling is automatic or even natural," and so he "must describe what it is like to want to believe in the fiction of sympathy, and what it's like to live in a world where sympathy is perhaps impossible" (180, 181). By arguing that the conventions of theater structure all sympathetic exchanges as a kind of spectacle of witnessing, Marshall attends to sympathy's darker psychosocial mechanism. Sympathy is about the individual mastery of desire as much as the emphatic exchange of feeling, about witnessing another's suffering in order to make oneself feel good, and thus about keeping individuals divided against one another according to the pursuit of individual happiness in the guise of making this pursuit a communal effort.

Godwin seems to know this when he turns the conversational ideal of his political justice into the violent detection of *Caleb Williams*, in which people are made to confess secrets regardless of whether or not they are true or even real. Haslam also dissociates himself from the coercive practice of William Pargeter, who would fix or *seize* the eye of his patients in order to placate them. I am reminded here of the traumatic encounter between the Wedding Guest and the Mariner, wherein the work of moral management is instead a kind of mesmeric encounter fixed by the Mariner's "glittering eye" (3, 17). At once conscious and unconscious, the Wedding Guest cannot help but listen and the Mariner cannot help but confess what in *Christabel* Coleridge calls the "forced unconscious sympathy" (597) of intersubjective encounters. Haslam's attempt to avoid such seizures, that is to say, merely indicates a different kind of possession, in which one learns to enjoy mutual self-discovery not for the goal of transformation, but for the sake of the ongoing pleasure to be derived from the process. Coleridge's texts, like Godwin's novel, thus stage the primal scene of moral management as if to make Haslam confront in Pinel's or Pargeter's methods the political unconscious of his own: the desire to hold the patient's eye as the window to his soul. This psychiatric gaze indicates a more tenacious possession of bourgeois bodies and minds, the moral management of which had become especially urgent by the early 1800s.

In "Incipient Madness," the speaker's visits are compulsively repetitive, resulting in his complete identification with and fetishization of nature. But this one-sidedness takes another form, for in the text's final lines he speaks with a kind of psychotic common sense of a world where things are always at one with themselves because they exist only for and within themselves. This episode points forward rather uncannily to *The Prelude*'s various scenes of self-reflection: the infant at the mother's breast; Wordsworth looking over the prow of a boat into darkened waters; the Boy of Winander who hears his own voice "mimicked" in the voice of an owl; the gaze into dark waters that produces the traumatic eruption of a defaced body. These spots of time work by a simultaneous penetration of and resistance to vision that is at once enlightening and narcissistic. In a passage on the life of the poet used in MS. B of *The Ruined Cottage*, then removed from MS. D and transplanted to Book Three of *The Prelude*, where Wordsworth uses it to describe the first of two ecstatic ascensions to poetic vocation, Wordsworth writes of his time at Cambridge,

> I had a world about me—'twas my own;
> I made it, for it only lived to me,
> And to the God who sees into the heart.
> Such sympathies, though rarely, were betrayed
> By outward gestures and by visible looks:
> Some called it madness—so indeed it was,
> If child-like fruitfulness in passing joy,
> If steady moods of thoughtfulness matured
> To inspiration, sort with such a name;
> If prophecy be madness. (*1805* 3.141–50)

Here, man's sympathy with himself, the internal sublation of his outward talk with God, marks the archetypal form of his daily communion with the visible earth that is the basis of a psychospiritual renovation. Together with Coleridge's idea of how imagination organizes and thus governs how good citizens learn to *internalize* permanently the ideas of church and state, the Wordsworthian program becomes the model for a Victorian ideal of social economy. This program is rooted in an oddly dissociative solitude. As Wordsworth says of his Arab dream in Book Five, one is "crazed/ By love and feeling, and internal thought/ Protracted among endless solitudes" (*1805* 5.144–6). But this narcissism seems right given Wordsworth's insistence on making pleasurable the discovery and diagnosis of psychopathology. Contrary to the fact that Wordsworth never writes the Romantic philosophic poem that was supposed to make the public feel better about itself, *The Prelude* ends up performing this function in the absence of *The Recluse*. His texts evolve to offer the pleasures of self-discovery, of exploring and refashioning the contours and planes of the post-Enlightenment self in order to conjure, like smoke in the Leyden jar or the crisis in Mesmer's salon, the effects of a core reaction—of a core, constitutive, authentic, and whole self that one knows to be there because one has created the aesthetics of a psychiatric experience that makes this appearance possible.

As Andrea Henderson notes, the varieties of subjectivity constructed in the Romantic period indicate how the psyche takes on a life of its own *because of* these constructions. Romantic interiority is merely a simulation that instead evokes the "notion of a heart or core in either society or the individual [that] is threatening because such a core becomes, in both cases, the centre of movement or circulation, a place of dangerous fluidity" (25). This is why David Hume suggests that the self is constituted less by the Lockean habit that produces a permanent sense of experience than from the necessary duration of habitual practice that manufactures this sense of permanence. In his *Treatise of Human Nature*, Hume writes: "there is no impression constant and invariable. Pain and pleasure, grief and joy, passions and sensations succeed each other, and never all exist at the same time. It cannot, therefore, be from any of these impressions, or from any other, that the idea of self is deriv'd; and consequently there is no such idea. . . . [M]ankind . . . [is] nothing but a bundle or collection of different perceptions, which succeed each other with an inconceivable rapidity, and are in perpetual flux and movement" (1:251–4). Whatever common sense emerges from this experience, Hume suggests, is quite by chance.

Wrestling with the arbitrariness of human nature was one of the crucibles of Romantic thought. In *Biographia Literaria*, Coleridge turns to German idealism to translate the mind's habitual impressions into a permanent record of experience. For Coleridge, the British empirical tradition, especially Hartley's associationism, was an "absolute *delirium*" (*Biographia* 1:111) that staged the mind's shifting palimpsest, to borrow De Quincey's metaphor, without revealing the soul's eternal form. Kant's idea of a transcendental apperception offered a schematic and disciplinary context that British sense-making eschewed but, for Coleridge, sorely lacked. Ironically, this scheme also encrypted a mode of sociability uncannily similar to Smith's imagining of it. In his third Critique, Kant appears to sublate Scottish Common Sense, and thus Humean and Smithean habit, as the *sensus communis* of that most difficult form of sympathetic agreement, aesthetic judgment. But the categorical imperative of *this* common sense is rather similar to the "invisible hand" of Smithean sympathy: both reflect an impulse to demand the other's assent to one's sense of things, yet to gather this consensus as if it were the most natural and unobtrusive event.

What was left, however, was to turn *this* practice into habit. The schema for this habit comes earlier in the eighteenth century. The exulting solitude of one's communion with nature in Akenside's *Pleasures of Imagination*, Joseph Warton's "The Enthusiast," or Thomas Warton's "The Pleasures of Melancholy" makes a spectacle of the mind's spectacular capacity to re-envision our environment. These texts typologize a feeling disposition toward the world and others that Romanticism then embodies as a dynamic economy of exchange between the self and world or between the self and others that eventually produces dynamic psychiatry. The business of this exchange is to get people habituated to feeling good about themselves, and thus about others and the world around them. This sociability and sociality seems doomed to remain haunted by the specters of its own transferential complexities, its failure to produce clear and optimal goals of self-understanding and communal dialogue. This unconscious undercurrent, not to mention the period's confrontation with the unconscious itself, always vexed and threatened to undo the psychological ties that bind, providing all the more reason to get British society in the habit of feeling good and thus addicted to the pleasures of moral management. The addiction itself took care of the unconscious desire by putting this desire to work in the name of building a better British citizen. How desire and addiction feed (upon) one another evokes Scull's point that the failure of psychiatry paradoxically ensured that the discipline survived on the breakdown of minds. Eventually pharmacology (as De Quincey already knew in 1821) would know how to feed this addiction differently, bypassing the business of moral management by putting the drug of psychiatry where it profits most: right on the pulses and into the veins of feeling itself. Romantic texts stage both the production and effects of this pleasurable psychiatric consciousness at once equivocally and unequivocally: by asking if, in the end, the "this" that "it" was for really matters at all.

NOTES

I wish to thank Michelle Faubert and Tom Schmid for their very kind invitation to present this work in this forum, and Faubert for including this paper in her session at the 2007 CSECS conference in Winnipeg. I thank Allan Ingram and his cohorts at Northumbria University for their enthusiastic response to an earlier version of this paper I gave as the first paper in the second series of lectures offered by the "Beyond Depression" Leverhulme-funded research project in September 2008. And I also thank the participants in the second "Discursive Identities" Workshop in Munich, also in September 2008, especially Gerold Sedlmayer, for their very helpful feedback. Finally, I thank the Social Sciences and Humanities Research Council of Canada for funding that made possible the research and writing of this material.

1. The 1980s and 1990s saw a surge in work on the history of psychiatry in the wake of foundational research by Ellenberger's *The Discovery of the Unconscious* (1970), Hunter and Macalpine's *Three Hundred Years of Psychiatry* (1963), and later Porter's *Mind Forg'd Manacles* (1987). See also Alexander and Selesnick's *The History of Psychiatry* (1966). Scull is not necessarily indicting these authors, but rather shows a general trend to shore up discursive and institutional authority.

2. Here I note the influence of Foucault's *Madness and Civilization* (1965), an abridged form of the original French publication, *Folie et Deraison: Histoire de la Folie a L'Age Classique* (1964), the whole of which has since been translated as *History of Madness* (2006). See also Dörner.

3. Jacques Khalip argues that the "trancelike inhumanism of the speargrass vision that concludes" Wordsworth's *The Ruined Cottage*, the central text of my discussion in this essay, "evokes a disastrous reticence that suffuses Wordsworth's thought," and reads the ruined cottage itself as "the place where Wordsworth explores the hospitality of dwelling in the rubble of disaster" ("The Ruin of Things" 4). I set aside this resistance to psychiatry to isolate the poem's testament to the addictive necessity of moral management.

4. Examining the rise of what came to be known as moral "therapy" or "treatment" of the insane at the York Retreat, Louis Charland highlights the problem with defining the word "moral" itself, which came to signify the "psychological" or "non-bodily" treatment of the mentally ill. It thus stressed extending to patients the same sense of moral autonomy granted to rational individuals. Yet because religious and social regimens were deployed to implement the treatment, it also signaled the management of ethical behavior, and thus implied a certain social morality. As Charland notes, the question now, as then, is essentially "philosophical": "moral treatment was unique because of the manner in which it fused affective and ethical considerations under the aegis of an overriding commitment to benevolence" (62).

5. For a discussion of the historical shift toward happiness as a "natural right," signaled in Locke's writings, see McMahon 197–252.

6. Speaking of the new discipline of "happiness studies," which combines cognitive science research and New Age wisdom, Žižek writes:

> [This] combination of cognitive science and Buddhism...is here given an ethical twist: what is offered in the guise of scientific research is a new morality that one is tempted to call *biomorali-ty*—the true counterpart to today's biopolitics. And indeed, was it not the Dalai Lama himself who wrote, "The purpose of life is to be happy"? This is *not true* of psychoanalysis, one should add. (45)

7. Alexander and Selesnick define a "Romantic reaction" (133–49) to the Enlightenment spirit of medical and scientific inquiry in which "there was a movement away from reason toward emotion and faith," a "swing toward mysticism [that] is often regarded as retrogressive" (133). They thus argue that "the optimistic and victorious spirit of rationalism yielded rapidly to disillusionment, and reason was dethroned by the rediscovery of the irrational depth of the human psyche" (133). Ellenberger's view of Romanticism is rather more nuanced and interdisciplinary, but essentially all three writers distinguish between Enlightenment rationality, scientific enquiry, and a materialist concern to locate the neurological sources of insanity, and a more speculative and philosophical Romantic enquiry into the nature of the psyche. The division does not get resolved, then, until the later nineteenth century, when neurological research, having advanced toward its original Enlightenment goal to produce neuropsychiatry, meets a more inventive but eclectic Romantic concern with psychic dynamics to produce what we have come to know as "dynamic psychiatry," a term that emerged with specific relevance in the late nineteenth century. Tellingly, Alexander, Selesnick, and Ellenberger rarely mention John Haslam, who is much more central to Porter's histories and whom I go on to discuss.

8. Alexander and Selesnick see Reil's *Rhapsodien über die Anwendung der psychischen Kurmethode auf Geisteszerrüttung* (1803) as the "first systematic treatise of psychotherapy." Reil was "more experimental and intuitive than his contemporaries," but was "entirely convinced...that mental disease is a psychological phenomenon, the cause of which requires psychological methods of treatment" (135).

9. Here I am thinking of Coleridge's *Christabel*, in which the speaker describes Geraldine as "A sight to dream of, not to tell" (247), or Shelley's *The Triumph of Life*, in which the speaker describes his waking dream as "thoughts which must r emain untold" (21). In *Romantic Psychoanalysis* I argue that Romantic literature, specifically poetry, invents the psychoanalytic scene as a literary response to the dangers

of enlightenment. For treatments of both Hogg and Godwin, see my "'the clearest light of reason'" and "Speaking of William Godwin's *Caleb Williams*."

10. See Fulford, who explores the impact of the Mesmeric "mania" or "crisis" on pre- and post-Revolutionary England.

11. Haslam's book was expanded for its second edition in 1809 as *Observations on Madness and Melancholy*. Perhaps its most important predecessor was William Battie's 1758 *Treatise on Madness*, the first sustained document of its kind.

12. See, for instance, De Quincey's 1821 *Confessions of an English Opium-Eater* or his 1840 article "The Opium and the China Question."

13. MS. A includes "Argument for Suicide," "Old Man Travelling, Animal Tranquillity and Decay," "Description of a Beggar," "Yet Once Again," "The Baker's Cart" fragment, "Incipient Madness," and the first partial manuscript version of "The Ruined Cottage." The Racedown Notebook contains work on "The Ruined Cottage" from between March and June 1797. These passages correspond to the conclusion of MS. B (499–513) and MS. B (321–325), in which Margaret finds the money left by her husband. I use James Butler's edition of the Cornell Wordsworth's *The Ruined Cottage* and *The Pedlar* for references to "The Baker's Cart," "Incipient Madness," and MSS. A, B, and D of "The Ruined Cottage." Unless otherwise specified, all references to "The Ruined Cottage" are from MS. D.

14. I set aside the issues of gender and class here to focus more broadly on moral management. See Swann and my discussion of the poem in *Romantic Psychoanalysis* (85–91), where I also discuss the work of transference in the encounter between the pedlar and speaker.

15. Essentially this meant treating the working class like children. Ironically, as with modern debates about using drugs to monitor children's unruly behavior, the nineteenth century became concerned that opium was a common ingredient of various children's prescriptions, such as Batley's Sedative Solution, Mother Bailey's Quieting Syrup, and especially Godfrey's Cordial (a mixture of opium, treacle, water, and spices), which were used to "quiet" children (see Wohl 34–5).

16. Mounting concern about intemperance in the eighteenth century was eventually taken up as part of a broader push toward social reform in the nineteenth century. Although churches and religious groups had earlier shouldered the burden of promoting abstinence, the origins of a formal temperance movement are American: the American Temperance Society was founded in 1826. In Europe the first such organization was the Ulster Temperance Society (1829), after which the movement quickly spread to Scotland and Britain, where the British and Foreign Temperance Society was founded in London in 1831. Temperance took its most extreme, one might say

fundamentalist, form as teetotalism. An early promoter was philanthropist Joseph Livesey (1794–1884), who started a temperance movement in Preston and who demanded a pledge of total abstinence from his members.

17. See Porter's Introduction to Haslam's *Illustrations of Madness.*

WORKS CITED

Alexander, Franz, and Sheldon T. Selesnick. *The History of Psychiatry: An Evaluation of Psychiatric Thought from Prehistoric Times to the Present.* New York: Harper and Row, 1966. Print.

Barrell, John. *Imagining the King's Death: Figurative Treason, Fantasies of Regicide, 1793–1796.* Oxford: Oxford UP, 2000. Print.

Charland, Louis. "Benevolent Theory: Moral Treatment at the York Retreat." *History of Psychiatry* 18.1 (2007): 61–80. Print.

Coleridge, Samuel Taylor. *Biographia Literaria.* Ed. James Engell and W. Jackson Bate. Princeton, NJ: Princeton UP, 1983. Print.

———. *The Collected Notebooks of Samuel Taylor Coleridge.* Ed. Kathleen Coburn and Merton Christensen. 4 vols. New York: Bollingen Series: Pantheon Books, 1957–1990. Print.

De Quincey, Thomas. *Confessions of an English Opium-Eater and Other Writings.* Ed. Grevel Lindop. Oxford: Oxford UP, 1985; rev. ed. 1998. Print.

Dörner, Klaus. *Madmen and the Bourgeoisie.* Trans. Joachim Neugroschel and Jean Steinberg. Oxford: Blackwell, 1981. Print.

Ellenberger, Henri F. *The Discovery of the Unconscious: The History and Evolution of Dynamic Psychiatry.* New York: Basic Books, 1970. Print.

Faflak, Joel. *Romantic Psychoanalysis: The Burden of the Mystery.* Albany: Suny, 2008. Print.

Faubert, Michelle. *Rhyming Reason: The Poetry of Romantic-Era Psychologists.* London: Pickering & Chatto, 2009. Print.

Fulford, Tim. "Conducting the Vital Fluid: The Politics and Poetics of Mesmerism in the 1790s." *Studies in Romanticism* 43 (Spring 2004): 57–78. Pri nt.

Haslam, John. *Observations on Madness and Melancholy.* 2nd ed. London: [n.pub.], 1809. Print.

Henderson, Andrea. *Romantic Identities: Varieties of Subjectivity, 1774–1830.* Cambridge: Cambridge UP, 1996. Print.

Hill, George Nesse. *An Essay on the Prevention and Cure of Insanity; With Observations on the Rules for the Detection of Pretenders to Madness.* London: Longman, Hurst, Rees, Orme & Brown, 1814. Print.

Hume, David. *A Treatise of Human Nature.* Ed. L. A. Selby-Bigge. 2nd ed. Oxford: Clarendon Press, 1978. Print.

Hunter, Richard, and Ida Macalpine, eds. *Three Hundred Years of Psychiatry 1535–1860.* London: Oxford UP, 1963. Print.

Khalip, Jacques. "The Ruin of Things." *Romantic Differences*. Ed. Theresa Kelley. *Romantic Circles Praxis* (forthcoming). Web.

Leask, Nigel. *British Romantic Writers and the East: Anxieties of Empire*. Cambridge: Cambridge UP, 1992. Print.

Malthus, Thomas. *An Essay on the Principle of Population, or, A View of its Past and Present Effects on Human Happiness: With an Inquiry into our Prospects Respecting the Future Removal or Migration of the Evils which it Occasions*. 2nd ed. London: J. Johnson, 1806. Print.

Marshall, David. *The Figure of Theatre: Shaftesbury, Defoe, Adam Smith, and George Eliot*. New York: Columbia UP, 1988. Print.

McMahon, Darrin M. *Happiness: A History*. New York: Grove Press, 2006. Print.

Porter, Roy. Introduction. *Illustrations of Madness*, by John Haslam. 1810 London: Routledge, 1988. xi–xlvii. Print.

———. *Mind Forg'd Manacles: A History of Madness in England from the Restoration to the Regency*. London: Athlone, 1987. Print.

———. *A Social History of Madness: Stories of the Insane*. London: Weidenfeld and Nicolson, 1987. Print.

Rajan, Tilottama. *Dark Interpreter: The Discourse of Romanticism*. Ithaca, NY: Cornell UP, 1980. Print.

Scull, Andrew. "Psychiatry and Its Historians." *History of Psychiatry* 2 (1991): 239–50. Print.

———. "Psychiatry and Social Control in the Nineteenth and Twentieth Centuries." *History of Psychiatry* 2 (1991): 149–69. Print.

Shuttleworth, Sally. "'The malady of thought': Embodied Memory in Victorian Psychology and the Novel." *Memory and Memorials, 1789–1914: Literary and Cultural Perspectives*. Ed. Matthew Campbell, Jacqueline M. Labbe, and Sally Shuttleworth. New York: Routledge, 2000. 26–59. Print.

Trotter, Thomas. *A View of the Nervous Temperament*. London: Longman, 1807; rpt. New York: Arno Press, 1978.

Wohl, Anthony S. *Endangered Lives: Public Health in Victorian Britain*. London: J. M. Dent & Sons Ltd., 1983.

Woodman, Ross. *Sanity, Madness, Transformation: The Psyche in Romanticism*. Ed. Joel Faflak. Toronto: U of Toronto P, 2007. Print.

Wordsworth, William. *The Prelude: 1799, 1805, 1850*. Ed. Jonathan Wordsworth, M. H. Abrams, and Stephen Gill. New York: W. W. Norton, 1979. Print.

———. *The Ruined Cottage* and *The Pedlar*. Ed. James Butler. Ithaca, NY: Cornell UP, 1979. Print.

———. *The Poetical Works of William Wordsworth*. Vol. 5. Ed. Ernest de Selincourt and Helen Darbishire. Oxford: Clarendon Press, 1959. Print.

Žižek, Slavoj. *In Defense of Lost Causes*. New York: Verso, 2008. Print.

CHAPTER FOUR

JOHN FERRIAR'S PSYCHOLOGY, JAMES HOGG'S *JUSTIFIED SINNER*, AND THE GAY SCIENCE OF HORROR WRITING

Michelle Faubert

Such recent works as Frederick Burwick's *Poetic Madness and the Romantic Imagination*, Jennifer Ford's *Coleridge on Dreaming: Romanticism, Dreams and the Medical Imagination*, David Vallins's *Coleridge and the Psychology of Romanticism: Feeling and Thought*, John Beer's *Romantic Consciousness: Blake to Mary Shelley*, and Joel Faflak's *Romantic Psychoanalysis: The Burden of the Mystery* document well Romantic-era writers' fascination with psychology and madness. Other recent studies on Romanticism and psychology, such as Alan Richardson's *British Romanticism and the Science of the Mind* and Neil Vickers's *Coleridge and the Doctors*, demonstrate the Romantics' familiarity with such topics as neuroscience, nerve theory, hypochondria, the psychology of dreams, Hartleyan associationism, and Kantian psychology, and link these topics to the Romantics' philosophical researches into the workings of society, the construction of language, and other weighty matters. Yet, Romantic-era psychologist John Ferriar's influential psychological works—with which the young S. T. Coleridge was familiar, as Neil Vickers has shown ("Beddoes" 74), and with which, I will suggest, James Hogg may also have been conversant—demonstrate that Romantic writers also valued psychological knowledge for its entertaining qualities. Ferriar argues in several of his texts that the products of his scientific inquiry should be used for literary delight. In his influential psychological text *An Essay Towards a Theory of Apparitions*, Ferriar devises a mechanics of horror based on his theory that readers revel in the very state of unreason and mental confusion into which a deftly illogical narrative or poem can immerse them, particularly when the subject matter is psychological. Hogg seems to give fictional life to Ferriar's complex theory in *The Private Memoirs and Confessions of a Justified Sinner*. Taken together, these texts reveal how discoveries from the new Romantic-era field of psychology could be employed to produce readerly pleasure.[1]

Ferriar's groundbreaking theory about the deeply psychological nature of horror writing is vital to the consideration of Hogg's *Private Memoirs and Confessions of a Justified Sinner* for several reasons. To begin with, Ferriar's work suggests that the lack of narrative closure in Hogg's novel may signify more than its roots in the literary tradition of the Gothic, to which recent critics have pointed (Fielding; Horstmann-Guthrie; Redekop). Narrative destabilization—which is extreme in Hogg's novel—may denote extraliterary influences. In *An Essay Towards a Theory of Apparitions*, Ferriar employs this tactic deftly while beckoning his fellow Scots to write literary texts that make use of his scientific discoveries and, a little more than a decade later, Hogg, a Highland author, did so. The very features of the novel that have been attributed to Hogg's *naïveté* and lack of formal education, aspects of Hogg's reception that Nelson Smith discusses in his critical study of the author's writing and life, may be understood as Hogg's response to Ferriar's radical theories regarding how to import psychological discoveries into literature, and, as such, these features may indicate Hogg's sophistication, both with regard to the complexity and cultural status of his research and influences and his clever deployment of Ferriar's methods. While several Romantic-era psychologists focused on the practical uses of pleasure, including literarily produced pleasure, for the governance of the psychology of the masses,[2] Ferriar sought to establish quite a different relationship between psychology, literature, and pleasure: he insists that psychology and the dramatic reproduction in readers of its signature subject, unreason, may be harnessed by literary writers to produce a piquant thrill of horror.

Hogg draws attention to narrative technique in the novel by layering voices. Set in early eighteenth-century Scotland, the novel contains a fictional editor who claims to have discovered in the grave of a young suicide the memoirs that comprise the narrative within the larger frame of his story. The "justified sinner" of the title, Robert

Wringhim, is a Calvinist who believes that he is one of the elect who are saved for all eternity, regardless of their earthly actions. His belief and ruthless judgment of the (in his view) damned who surround him drive Wringhim to commit fratricide and a host of other murders and crimes, all at the urging of an evil friend, Gil-Martin, who may be the devil incarnate or Robert's double. The real identity of this character is impossible to determine, however, because of logical contradictions within the narrative. Such paradoxical messages and contradictory details have long frustrated critics of the novel, who have struggled to explain the significance of such apparently sloppy intrusions of illogicality in an otherwise deftly managed and complex tale (Horstmann-Guthrie 63). I contend that Hogg intentionally includes narrative contradictions in his novel to defy logically closed explanations for its mysteries, and that he may have been inspired by Ferriar's text to create his disturbingly inconclusive tale. The narrative is so evocative of Ferriar's text on hallucinations and so steeped in psychological subject matter—such as religious obsession or "enthusiasm," mob madness, hallucinations, and "maternal impressions"—that Hogg seems to be using the novel to dramatize his fellow Scot's directions regarding the use of psychological subject matter in the literature of horror. Hogg challenges his readers to appreciate the novel for the weird pleasure it can afford by relaying a tale about strange psychological phenomena, proffering some possible contemporary psychological insights that would seem to resolve the mad conundrums he presents, and then undercutting these psychological interpretations. Hogg thereby refuses to provide readers with an escape route into the comfortable, if boring, realm of reason in which they formerly believed themselves to belong, and all the more so in this period of the birth of psychology. In so doing, Hogg reproduces in readers the mental confusion that the often insane characters in the novel convey; he convinces readers that their powers of reason are weak, just as the characters in the novel flounder upon witnessing what is logically impossible. Through narrative technique, then, Hogg blurs the boundary between the Gothic world of madness in the narrative and the world that readers occupy, which creates a radically different readerly horror that is intense because it is personal.

John Ferriar (1761–1815) was born in Scotland, finished his MD degree at Edinburgh University, and later established himself as one of the premier physicians in Manchester (Webb), partly through such publications as his thesis, *Tentamen medicum, inaugurale, de variola*[3], and his most successful psychological text, *Medical Histories and Reflections*. Although scholars seldom discuss his work today, he was an important influence on nineteenth-century culture. Ferriar introduced the term "hysterical conversion," which suggests his influence on psychoanalytic theory because the term was later adopted by Sigmund Freud and established as a hallmark of his theories about neuroses (Hunter and Macalpine 543). Another connection to Freud appears in Ferriar's work on dream interpretation, *The Theory of Dreams in Which an Inquiry Is Made into the Powers and Faculties of the Human Mind, as They Are Illustrated in the Most Remarkable Dreams Recorded in Sacred and Profane History*, which develops the idea of different levels of consciousness and the motivations that rule each. Ferriar writes That "if vice peeps out" when we are awake,

> it accommodates itself to the opinion of men, and is abashed; and veiling its passions, it does not entirely give itself to its impulse, but restrains and contends with it, but in sleep flying beyond opinions and laws, and transgressing all modesty and shame, it excites every lust and stirs up evil propensities. (3)

In psychoanalytic terms, the superego rules our waking actions, but our dreams are guided by the id. In the Romantic era, Ferriar's influence extended beyond the world of psychology: he was equally well known for his contributions to the literary world of Romantic-era Britain via his membership in the Manchester Literary Society, to which he presented several papers on medicine, psychology, and literature. One of these papers covers a topic pertinent to the argument of the present essay: "Of Popular Illusions, and Particularly of Medical Demonology" investigates the overlap between the supernatural and psychological realms. The first words of the essay indicate that Ferriar considered these topics to be entertaining: "There are two classes of readers, who will probably expect little entertainment from the subject of this essay; those who are not acquainted with it as a branch of literature, will think it an idle talk to attack the forgotten follies of the nursery" (31–2). Yet the most significant text that Ferriar published out of his involvement with this literary society was a monograph called *Illustrations of Sterne: With Other Essays and Verses*, an expansion of a lecture in which he traces the influence of early French romances on Laurence Sterne's *Tristram Shandy*. Notably, Ferriar also links several of Sterne's sources to Robert Burton's influential psychological work *Anatomy of Melancholy* ("Illustrations of Sterne," e.g. 111). This detail, coupled with the fact that he signs himself "John Ferriar, MD" on the title page, suggests that here, too, Ferriar endeavored to apply his psychological knowledge to the literary realm and thereby integrate his audience's experiences of both. Nor did Ferrer limit himself to scientific prose to achieve this union, as he illustrates the relationship between literature and mental health in his humorous epistolary poem about obsessive book collecting, *The Bibliomania, An Epistle, to Richard Heber, Esq.* As I will explain with reference to *An Essay Towards a Theory of Apparitions*, the Scottish psychologist reveals that the fields of literature and psychology are integrally related in the production of readerly pleasure.

Ferrier's texts on hallucinations (*An Essay Towards a Theory of Apparitions*) and dreams (*The Theory of Dreams*) present psychological phenomena as a fund of amusing subject matter for the literary writer and a source of enjoyment for readers who, inspired by the text, reflect upon their own mental states. Ferrier states clearly in the Preface to *The Theory of Dreams* that he wrote it to provide pleasure to readers first and information only secondarily: "That the subject may afford some little entertainment, and even instruction to the reader, is the Author's earnest hope" (v). When he echoes this sentiment by writing that he authored his work to help readers "retire from the terrible events of history," Ferrier reveals that he wrote this scientific text to produce delight in the reader. He introduces his text on hallucinations in a similar way. *An Essay Towards a Theory of Apparitions* is not, as one might expect, a guidebook on how to avoid a mental phenomenon that most people would consider to be undesirable and an established symptom of insanity. On the contrary, this early psychologist claims that reading ghost stories and other works that stimulate our sense of the supernatural results in hallucinations (e.g. 102), and he then proceeds to fill his text with impressive tales of phantoms and the paranormal, which, presumably, will cause readers to hallucinate. Ferrier's text is both a manual and the means for generating hallucinations through ghost stories:

> a great convenience will be found in my system; apparitions may be evoked, in open day....Nay, a person rightly prepared may see ghosts, while seated comfortably by his library-fire, in as much perfection, as amidst broken tombs, nodding ruins, and awe-inspiring ivy. (viii)

He goes on to argue that the significance of these scientific efforts is not some lofty experimental design, but simply amusement:

> But when I consider the delight with which stories of apparitions are received by persons of all ages, and of the most various kinds of knowledge and ability, I cannot help feeling some degree of complacency, in offering to the makers and readers of such stories, a view of

the subject, which may extend their enjoyment far beyond its former limits. (vi)

The psychologist implies that hallucinations are fun, pleasure is a worthy end of its own, and literature should endeavor to reach this goal in two connected ways: through the exploration of psychological subject matter and the production of unreason in the audience through supernatural stories, which is manifest as hallucinations. Put simply, Ferriar presents his psychological treatise on "spectral delusions" (14) as entertainment: "Take courage, then, good reader, and knock at the portal of my enchanted castle, which will be opened to you, not by a grinning demon, but by a very civil person, in a black velvet cap, with whom you may pass an hour not disagreeably" (ix). By suggesting that readers may divert themselves with hallucinations and helping to produce them in this text, Ferriar emphasizes that writers may create readerly pleasure by constructing in their audiences a state of unreason.

With pleasure as the objective, Ferriar presents his psychological texts as literary and encourages literary writers to make their own texts psychological through subject matter and readerly affect. To illustrate his point, Ferriar compares his ghost stories to the most famous Gothic tales of the Romantic period and argues that his psychological tales are superior, thereby implying that psychology and literature are so integrally related that one realm suffers if it does not sufficiently reflect the other. He writes, "It has given me pain to see the most fearful and ghastly commencements of a tale of horror reduced to mere common events, at the winding up of the book" (vi). The typical conclusions to Ann Radcliffe's Gothic tales, in which all of the preceding mysterious events are explained as ordinary and rationally comprehensible, are ready examples of Ferriar's complaint. The Scottish psychologist promises to maintain a level of mystery in his ghost stories, pledging later, "The highest flights of imagination may now be indulged, on this subject, although no loop-hole should be left for mortifying explanations, and for those modifications of terror, which completely baulk the reader's curiosity, and disgust him with a second reading" (vii). Here, Ferriar underscores that, far from being desirable, logical explanation in a tale of horror "modif[ies]" the reader's "terror," "disgust[s] him," and destroys the agreeable feeling of "curiosity" produced by its irrationality.

Ferriar's desire to entertain by providing his audience with enjoyment of the mysterious realm of the irrational will surprise readers even today, since typically, scientific works are dry and fact-based. The common assumption is that an apparent desire to entertain can make the scientific writer's facts seem fictional and threaten his or her authority. Thus, our knowledge that *An Essay Towards a Theory of Apparitions* is a text about hallucinations by a psychologist may lead to the hasty conclusion that Ferriar will illustrate how all ghosts are merely the product of predictable physical stimuli and response, and that he will provide a natural explanation for apparitions that demystifies the fascinating subject in the style of Radcliffe's conclusions. This assumption would appear to be supported by Ferriar's own concluding avowal, "I have thus presented to the reader, those facts which have afforded, to my own mind, a satisfactory explanation of such relations of spectral appearances, as cannot be refused of credit" (137), and his intervening discussion of ghosts as the "spectral delusions" born of "latent lunacy" (14, 111), a psychological account of ghosts that might be understood as a "mortifying explanation" of them, or a scientific description of their banal mental sources that erases their mystery. However, this supposition regarding Ferriar's conventional scientific treatment of hallucinations leads to this question: what, then, does Ferriar mean in his early statements about the "disgust[ing]" nature of logical explanations for ghost stories? The answer to this seeming impasse illustrates Ferriar's most convincing argument about how the practical field of psychology gives pleasure: he presents the very subject of psychology as a field of great mystery and its discoveries as conducive to astonishment, rather than the cure for it. With specific reference to fiction, he suggests the creative potential for the psychological phenomena that he details in this text: "The subject of *latent lunacy* is an untouched field, which would afford the richest harvest to a skilful and diligent observer" (111–12). Additionally, Ferriar presents throughout the text several tales of apparitions that he does not in fact logically illuminate with psychological explanations, despite his assertions to the contrary.[4] Considered in combination with his declaration about the power of psychological subject matter to enrich literature, this circumstance shows that Ferriar is more interested in diverting his readers through psychological subject matter, no matter how illogical it is, than spreading scientific knowledge, the coinage of reason. Hogg, in turn, seems to have accepted his fellow Scot's advice to reap a "rich[ ] harvest" from the field of psychology in his production of the literary granary that is *The Private Memoirs and Confessions of a Justified Sinner*, to expand upon Ferriar's metaphor. By incorporating psychological subject matter into the novel and reproducing a state of irrationality in his readers by denying logical narrative closure to them, Hogg uses Ferriaran methods to create pleasurable fear in his audience.

Hogg illustrates that the most terrifying narrative effects are a combination of the scientifically explicable and the supernatural by adopting the same image that Ferriar uses in his psychological text about how to create thrilling tales of horror through scientific means. In order to afford his readers the "delight" with which he knows "stories of apparitions are received by persons of all ages" (*Apparitions* vi), Ferriar regales his audience with the history of the "Giant of the Broken" in Germany, known as "the 'nursing mother' of ghosts," he claims (21–3). According to Ferriar's naturalistic explanation of the apparition, if the conditions are right in this mountain range—if the hour is very early, the atmosphere is misty, and the sun is at the perfect angle—then the mountain climber "will see the singular spectacle of his own shadow extending to the length of five or six hundred feet, at the distance of about two miles before him" (footnote on 27). Hogg seems to apply Ferriar's advice to create readerly "delight" by refusing to provide "mortifying" logical explanations for his own treatment of a "Giant of the Broken"-type apparition in *The Private Memoirs and Confessions of a Justified Sinner*. In Hogg's novel, George Colwan, the older brother of the "justified sinner," Robert Wringhim, sees the gigantic form of his madly religious brother while walking in the misty mountains of Scotland early in the morning. George sees this terrifying vision upon arising "very early...to make an excursion to the top of Arthur's Seat," the volcanic mountain to the east of Edinburgh that is a famous natural vista (77): "What an apparition was there presented to his view! He saw, delineated in the cloud, the shoulders, arms, and features of a human being of the most dreadful aspect. The face was the face of his brother, but dilated to twenty times the natural size," such that even the utterly sensible George "conceived it to be a spirit.... He was farther confirmed in the belief that it was a malignant spirit, on perceiving that it approached him across the front of a precipice, where there was not footing for thing of mortal frame" (79–80). George then springs away from the horrifying vision and collides with the real form of his brother. Even during later meditation upon the occurrence, George "could not get quit of a conviction that he was haunted by some evil genius in the shape of his brother.... In no other way could he account for the apparition that he saw that morning on the face of the rock" (82). At this point in the novel, readers cannot imagine the enormous apparition to be anything but a kind of spirit, either, for Hogg does not provide a natural explanation for the strange event until later in the narrative and in the words of a very minor character: a friend of George's father, Adam Gordon (83). By delaying such scientific explanations and interspersing them with

supernatural events that are truly inexplicable—such as the appearance of "George" (probably Gil-Martin, supernaturally transformed)
to Mrs. Logan and Arabella (Bell) Calvert after he is dead and buried (108–10)—Hogg replicates Ferriar's valorization of the irrational
over the scientific, or the mysterious and entertaining over the merely
informative.

Hogg is even prepared for the possibility that his readers are familiar with either Ferriar's text or, through other sources, the scientific
explanation for this "apparition," and he takes care to guide his readers' responses to it. Indeed, a few pages before this scene, the rational, scholarly Editor of George's memoirs comments upon a similarly
"supernatural" event—a bright halo over the head of George—and
George's realization of its natural cause: "the better the works of
nature are understood, the more they will be ever admired. That was
a scene that would have entranced the man of science with delight"
(78).[5] Again in keeping with Ferriar's advice in *An Essay Towards a
Theory of Apparitions*, Hogg directs his readers toward enjoyment and
"delight," even in the spirit of scientific inquiry, and puts into effect
Ferriar's complex formula for a thrilling horror story: suggest a scientific explanation to build up readers' expectations of logical closure
and then deny the same to produce disorientation and confusion.

Critical debate regarding Hogg's source for this image rages.
In his informative article "Dark Interpreter: Literary Uses of the
Brocken Spectre from Coleridge to Pynchon," Sebastian Mitchell
proffers several potential sources for Hogg's knowledge of the
Brocken Spectre, as the phenomenon is commonly called. Mitchell
notes that "The Scottish scientist, David Brewster, provided the
key popular scientific account for the Spectre for an Anglophone
audience in this period in *Letters on Natural Magic Addressed to Sir
Walter Scott Bart*" and adds that Hogg knew Brewster, a fellow res-
ident of Edinburgh (171, 177), but since the latter published his
account in 1832—eight years after Hogg published his novel—the
influence seems less certain. Mitchell also mentions that, for his part,
Coleridge knew of the phenomenon as early as 1799 and included
a reference to it in his poem "Constancy to an Ideal Object," which
he composed between 1804 and 1807; however, Coleridge did not
publish the poem until 1828—again, after Hogg published his
novel—which undermines the theory that Coleridge's poem may
have been Hogg's source (172).[6] Mitchell's argument that Coleridge
had read John Haygarth's description of a Brocken Spectre in the
Memoirs of the Literary and Philosophical Society of Manchester, in
which "Haygarth describes how he saw his shadow and a glory in the

vale of Clwyd in February 1780" (172), may implicate Haygarth as a possible source for Hogg, but this evidence suggests a Ferriaran connection as well. Ferriar, who was also a member of the society, may have become aware of the Brocken Spectre through Haygarth's work and, since Haygarth describes it in a Scottish context, the tale may have gained some national stature in those northern climes, despite the English locale of the journal. Ferriar's influential status as a psychologist, his Scottish heritage, and the date of publication of his text on apparitions (eleven years before Hogg published his novel) are enough reason to suggest that Hogg adapted this image of the mountain ghost from Ferriar's work. The case for a link between the two texts gains credence upon consideration that Hogg's use of the image is so like Ferriar's and explains so well an aspect of the novelist's work that has always mystified critics.

If Ferriar's treatment of the Brocken Spectre may be viewed as a metonymic illustration of his general purpose in *An Essay Towards a Theory of Apparitions*, then Hogg's use of the image may function in a similar manner. Mitchell suggests as much when he claims that "most substantial literary examinations of the apparition draw directly upon both its rational and irrational aspects" in order to create the same narrative effects (171), with the exception of Sir Walter Scott's use of the image in *The Antiquary*, which alludes only to the scientific significance of the Brocken Spectre (174). Even though Scott's novel may be cited as another likely source for Hogg, the former's mundane use of the image suggests otherwise. Hogg and Ferriar go a step farther than does Scott in that they use the Brocken Spectre as a scientifically explicable phenomenon that the ultimately irrational framework of their texts subsumes, thereby making it an illustration of how scientific knowledge must be subordinated to the goal of creating creepy psychological thrills for readers. Both Hogg and Ferriar raise the specter, so to speak, of science and naturalistic explanations for seemingly supernatural occurrences, only to undermine these same explanations by engulfing them with rationally inexplicable tales. In this way, the authors disorient their readers, producing a state of confusion that replicates the emotions of the characters in their tales of horror, and thereby blur the boundary between fact and fiction.

Ferriar valorizes mystery and even readerly confusion as conducive to the audience's pleasure in a work of horror when he writes that "The highest flights of imagination may now be indulged, on this subject, although no loop-hole should be left for mortifying explanations, and for those modifications of terror, which completely baulk the reader's curiosity, and disgust him with a second reading" (*Apparitions* vii). Thus, even though Ferriar presents his text on apparitions as a psychological treatise that will reveal how "latent lunacy" and hallucinations create ghosts—a coy hint that he will "disgust" his readers, as he puts it, by explaining in rational terms the reasons for the many ghost stories he includes in the text—he refuses to provide rational explanations, psychological or otherwise, for many of his ghost stories. For example, Ferriar presents as an instance of what "is known in the North of Scotland" as "'Second-Sight'" (63–4) a creepy tale about "Dr. [John] Donne," who saw a vision of his wife carrying a dead child while he was in Paris and she in London, only to discover on his return home that their baby had died in his absence. Nor does Ferriar attempt to explain this phenomenon with recourse to psychological knowledge, his field of expertise. The disjunction between his promises to explain odd mental phenomena in a scientific way and the illogical narrative that he really provides in this text creates a state of confusion in readers, who grope for stability by using their reason. They are promised rational satisfaction, only to be denied it. They wade into the uncomfortable subject of insanity, confident that the new science of psychology will guarantee an explanation of this disturbing world, only to find that the mental confusion that they study is their own.

Hogg's frequent references to one of the flourishing new sciences in the Romantic period, psychology, and its main area of study, insanity and other mysteries of the mind, may be viewed as more than the novelist's way to capitalize on a popular Gothic topic.[7] Hogg gestures to the realm of psychology in order to tease readers with the possibility of a scientific explanation for the mental confusion into which he is, in fact, in the process of thrusting them. Hogg refers to some of the hottest topics in Romantic psychology in the course of his Gothic novel. For instance, he makes reference to the field of phrenology in the scene in which Mrs. Logan meets Bell Calvert, remarking that the latter "viewed Mrs. Logan with a stern, steady gaze, as if reading her features as a margin to her intellect" (92). This prostitute seems to be submitting her visitor to a phrenological study: Romantic-era phrenology, or the science of reading cranial bumps and facial features as an index to the mind, was "designed to reveal the inner man from outer signs," Richard Hunter and Ida Macalpine explain (712). Anne Mellor elaborates that this practice was the "more empirical offspring" of the physiognomy of Johann Caspar Lavater, who studied the whole body to discover how the psychological and spiritual elements of the subject expressed itself in the body; phrenology, as developed by Lavater's student Franz Joseph Gall and Gall's student Johann Gaspar Spurzheim, focused specifically on the head and less stringently on the role of the spirit in forming the outer person (53).[8] By suggesting that an uneducated prostitute may be engaged in cutting-edge phrenological inquiry, Hogg destabilizes common notions of authority, and these are further undermined by the end of the novel, which explodes all of the potential psychological interpretations of the textual mysteries. Hogg also destabilizes authority here by indicating that it may be found where the audience is not likely to look (for who would suppose that a prostitute is informed about the latest psychological theories?) and, in this way, he offers a clue to interpreting the text. That is to say, Hogg may warn his readers not to discount the extent to which he—the model for the "Ettrick shepherd" who, in the *Blackwood's* series called "*Noctes Ambrosianae*," was often characterized as an "unsophisticated, part-buffoon...who drank heavily" (Smith 15)—organizes his tale and controls readers' reactions. Prejudiced by the popular perception of Hogg as an uneducated clown, readers may be inclined to attribute the contradictions within the novel to the author's lack of sophistication and logical control of the narrative, a reaction that Hogg coyly confirms by presenting the "Hogg" character in the novel as confused and bumbling. However, Hogg's attribution of subtle insights and psychological inquiry to a prostitute reminds readers that they must prepare to reconsider their comfortable assumptions about where authority lies—as well as where it may not be found.

Bell Calvert is also the mouthpiece for Hogg's remarks upon one of the greatest debates in eighteenth-century Scottish Enlightenment psychology, a debate that raged between the skeptical philosophers (influenced by David Hume and his seminal text, *A Treatise of Human Nature*) and their opponents, the Common Sense philosophers, such as Dugald Stewart and James Beattie. Humean psychology challenged its students to approach all phenomena skeptically, demanding proof and evidence, and even going so far as to assert that since humans cannot verify the existence of the outer world beyond a shadow of a doubt, they must submit to the possibility of its non-existence. James Beattie, professor of Moral Philosophy at Marischal College in Scotland and poet of the much-loved autobiographical poem *The Minstrel*, answers, "We cannot prove by argument, that bodies exist, or that we ourselves exist; nor is it necessary that we should: for the thing is self-evident, and the constitution of our nature makes it impossible for us to entertain any doubt concerning this matter" (*Elements of Moral Science* 48). Beattie then asserts that Hume and his successors

> came at last to affirm, that the soul perceives nothing but its own ideas; and that . . . the whole universe which we see around us, has no existence but in the mind that perceives it. Never were reason and language more abused than by this extravagant theory. . . . We perceive outward things themselves, and believe that they exist, and are what they appear to be. This is the language of common sense, and the belief of all mankind. (50)

Meanwhile, in Hogg's novel, this heady debate is summed up in the words of an aging prostitute: Bell asks, "We have nothing on earth but our senses to depend upon: if these deceive us, what are we to do [?]" (107). Beattie himself did not articulate the philosophical debate better. Again, Hogg undermines his audience's understanding by confounding expectations about where authority lies, even as he weaves psychological insights into a text that may, upon a casual reading, seem to be an unrefined, chaotic, and superstitious yarn.

In addition to this reference to an eighteenth-century psychological debate, Hogg evokes a field of inquiry that was gaining momentum in the early nineteenth century: the psychology of mobs. The most influential text on mob madness—Charles Mackay's *Extraordinary Popular Delusions and the Madness of Crowds*—reveals the social and mental chaos that can ensue when a crowd of people become agitated together, but, notably, Mackay published this text in the early Victorian period and it focuses mainly on marketplace madness. Two possible eighteenth-century influences on Hogg's thinking about mob madness are David Hume and Robert Whytt. In *Literature and Medicine in Nineteenth-Century Britain*, Janice Caldwell notes,

> Hume wrote in *A Treatise of Human Nature* that there "is a transition of passion" in any act of social sympathy, in which we not only imagine the experience of the other, but feel it on our nerves: "As in strings equally wound up, the motion of one communicates itself to the rest; so all the affections readily pass from one person to another, and beget correspondent movements in every human creature."

Caldwell continues: "fears of social contamination inevitably arose. The Earl of Shaftesbury . . . extolled sympathy within gentlemanly fellowship, but mistrusted sympathetic contact with the mob, whose 'very looks' could be 'infectious'; passion and panic might spread 'from face to face'" (32).[9] Hogg capitalizes on the fears raised by the Earl of Shaftesbury's theory about crowds by representing insanity as infectious. When Robert's crowd challenges the party with which George is drinking as dishonorable, the accusation "actually roused the party to temporary madness" (68). And when Mrs. Logan and Bell discover that they have both, inexplicably, witnessed the dead George walk alongside Robert, they fall into hysterical fits that are, apparently, contagious:

> Their looks encountered, and there was an unearthly amazement that gleamed from each, which, meeting together, caught real fire and returned the flame to their heated imaginations, till the two associates became like two statues, with their hands spread, their eyes fixed, and their chops fallen down upon their bosoms. An old woman who kept the lodging-house...chanced to enter at this crisis with some cordial; and, seeing the state of her lodgers, she caught the infection, and fell into the same rigid and statue-like appearance. (109)

Hogg continues the scene in the same humorous and enlightening vein. Bell notes of Robert's mystery friend,

> "It can be none other than he. But, no, it is impossible! I saw him stabbed through and through the heart; I saw him...groan away his soul. Yet, if it is not he, who can it be?"
> "It is he!" cried Mrs. Logan, hysterically.
> "Yes, yes, it is he!" cried the landlady in unison.
> "It is who?" said Mrs. Calvert; "whom do you mean, mistress?"
> "Oh, I don't know! I don't know! I was affrighted."
> "Hold your peace, then, till you recover your senses..." [and] Mrs. Calvert turned the latter gently and civilly out of the apartment, observing that there seemed to be some infection in the air of the room. (109–10)

For the third time, this prostitute, fresh out of prison, reveals an extraordinary degree of psychological perspicacity. By investing a prostitute with cutting-edge psychological insight that Romantic readers would expect only from scholars and professionals in the study of the mind, Hogg undercuts the authority of science as the key to solving the mysteries in the novel even as he proffers it as the stable ground for which readers grope. By so doing, Hogg echoes Ferriar's technique in *Essay Towards a Theory of Apparitions*, in which the scientist implies that his scientific text will provide a psychological explanation for the ghost stories he provides and then—in accordance with his assertion that such explanations destroy the enjoyment that tales of horror create—refuses to provide the promised rationalization. The effect on readers, in both texts, is mental confusion, the destabilization of reason, and the eerie thrill of temporary insanity, which replicates the psychological instability that afflicts many characters in tales of horror, including Hogg's own.

Hogg also undercuts authority in this novel through the character of Reverend Wringhim, a Calvinist clergyman who uses psychological insight to bolster his falsehoods about his very unclerical transgressions. In a conversation with John Barnet, his servant, the clergyman counters the latter's suggestion that young Robert may be taken for his bastard son because of their strong resemblance:

> "[T]here are many reasons for such likenesses, besides that of consanguinity. They depend much on the thoughts and affections of the mother; and, it is probable, that that mother of this boy, being deserted by her worthless husband, having turned her thoughts on me, as likely to be her protector, may have caused this striking resemblance." (123–4)

Here, Reverend Wringhim employs his knowledge of the contemporary theory of "maternal impressions" in an effort to deceive his old servant about his sexual sins. The Reverend alludes to the psychological theory that a "fetus can be affected by its mother's desires, fears, experiences" (Mazzoni ix) to the extent that the baby may resemble that about which the mother thought intensely when pregnant. The most famous example of this theory concerns Joseph Merrick, better known as "the elephant man." His Victorian contemporaries believed that his physical deformities were the product of his mother's traumatized reaction to a raging circus elephant that threatened her while she was pregnant with Merrick. In his reference to this theory, Hogg again undercuts the reliability of the scientific explanations that he presents in the novel by framing them as part of a deception that an unreliable authority figure concocts. By destabilizing the realm of the rational, Hogg follows Ferriar's advice regarding how to create the readerly confusion that is so essential to the pleasures that tales of horror may afford.

Hogg encourages (especially Scottish) readers to reconsider their trust in authority by casting the staunchest Calvinists as liars, evil, or insane.[10] After all, the principal line of psychological inquiry in the text concerns whether Robert Wringhim is afflicted with religious enthusiasm or is the victim of demonic possession. When Robert tells

of his "singular delusion that...[he] was two persons," which made
him suspect that he was "deranged in...[his] intellect" (159), the
novel appears to be a psychological thriller about religious mania.
As Hunter notes of the text, "It is interested in subjectivity and psychological states of fear and division, in the externalization of mental
conflicts through acts of murder and violence, and in the presenta-
tion of paranoia as a product of religious obsessiveness" (31). Since
André Gide celebrated Hogg's psychological insight in his introduction to a 1948 reprint of the novel (Smith 145), many critics, such
as Penny Fielding and Allan Beveridge, have focused on the novel's theme of insanity.[11] Several of these critics maintain that their
psychological readings illuminate how Robert may be understood
as experiencing mental delusions of some sort; Hunter comments,
these "psychological readings...are plausible because of the novel's
studied refusal to secure evidence concerning the identity, or even
the existence, of Gil-Martin. Robert himself notes how the various
accounts of his companion given to his parents 'all described him
differently,'" which, Hunter insists, presents the possibility that Gil-
Martin is merely a "projection of Robert's damaged mind" (140, 37).
I contend, however, that Gil-Martin's very appearance to others (indicated in the quotation from the book that Hunter provides in the
above passage) illustrates that Gil-Martin cannot be a mere creature
of Robert's diseased imagination, in which case Robert is not mad,
but possessed. Alternatively, all of the characters who see Gil-Martin
may be regarded as delusional. This interpretation contributes to the
theme of "contagious madness," or mob madness, and, in turn, to a
reading of the novel as a whole that adds to its destabilizing effects in
a radical way: if, indeed, almost every character in the novel is insane
(for most of them see Gil-Martin), then the very concept of madness must be redefined, for the present definition makes sense only
where there is difference and abnormality. This analysis of the novel
is bolstered upon consideration that it is the only one that accounts
for most of the tale's contradictions, making it logically consistent (at
least until the second installment of the Editor's narrative). However,
this interpretation is the most unbalancing of all, for it creates a kind
of paradox in which the only way to establish the narrative as logical
is by understanding its fictional world as insane—one in which hallucinations are normal, which the very concept of madness and the
validity of psychology.

   In the final analysis, though, even this radical interpretation of the
text as depicting a "world gone mad" fails to frame the events in a
perfectly logical manner, since the Editor's closing comments upon

the memoirs and the supposed suicide of Robert imply strongly that Gil-Martin is real. Quoting from a real-life letter that Hogg published in *Blackwood's* (which I will discuss in greater detail momentarily), the Editor reveals that a witness—completely ignorant of Robert's identity and therefore unprejudiced—"*could almost give his oath* that he saw two people busily engaged at the hay-rick" (223; Hogg's emphasis); additionally, both the letter-writing real-life Hogg and this witness confirm that the suicide itself is "rather a singular circumstance" (224) or well-nigh impossible because "these ropes are so brittle, being made of green hay, that they will scarcely bear to be bound over the rick," much less hold a grown man (223, 224). Hogg's repeated insistence upon the weakness of the rope and the witness's attestation that he saw the two men "going round it [i.e. the hay-rick] and round it" leads to one conclusion: after a lengthy chase around the hay-rick, Gil-Martin killed Robert and arranged the corpse to look like a suicide. And if Gil-Martin is real, he is certainly supernatural, since he has the ability to adopt anyone's appearance—not to mention that he would have had to suspend Robert's body from the hay-rick supernaturally, given the weakness of the green hay. Disturbingly, if Gil-Martin is supernatural, then, again, the readers' rationality is superfluous because it equips them to understand the natural world alone. Hogg even undercuts the strongest instance of how psychological insight may explain most of the logical contradictions in the novel: the concept of "infectious" or mob madness may explain why many characters see Gil-Martin, but Hogg's insistence on the paltry powers of reason and mockery of scientific knowledge undermine such logical interpretations. Unreason rules both the world of the novel and readers' experiences. Their reason and logic serve them but poorly as they struggle to comprehend this disturbing tale of madness and the supernatural.

When Hogg's narrative suggests that insanity may be at the root of the many mysteries in the novel, readers expect to find logical resolution in the psychological knowledge to which it gestures frequently. However, the author presents this knowledge in contexts that consistently undercut it, thereby damning it to failure as the basis for explication. Just as the characters within the novel are denied the security that the realm of science and rationality offer, readers remain in a state of unreason. Hogg further accomplishes an elision between our reality and the fictional world by including the *Blackwood's* letter in the novel, which envelops readers in a world of unreason and irrationality—a Gothic-like realm where madness rules. Hogg thus constructs his narrative according to the mechanics of horror that Ferriar elucidates in his psychological text on apparitions. There, Ferriar suggests that such readerly affect is linked to the denial of rational, and specifically psychological, explanation; similarly, by first encouraging our belief in the stable world of science and rationality and then denying the efficacy of reason, Hogg thrusts readers into an irrational and/or supernatural world that reels chaotically beyond their ability to comprehend it and predict its outcomes. Like the mirrors of a fun house that reflect the subject as distorted, the novel reveals readers' understandings as warped.

Ferriar claims that his narrative methods produce fear and "delight" in readers, and Hogg attempts to produce the same readerly affect through his novel. However, this radical approach to the mechanics of horror also victimizes readers, and they have not always responded positively. As Ulrike Horstmann-Guthrie notes about the most voluble and influential champion of Hogg's novel after it had faded from critical notice, even Gide complained that "'the fantastic part' [of the novel] is not 'always psychologically explicable, without having recourse to the supernatural'" (63), a response that shows both Gide's inability to succumb to confusion and his disbelief that logical chaos is a legitimate and productive readerly response. I maintain that Gide and others who damn Hogg for his refusal to force the tale into some kind of logical framework condemn themselves to a limited experience of the reactions that Hogg means to evoke in his readers. What Fielding asserts about Hogg's short story "Cousin Mattie" may also be said of *The Private Memoirs and Confessions of a Justified Sinner*: "The story refuses to privilege any one exegetic discourse, rather working to stave off the voyeuristic and taxonomic attentions of observers such as the narrator or an analytically-inclined reader" (16). Taking his cue from Ferriar's *An Essay Towards a Theory of Apparitions*, Hogg works to increase the pleasure that tales of horror and the supernatural produce in readers; he attempts to "extend their enjoyment far beyond its former limits," as Ferriar says of his own purpose (*Apparitions* vi), by introducing a radical narrative technique in his Gothic tale that incorporates readers into its world of unreason and blurs the line between fiction and reality. The resulting readerly disequilibrium, then, is the fun of psychology, the *jouissance* of using it to confirm the power of unreason, which is the very realm that psychology claims to control.

In denying readers the usual means of interpreting and mastering his narrative through logic and empirical proof, Hogg encourages them to cast for a reliable narrator to guide them through the dark passages of the tale and then, trickster-like, establishes these authorities as deeply untrustworthy. Just as he uses psychological subject matter to produce a particular mental response in his readers, Hogg uses subtle narrative means to disorient them. The Editor confirms the wisdom of consulting others to establish the truth when inscrutability reigns by identifying the "sequel" of Wringhim's memoirs as "a thing so extraordinary, so unprecedented, and so far out of the common course of human events, that if there were not hundreds of living witnesses to attest the truth of it, I would not bid any rational being to believe it" (222). Moreover, the fictional Editor who frames Wringhim's memoirs with his own account of the events presents himself as rational and scientific (Smith 153; Horstmann-Guthrie 66), which positions him as an authority and trustworthy, much as the psychologist's voice does in Ferriar's text. Claiming to provide readers with all of the information that they need to solve the mystery of the young suicide and the murders associated with him, the Editor notes that he relies for his portion of the narrative on local "tradition," "parish registers," and other texts that may be taken as good evidence of his claims (49). However, as Horstmann-Guthrie notes, "The end of 'The Editor's Narrative' leaves a number of questions unresolved, while references to 'the narrative of one who knew all the circumstances'…imply a promise that the Sinner's memoir will throw light upon events which have so far remained enigmatic," a promise that is not fulfilled (69). The Editor confesses that he does not understand the significance of this narrative, either (232), leaving readers to flounder for logical meaning on their own. By the end of the novel, Hogg himself removes readers' last hope to be enlightened by an authority who has some objectivity and control over the narrative by intimating that he, the author of this fiction, is unreliable: with his own name and real occupation as a shepherd and poet, Hogg appears as a semi-fictional character in the novel and gives the Editor of the narrative such poor directions to the grave of Wringhim that "Hogg's" neighbors "testif[y]…great surprise at such a singular blunder," since the shepherd "herded the very ground where the grave is, and saw both hills from his own window" (228). Upon discovering this strong proof of "Hogg's" undependability, readers suspect that the author shirks all responsibility for resolving his own tale in a comprehensible way, which thrusts them into a state of confusion, convinced only of the futility of attempting to comprehend Hogg's tale logically. In short, readers are again ushered into a state of unreason, a realm where their rational abilities cannot aid them, and, as such, they partake in the Gothic atmosphere of insanity and chaos. Hogg's strange technique of including himself as a character in the novel only adds to his readers' confusion, for it blends fact and fiction, as does the Editor's reference to an "extract from an authentic letter, published in *Blackwood's Magazine* for August, 1823" in the text of the novel, since this letter really did appear in the journal a year before Hogg published *The Private Memoirs and Confessions of a Justified Sinner* (222). This situation further interweaves the world outside of the novel with the illogical and fictional world of the narrative, which either lends an air of reality to this impossible tale or surreality to readers' lived experiences, especially if they had read the 1823 letter in *Blackwood's*, completely unaware that they were being ensnared in a fictional narrative soon to be published. Again, the boundary between fact and fiction fades, and "Hogg"/Hogg condemns readers to a state of mental chaos that is matched throughout the novel in almost all of its major characters.

Through the use of psychological subject matter and his own psychological insight into ways of manipulating readers' experiences of a text, the writer can create a uniquely horrifying reading experience. Ghost stories and the Gothic produce feelings of horror that "delight" readers, Ferriar claims in *An Essay Towards a Theory of Apparitions*, but his original method of intensifying their horror through the use of psychological insight maximizes their pleasure. In *The Private Memoirs and Confessions of a Justified Sinner*, the novelist seems to heed Ferriar's complaint that, when writers reduce psychological terror and mystery to logically explicable events, narratives become devoid of pleasure and "disgust" their readers, as well as Ferriar's encomiums about the sheer joy of frightening tales and readerly unreason (*Apparitions* vi). By refusing to explain in rational terms the thrilling psychological mysteries his novel presents, Hogg indulges readers in the realm of unreason for the sheer pleasure of the creepy experience. The paradoxical and illogical characteristics of the narrative punish with frustration readers' efforts to search for a rational meaning or practical lesson behind the fictional events, and they reinforce the frightening implication behind every tale of horror: that unreason sometimes rules and this world may not be explained in empirical terms alone.

NOTES

1. Michael Donnelly calls the period 1790–1850 "the birth of psychiatry" (Donnelly viii); I call it "the birth of psychology," a term that I prefer to "psychiatry" because "psychology" was current in the period I study. David Hartley used the term in the 1750s, as did others before

him, according to the *Oxford English Dictionary* entry for "psychology," but it is arguable that the word was employed to signify only the concepts that were associated with it near the end of the eighteenth century in the work of Dugald Stewart and James Beattie. The issue of the proper terminology for early doctors of the mind is highly contentious. Porter explains that the word "psychiatry" was used by the late eighteenth century (ix), and Allen Thiher confirms that the German Dr. J. C. Reil popularized the word "psychiatry" (167)—although it is unlikely that the German document in which this information appeared would so immediately become known to, and its contents and terminology so quickly adopted by, British medical professionals. In *A Historical Dictionary of Psychiatry*, Edward Shorter confirms that the term originated in 1808 with Reil's work, and adds that "The use of the new term spread rather slowly," even in Germany (232–3). Thus, it seems safe to say that the doctors of the mind were not called "psychiatrists" in England.

2. In the prefatory matter to their literary texts, Romantic-era associationists Thomas Brown and Thomas Beddoes discuss how literature may be used to form the minds of readers in desirable, usually moral, ways. Beddoes does so in two texts, *The History of Isaac Jenkins, and Sarah His Wife, and Their Three Children* and his long poem *Alexander's Expedition down the Hydaspes and the Indus to the Indian Ocean*, and Brown expounds this message in his lengthy near-replication of Alexander Pope's *The Rape of the Lock*, called *The Paradise of Coquettes, a Poem in Nine Parts*. Both early psychologists maintain that literature may be a useful tool to form associations in the mind of the readers that will guide their future moral actions.

3. A rough translation of this title is "Inaugural Doctoral Trial, about Variola"; variola is smallpox.

4. For example, Ferriar recounts the creepy tale of a Scottish chieftain who foresaw the death of one of his friends, as well as that of a woman who saw herself in front of her for five years, but nowhere does the psychologist provide "a satisfactory explanation of such relations of spectral appearances, as cannot be refused of credit," as he claims at the close of the text (64–7, 137). Incidentally, the latter tale about the woman and her double also echoes strongly Hogg's novel about Robert Wringhim and his double, Gil-Martin.

5. Smith and Horstmann-Guthrie discuss the fictional Editor as a representative of rationality and empiricism.

6. Thomas De Quincey quotes Coleridge's poem in a footnote to "The Apparition of the Brocken," which is part of *Suspiria de Profundis* (1845). In this short meditation on the phenomenon, De Quincey uses the topic of the "famous Spectre of the Brocken" (202) to expand upon the idea of the externalization of dreams and other products of the mind, calling the "apparition" "the Dark Interpreter" (205).

7. The links between Gothic literature and psychology are well documented. The most relevant to the present project is Joel Faflak's "'the clearest light of reason': Making Sense of Hogg's Body of Evidence," which investigates the influence of Romantic-era psychology, especially Mesmerism, on Hogg's narrative. Some of the most recent studies on the general subject of the Gothic and psychology are Julia Reid's *Robert Louis Stevenson, Science, and the* Fin de Siècle; Raphael Ingelbien's "Gothic Genealogies: Dracula, Bowen's Court, and Anglo-Irish Psychology"; Steven Bruhm's "The Contemporary Gothic: Why We Need It"; William Veeder's "The Nurture of the Gothic, or, How Can a Text Be Both Popular and Subversive?"; Thomas Kullmann's "Nature and Psychology in *Melmoth the Wanderer* and *Wuthering Heights*"; Matthew Brennan's "Poe's Gothic Sublimity: Prose Style, Painting, and Mental Boundaries in 'The Fall of the House of Usher'"; David Punter's "Narrative and Psychology in Gothic Fiction"; Daniel Pick's "'Terrors of the Night': Dracula and 'Degeneration' in the Late Nineteenth Century"; and Mark Hennelly's "'Putting My Eye to the Keyhole': Gothic Vision in *The Monk*."

8. As Thomas Forster, who coined the term "phrenology," explains in *Sketch of the New Anatomy*, "The size and figure of the scull are conformable to that of the brain; hence the organs are indicated on the outside of the head.... Dissection has proved a determined relation between the external form and the development of the organs within the cranium" (19–20).

9. Caldwell quotes from Whytt's *Observations on the Nature, Causes, and Cure of those Disorders Which Have Been Called Nervous, Hypochondriac, or Hysteric* (213–14), and page 576 of Hume's text. In his references to mob madness, Hogg may also gesture to the work of Thomas Beddoes, an influential associationist and nerve theorist of the early Romantic period (and the father of Thomas Lovell Beddoes). In his educational text called *The History of Isaac Jenkins, and Sarah His Wife, and Their Three Children* from 1796, Beddoes maintains that he intends to educate the poor members of English society, especially impoverished youth, because he wants to counteract what he describes as the English propensity to form mobs, with which, he adds, Americans are not afflicted because they are properly educated (7).

10. Adrian Hunter notes that Hogg had a particular interest in, and aversion to, religious enthusiasm. In his introduction to the novel, Hunter cites a passage from a letter that Hogg wrote in 1832, in which the author "describes a sermon heard in London as 'the ravings of enthusiastic madness'" (13).

11. Additionally, Hunter draws attention to the psychoanalytic reading of the novel executed by Barbara Bloedé in "*The Confessions of a Justified Sinner*: The Paranoiac Nucleus," as well as the more

generally psychological interpretation of it in L. L. Lee's "The Devil's Figure: James Hogg's Justified Sinner."

WORKS CITED

Beattie, James. *Elements of Moral Science*. 1790–93. Philadelphia: Hopkins and Earle, 1809. Print.

———. "The Minstrel, or Progress of Genius." 1771–74. *Poems of Established Reputation*. Baltimore: Warner and Hanna, 1803. 57–92. Print.

Beddoes, Thomas. *The History of Isaac Jenkins, and Sarah His Wife, and Their Three Children*. Bristol: n.p., 1796. ESTC reel 4409, no. 15. Microfilm.

———.*Alexander's Expedition down the Hydaspes and the Indus to the Indian Ocean*. London: J. Edmunds, 1792. ESTC reel 3938, no. 3. Microfilm.

Beer, John. *Romantic Consciousness: Blake to Mary Shelley*. Basingstoke, UK: Palgrave Macmillan, 2003. Print.

Beveridge, Allan. "James Hogg and Abnormal Psychology: Some Background Notes." *Studies in Hogg and His World* 2 (1991): 91–4. Print.

Bloedé, Barbara. "*The Confessions of a Justified Sinner*: The Paranoiac Nucleus." *Papers Given at the First Conference of the James Hogg Society*. Ed. Gillian Hughes. Stirling, UK: The James Hogg Society, 1984. Print.

Brennan, Matthew C. "Poe's Gothic Sublimity: Prose Style, Painting, and Mental Boundaries in 'The Fall of the House of Usher.'" *Journal of Evolutionary Psychology* 11.3–4 (1990): 353–9. Print.

Brown, Thomas. *The Paradise of Coquettes, A Poem in Nine Parts*. London: John Murray, 1814. Print.

Bruhm, Steven. "The Contemporary Gothic: Why We Need It." *The Cambridge Companion to Gothic Fiction*. Ed. and intro. Jerrold E. Hogle. Cambridge: Cambridge UP, 2002. 259–76. Print.

Burwick, Frederick. *Poetic Madness and the Romantic Imagination*. University Park: Pennsylvania State UP, 1996. Print.

Caldwell, Janice. *Literature and Medicine in Nineteenth-Century Britain: From Mary Shelley to George Eliot*. Cambridge: Cambridge UP, 2004. Print.

De Quincey, Thomas. *Suspiria de Profundis*. 1845. In *Confessions of an English Opium-Eater*. Ed. Joel Faflak. Peterborough, Ontario: Broadview Press, 2009. 133–229. Print.

Donnelly, Michael. *Managing the Mind: A Study of Medical Psychology in Early Nineteenth-Century Britain*. London: Tavistock, 1983. Print.

Faflak, Joel. *Romantic Psychoanalysis: The Burden of the Mystery*. Albany: State U of New York P, 2008. Print.

———. "'The Clearest Light of Reason': Making Sense of Hogg's Body of Evidence." *Gothic Studies* 5.1 (2003): 94–110. Print.

Ferriar, John. *The Bibliomania, an Epistle, to Richard Heber, Esq*. 1812. Ed. Marc Vaulbert de Chantilly. London: The Vanity Press of Bethnal Green, 2001. 23–32. Print.

———. *An Essay Towards a Theory of Apparitions.* London: Cadell and Davies, 1813. Print.

———. "Illustrations of Sterne." *Illustrations of Sterne: With Other Essays and Verses.* 2nd ed. 2 vols. London: Cadell and Davies, 1812. Print.

———. *The Theory of Dreams in Which an Inquiry Is Made into the Powers and Faculties of the Human Mind, as They Are Illustrated in the Most Remarkable Dreams Recorded in Sacred and Profane History.* 2 Vols. Vol. 1. London: F. C. and J. Rivington, 1808. Print.

———. "Of Popular Illusions, and Particularly of Medical Demonology." *Memoirs of the Literary and Philosophical Society of Manchester.* 5 vols. Vol. 3. Warrington, UK: W. Eyres, 1785–1802. 23–116. Print.

———. *Medical Histories and Reflections.* Vol. 2. London: Cadell and Davies, 1795. Print.

———. *Medical Histories and Reflections.* Vol. 1. London: T. Cadell, 1792. Print.

———. *Tentamen medicum, inaugurale, de variola.* Edinburgh: Balfour and Smellie, 1781. Print.

Fielding, Penny. "Burial Letters: Death and Dreaming in Hogg's 'Cousin Mattie.'" *Studies in Hogg and His World* 16 (2005): 5–19. Print.

Ford, Jennifer. *Coleridge on Dreaming: Romanticism, Dreams and the Medical Imagination.* Cambridge: Cambridge UP, 1998. Print.

Forster, Thomas Ignatius Maria. *Sketch of the New Anatomy and Physiology of the Brain and Nervous System of Drs. Gall and Spurzheim, Considered as Comprehending a Complete System of Zoonomy, with Observations on Its Tendency to the Improvement of Education, of Punishment, and of the Treatment of Insanity. Reprinted from The Pamphleteer, with Additions.* London: Messrs. Law and Whittaker, 1815. Print.

Hall, Jason Y. "Gall's Phrenology: A Romantic Psychology." *Studies in Romanticism* 16.3 (1977): 305–17. Print.

Hennelly, Mark. "'Putting My Eye to the Keyhole': Gothic Vision in *The Monk*." *Journal of Evolutionary Psychology* 8.3–4 (1987): 289–305. Print.

Hogg, James. *The Private Memoirs and Confessions of a Justified Sinner.* 1824. Ed. and intro. Adrian Hunter. Peterborough, Ontario: Broadview Press, 2001. Print.

Horstmann-Guthrie, Ulrike. "Narrative Technique and Reader Manipulation in Hoffmann's *Elixiere* and Hogg's *Confessions*." *Proceedings of the Leeds Philosophical and Literary Society* 22.1 (1992): 62–74. Print.

Hume, David. *A Treatise of Human Nature.* 1739. Ed. L. A. Selby-Bigge. Oxford: Clarendon Press, 1951. Print.

Hunter, Adrian. Introduction. *The Private Memoirs and Confessions of a Justified Sinner.* 1824. By James Hogg. Ed. and intro. Adrian Hunter. Peterborough, Ontario: Broadview Press, 2001. 7–39. Print.

Hunter, Richard, and Ida Macalpine, eds. *Three Hundred Years of Psychiatry 1535–1860.* London: Oxford UP, 1963. Print.

Ingelbien, Raphael. "Gothic Genealogies: Dracula, Bowen's Court, and Anglo-Irish Psychology." *English Literary History* 70.4 (2003): 1089–1105. Print.

Kullmann, Thomas. "Nature and Psychology in *Melmoth the Wanderer* and *Wuthering Heights.*" *Exhibited by Candlelight: Sources and Developments in the Gothic Tradition.* Ed. Valeria Tinkler-Villani, Peter Davidson, and Jane Stevenson. Amsterdam: Rodopi, 1995. 99–106. Print.

Lee, L. L. "The Devil's Figure: James Hogg's Justified Sinner." *Studies in Scottish Literature* 3 (1965–6): 230–9. Print.

Mackay, Charles. *Extraordinary Popular Delusions and the Madness of Crowds.* 1841, 1852. New York: Harmony Books, 1980. Print.

Mazzoni, Cristina. *Maternal Impressions: Pregnancy and Childbirth in Literature and Theory.* Ithaca, NY: Cornell UP, 2002. Print.

Mellor, Anne K. "Physiognomy, Phrenology, and Blake's Visionary Heads." *Blake in His Time.* Ed. Robert N. Essick and Donald Ross Pearce. Bloomington: Indiana UP, 1978. 53–74. Print.

Miall, David S. "The Preceptor as Fiend: Radcliffe's Psychology of the Gothic." *Jane Austen and Mary Shelley and Their Sisters.* Ed. Laura Dabundo. Lanham, Maryland: UP of America, 2000. 31–43. Print.

Mitchell, Sebastian. "Dark Interpreter: Literary Uses of the Brocken Spectre from Coleridge to Pynchon." *The Dalhousie Review* 87.2 (2007): 167–87. Print.

Pick, Daniel. " 'Terrors of the Night': Dracula and 'Degeneration' in the Late Nineteenth Century." *Critical Quarterly* 30.4 (1988): 71–87. Print.

"Psychology." *The Oxford English Dictionary Online.* 2nd ed. 2008. Web. Apr. 12, 2008.

Punter, David. "Narrative and Psychology in Gothic Fiction." *Gothic Fictions: Prohibition/Transgression.* Ed. and afterword Kenneth W. Graham. New York: AMS, 1989. 1–27. Print.

Redekop, Magdalene. "Beyond Closure: Buried Alive with Hogg's Justified Sinner." *ELH (English Literary History)* 52.1 (1985): 159–84. Print.

Reid, Julia. *Robert Louis Stevenson, Science, and the* Fin de Siècle. New York: Palgrave Macmillan, 2006. Print.

Richardson, Alan. *British Romanticism and the Science of the Mind.* New York: Cambridge UP, 2001. Print.

Shorter, Edward. *A Historical Dictionary of Psychiatry.* Oxford: Oxford UP, 2005. Print.

Smith, Nelson C. *James Hogg.* Boston: Twayne Publishers, 1980. Print.

Thiher, Allen. *Revels in Madness: Insanity in Medicine and Literature.* Ann Arbor: U of Michigan P, 1999. Print.

Vallins, David. *Coleridge and the Psychology of Romanticism: Feeling and Thought.* Basingstoke, UK: Palgrave Macmillan, 2000. Print.

Veeder, William. "The Nurture of the Gothic, or, How Can a Text Be Both Popular and Subversive?" *Spectral Readings: Towards a Gothic Geography.*

Ed. and intro. Glennis Byron and David Punter. New York: Macmillan, 1999. 54–70. Print.

Vickers, Neil. *Coleridge and the Doctors.* Oxford: Clarendon Press, 2004. Print.

———. "Coleridge, Thomas Beddoes and Brunonian Medicine." *European Romantic Review* 8.1 (1997): 47–94. Print.

Webb, K. A. "Ferriar, John (1761–1815)." *Oxford Dictionary of National Biography.* 2004. Web. Jul. 11, 2005.

Whytt, Robert. *Observations on the Nature, Causes, and Cure of Those Disorders Which Have Been Called Nervous, Hypochondriac, or Hysteric.* Edinburgh: n.p., 1765. Print.

CHAPTER FIVE

"IT IS A PATH I HAVE PRAYED TO FOLLOW": THE PARADOXICAL PLEASURES OF ROMANTIC DISEASE

Clark Lawlor

INTRODUCTION

The beautiful Lady Mary! How could she die?–and of consumption! But it is a path I have prayed to follow. I would wish all I love to perish of that gentle disease. How glorious! To depart in the hey-day of the young blood–the heart all passion–the imagination all fire– amid the remembrances of happier days–in the fall of the year–and so be buried up forever in the gorgeous autumnal leaves!

—Edgar Allan Poe, "Metzengerstein" 20

Poe's well-known fictional comments seem to mirror the events and obsessions of his own life: notoriously psychoanalyzed by Marie Bonaparte, student of Freud, in her critical biography, Poe married or became amorously (not necessarily sexually) involved with consumptive women who suffered the fate and disease of his own beautiful but terminally ill mother. Bonaparte reads Poe as an individual psychoanalytic case study, but she ignores the fact that Poe's age took its cue from the Romantics and their culture in attributing pleasure to certain types of disease. This essay discusses the idea that illness—an often painful phenomenon and negatively construed experience—can paradoxically give pleasure to the beholder and even to the sufferer.

Consumption, phthisis or tabes (pulmonary tuberculosis), is an obvious, although by no means exclusive, instance of a disease that might be regarded, consciously or unconsciously, as a positive aspect of the self, or at least of someone else's self. In contrast with Sander Gilman's postmodern theoretical model of disease as the Other that threatens to dissolve the boundaries of the self, certain illnesses (I am using this word interchangeably with "disease," despite the various attempts to argue that "disease" refers to the biological construct and "illness" to the cultural construct) seem to act as bolsters to one's sense of self, as a perverse kind of cultural capital (to adapt Pierre Bourdieu's formulation).[1] Melancholy is another Romantic condition that has a long prehistory of pleasurable associations, a major one for Romantic writers being the pseudo-Aristotelian link (via Marsilio Ficino) with genius.[2] This essay, however, will focus on the case of consumption, primarily in relation to the consumptive poets Mary Tighe and the famous (in their time) Davidson sisters, Lucretia and Margaret, examining how the pleasures of disease figured in terms of their art, their lives, and their critical reception. By examining these lesser-known female poets, I intend to elucidate the complex construction of pleasure and disease between different "actors" in the poetic domain. Pleasure circulates in an apparently perverse—because grounded in the consumption of the disease consumption—exchange between poet, critic, and reading public. Previous discussions of consumption have noted its fashionability, but not explicitly examined in any detail the role of pleasure and its production among different groups in such fashionability. Before I discuss Tighe and the Davidsons, a more general consideration of the status of Sensibility and the prehistory of consumption is in order as a means of interrogating how disease could be more than merely a secondary gain for a poet.

One way to approach the question of Romantic pleasure in disease is via the culture—both medical and literary—of Sensibility, a key component of Romanticism that, until relatively recently, critics have viewed as a shallow and feminized literary cult that had little bearing on "deep" Romanticism. I have argued, following George Rousseau's work on nerves, spirits, and fibers, that Sensibility is a movement propelled by the new ideas about the nerves propagated first by Thomas Willis in the late seventeenth century and then by Albrecht von Haller in the mid-eighteenth century. When the body and mind were reconceptualized as a symbiotic entity bound by the physical structure of the nervous system, one not always open to conscious control, the role of the nerves as transmitters of external stimuli ensured that the body was always bound to be indicative of the activities of the mind.

People with finer nerves were more inclined to be receptive to the beauties or horrors of the world beyond the body. Thus poets were thought to be the most delicate of individuals, "hypersensitive to external stimuli, closely allying the twin states of pleasure and pain" (Lawlor, "Poetry" 50). Akenside's "The Pleasures of Imagination" describes the poet-figure Memnon's harp strings as "the finer organs of the mind," which ensure that any sensory input from the world around him "Thrills thro' imagination's tender frame,/ From nerve to nerve."[3] The poet's Sensibility was at an extreme end of the spectrum, with the cloddish and thick-nerved peasant or slave at the other. By the Romantic period, John Brown's ideas of excitability, of over- and understimulation of the nervous system, had modified the idea of Sensibility into a more intense state than before, paving the way for the rise of the image of the Romantic poet oscillating between the extremes of inspired hyperactivity and despairing exhaustion, plea- sure and pain (Lawlor, *Consumption* 114).

In order to understand how a killer disease like consumption might bring pleasure and how it might relate to Romantic Sensibility, it is first necessary to visit the origins of consumption in two discourses: as the disease of the Good Christian Death, and as the disease of love. Consumption had become the disease of the good Christian in the medieval *Ars Moriendi* and even earlier because its symptoms, or the "narrative" of the disease itself in biological terms, suited the dis- cursive necessities of the Christian's preparation for—and execution of—his or her own death (Lawlor, *Consumption* 28–40).[4] Because consumption was usually chronic (unless galloping), it gave time for the dying persons to order their affairs with God and Man; because there was no taint of lunacy and supposedly no agonizing pain (because there are few nerves in the lungs, comparatively speaking) in consumption, it allowed the believers to face their Maker *compos mentis*. This lack of pain was also an attractive prospect to the prob- ably terrified patient and potentially even a sign of God's favor to the Christian who had been given such a "golden disease," as Bunyan had put it (323, 302). Those of a Calvinist tendency might regard consumption as a sign of election, "*La mort des élus*," or the death of the elect.[5] Moreover, consumption thinned and wasted the sufferer: consumption might be a visible symbol of both the individual's moral restraint and lack of visceral greed and, in the process of wasting, enact the movement away from the material and toward the spiritual. The exemplary priests John Donne and George Herbert were both wasted, even skeletal, by the time they died of consumption: Donne in particular had preached a sermon in St. Paul's while notoriously

thin, and had been pronounced to be giving his own funeral speech
(Walton 74–5). In the early modern tradition and later in the eighteenth century, consumption had been considered the disease of the
Good Death. Thomas Browne's letter describing the easy and soft
death of a friend from consumption proved to be tremendously popular with readers well into the nineteenth century, not least because
consumption continued to kill people in very large numbers throughout these centuries (Browne 177–96).

At least from classical times, consumption also figured as the disease of love, and a consequence of love melancholy. Consumption was
said to visit lovers because of the "non-natural" factor of emotional
turmoil playing itself out on the body, as Gideon Harvey's chapter
"Of an Amorous Consumption" explains in his *Morbus Anglicus: or
the Anatomy of Consumptions. Containing methods of curing all consumptions, coughs, and spitting of blood ...To which are added, some
brief discourses of melancholy, madness, and distraction occasioned by
love* (1660; 39). Heartbreak, after all, was taken seriously as a literal
illness in the early modern period. Love melancholy was predicated
on the absence of the desired object; the good news was that cure
could easily be effected by the pining lover achieving union with his
or her beloved. Again, the symptoms of the disease "narrative" suited
that of the lover. The consumptive and wasting lover, male or female,
would be authenticated by this very disease—what better proof of
one's suffering for love? Luckily, these physical signs were largely
aesthetic and beautifying. For women, this involved the alternating
paleness and hectic flush of the cheeks, bodily manifestations of consumption that mapped well onto the traditional features of female
beauty. The wasting of the body in both men and women was an
enactment of the power of love to purify the body of its gross matter
(especially in the neo-Platonic tradition of progression from earthly
to heavenly love) and, as a by-product, might beautify the woman
still further. Again, the painlessness of consumption allowed lovers
to go about complaining of their lot, and indeed to continue their
love affairs, amours usually frustrated for the convenience of narrative pleasure. The chronic nature of consumption also allowed the
sustained composition of literature: a speedy disease like the plague
or cholera might leave no time for such luxuries. Literary productivity
was a happy and crucial side effect of consumption's slow process.

With the advent of the new nerve theory of the eighteenth century
and the rise of Sensibility—a phenomenon driven by these new medical ideas—consumption's two discourses of religion and love were
pushed closer together. George Cheyne, along with other medics,

had stated that those refined and thin-nerved sufferers of diseases of the nerves or "the English Malady" would, unless treated, segue naturally into "a real sensible *Phthisis Pulmonum*" (185–7). Cheyne had treated Samuel Richardson for his nervous "Hyp," so it is no coincidence that Richardson's character Clarissa Harlowe manifests aspects of both discourses as she suffers a love melancholy that is displaced neo-Platonically (through her rape) into a religious melancholy. The ensuing nervous consumption both kills her and symbolizes her reinvention from broken-hearted lover who has lost the earthly object of her desire (unworthy though he turns out to be) into a religious martyr in the manner of a John Donne: witness her elaborate preparation for death, very much based on Donne's notorious efforts. Both Donne and Clarissa prepare their own coffins and keep them in their homes, and both consumptives adopt a pious disregard for earthly matters as they turn toward the next world. Clarissa's peculiarly devout Sensibility (in all senses of the word) paved the way for later sentimental heroines—Romantic and Victorian—and their exemplary and authoritative moral status. Such a model affected the construction of the poets I will be examining later: Mary Tighe and Lucretia and Margaret Davidson.

By the time of the Romantic period, and with the aid of the influential Clarissa among many others, one strain of popular opinion had it that to be consumptive was beautiful and poetic. As Shelley said to Keats: "This consumption is a disease particularly fond of people who write such good verses as you have done, and with the assistance of an English winter it can often indulge its selection;—I do not think that young and amiable poets are at all bound to gratify its taste; they have entered into no bond with the Muses to that effect" (220–1). Doctors agreed: Thomas Young argued that "there is some reason to conjecture, that the enthusiasm of genius, as well as of passion, and the delicate sensibility, which leads to a successful cultivation of the fine arts, have never been developed in greater perfection, than where the constitution has been decidedly marked by that character, which is ... often evidently observable in the victims of pulmonary consumption" (43). The vogue of the "genteel, linear, consumptive make, now or lately so much in request," as Thomas Beddoes put it at the turn of the century, was evidence that literature provided a template for real-life behavior, as well as vice versa (214).

Consumption, therefore, had become linked with pleasure in the Romantic period from at least two perspectives: that of the individual sufferer, who might accrue "cultural capital" from its poetic or beautiful qualities, and that of the beholder of the sufferer, who might be uplifted, inspired spiritually, or even sexually attracted (as with Poe) by the vision or works of the consumptive. The pleasure of the consumptive sufferers themselves generally occurred in the early stages of the disease, since the realities of approaching death and increasingly uncomfortable symptoms in later stages would dampen any sense of Romantic inspiration (the pun on breath is intentional), although in some cases it does appear that the sufferer was only mildly aware of the condition right up till the last moments of his or her life. The pleasure of the beholder depended partly on the gender of the consumptive and the spectator: beautiful dying women were a popular preoccupation with men of this period, and both sexes could draw consolation from the beatifying effects of this spiritual disease. Here I will examine female poets who can illustrate the pleasures and pains of consumption from these different viewpoints.

These poets are the Irish Mary Tighe, an influence on Keats via her *Psyche*, and the famous American Davidson sisters, Lucretia and Margaret, who were notoriously linked to Poe's condemnation of their poetry even as he lauded their persons. All these female poets died young—very young in the case of the Davidsons—of consumption. In these instances, however, it seems critics and readers both male and female relished the mythology of the consumptive poet, whereas the poets themselves had no such delusions. Despite their knowledge of consumptive reality, these poets were able to manipulate their audience's awareness of consumption as the mark of the authentic poet by working it into their poetry.

MARY TIGHE AND THE CONSEQUENCES
OF PLEASURE

Irish poet Mary Tighe (1772–1810) was raised in County Wicklow and died of consumption at her poetic cousin William Tighe's home at Woodstock, County Kilkenny. Mary endured an unhappy marriage with her other, more practical, cousin Henry Tighe, a politician. She seems to have contracted her consumption around 1802, suffering greatly and clearly unpleasurably until her death eight years later. The pleasures of consumption in Tighe's writing were not those of a Poe character: she seems to have been oppressed more than was typical by the disease, and reflects this in most of her personal poetry. In Tighe—unlike the work of Lucretia Davidson—we find the pleasures of consumption largely generated by popular demand for an image of consumptive femininity, although there is always the general sense that consumption authenticates Tighe as a poet.

Her major work, *Psyche, with Other Poems. By the Late Mrs Henry Tighe* (1811), was circulated among friends and family in 1795, although it was not published for general viewing—edited by her cousin William—until the year after her death. Both the eponymous Psyche and her lover exhibit consumptive symptoms that are generated through the vicissitudes of love. The other poems that accompanied *Psyche* in this volume are of special interest to the student of consumptive poetry, pleasurable or otherwise, because they are a literary testament to Tighe's personal experience of consumption, although they rework this raw narrative material of disease in various ways and through different genres. These poems are not odes in praise of consumption and the genius it visits on the poet, and do not conform to the glamour of the disease as in the more clichéd depiction in *Psyche;* rather, Tighe presents a poetic representation of the suffering poet that serves to generate and vindicate her poetry. This is a perverse kind of pleasure, but no more perverse than the pleasure the male critics took in such a spectacle.

In her poem "Pleasure," Tighe partly blames her disease on her high-society life when younger, although her biographers and critics largely ascribe it to her hyper-femininity. "Pleasure" is a poem in which, ironically, like the Beddoesian rants against the modern female lifestyle, Tighe cites her previous high-society glamour in Dublin and London as the cause of her present consumptive condition: her personal and poetic illness narrative coincides with the medical one (*Keats and Mary Tighe* 262–5). The "syren Pleasure" has urged her to "suck sweet poison from...[its] velvet lip" and has "in opiate charms my virtue steep[ed]," silencing "Reason and Conscience" (1, 4–6). She has "with dear purchase seize[d] each glittering toy" presented to her in Pleasure's "faithless dreams" (10). The dreams refer to the tensions generated by her religious upbringing and the giddy world of her youth, especially in the later 1780s when she formed an attachment to her cousin Henry Tighe, a relationship that she was soon to regret. Her first ominous cough came roughly a year after she became involved with Henry, although this did not stop her regular shuttling back and forth between England and Ireland (*Works* 4–6).

Tighe's autobiographical narrator compares the consequence of this indulgence to the fate of "the charmed mariner," who is lured to "poisoned Senegal's ill-omened tide" in which the dazzling and luxuriant view of land hides the "deadly vapours" and "rank infected ground" (*Works* 27–8, 53, 55). Like slow-creeping yet beautiful consumption, whose sight gives pleasure but whose touch brings eventual death, "Deceitful calms deal subtle death around":

> Even as they gaze their vital powers decay,
> Their wasted health and vigour melt away;
> Till quite extinct the animating fire,
> Pale, ghastly victims, they at last expire. (57–60)

As Alan Bewell has shown in his *Romanticism and Colonial Disease*, consumption of the privileged Romantic type was primarily regarded as disease of the white, upper-class European, but here Tighe highlights the dangers of European civilization by drawing on a colonial disease mythology in which beautiful vistas and lush vegetation hide diseases fatal to the European, even as Europeans brought the "white plague" of consumption to the inhabitants of those lands. Pleasure has also transformed Mary into a pale consumptive whose vital energy or "animating fire" is on the verge of expiring, true to the medical theory of Romantic Vitalism (Lawlor, *Consumption* 114).[6] These are the final lines of the poem; no gloss is needed to explain that the sailors reflect Tighe's own self-image and disease. The opening part of the poem merely introduces her own instance of deception by Pleasure and then goes on to warn others, "the young and innocent" as she herself was then, about the Siren hazards of this foe "whose breath can blast." As with a seductive but miasmatic foreign shore like Senegal, people do well to shun contact with the dangerous pleasures of fashionable London life.

Tighe's poem does not overly condemn herself or the sailors, however: all are unwary "victims" of Pleasure's illusory "magic charms." Senegal is a blank imaginative space in which the European can unrestrainedly fantasize about the bounties it holds, while the pleasurable social spaces of the European city hold a similar attraction for young women who are not warned about the paradoxical pains of pleasure (although medics like Thomas Beddoes who had fulminated constantly in their writings against the fashionable female lifestyle would beg to differ). Excessive economic consumption of luxury in Britain or Senegal results in the eponymous disease: in both cases the "goods" are tainted by some deceptive flaw. Nor does the poem work on only a single level: Tighe has been seduced and deceived not only by a lifestyle, but also by a particular man—her husband. As I have shown, female disappointment in love was traditionally a cause of consumptive love melancholy, even if in this instance the problem occurs after Mary's marriage rather than before. Luxury and love combine to cause Mary's consumption, leaving her neither young nor innocent. Understandably, her husband is a shady figure in her poetry, social mores being strict in such a "polite" society. Instead the focus is usually on redeeming and safe female friendship that struggles against the onset of consumption.

CONSTRUCTING THE CONSUMPTIVE IMAGE:
CONSUMING CRITICS AND POETS

Contemporary reviews of Tighe (all posthumous) tend to concentrate on *Psyche*, a narrative poem written in Spenserian stanzas, which follows the trials of the eponymous heroine. Critics were not slow to read *Psyche* against the consumptive condition of the authoress. Although generally enthusiastic, *The British Review* complains that "the author seems to have been infected by the languor" (Anon. 287) that is described in the following lines:

> But melancholy poisons all her joys,
> And secret sorrows all her hopes depress,
> Consuming languor every bliss destroys,
> And sad she droops, repining, comfortless.
> (*Psyche, with Other Poems* 38, ll. 514–17)

Tighe evidently transferred her own consumptive pains, rather than pleasures at this point, into the love melancholy of her heroine. The *Quarterly Review* also notes "the not uncommon intervention of languor" within the "descriptive energy" of Tighe's *Psyche* (Anon. 478). The *British Review* uses the language of disease to link both the author and the text: the one "infects" the other. The cult of the author was developing in this period, and the medical theory of the day did nothing to discourage biographical readings, stating clearly the direct connection between mind and body. Tighe's apparent expression of her own consumptive experience, and feelings about it, disturbed the healthy narrative that at least some of the more sanitary critics apparently wished to build—although in practice an "unhealthy" early death made better copy for the literary journals.

Both Psyche and her lover exhibit consumptive symptoms that are generated through the agonies of love. Again, the *British Review* cites these extracts from *Psyche*: "More sweet than health's fresh bloom the wan hue seemed/ Which set upon her pallid cheek" (Anon. 293; *Psyche, with Other Poems* 173, ll. 505–6). The fashion of consumptive femininity, against which Beddoes and Trotter had railed, is evident here, where Psyche's pale and interesting look is preferable to robust good health. One of the sources of pleasure in consumption for a woman (at least theoretically) was the "hectic flush," the alternating flush and pallor of the cheeks caused by the illness that so nicely corresponded with classical definitions of female beauty.

The contrast between this idealized representation and Tighe's self-image in her more personal poetry is striking: it was one thing to represent cultural stereotypes of pleasurable disease and quite another to describe the experience of one's own debilitating condition. Part of the problem here is the inherent variability and instability of disease "narrative" or pattern of symptoms in consumption. Sometimes the disease could be gentle and easy, but it could also be a chokingly awful way to die. The reader finds both kinds of representations in literature, but there is a tendency to follow the more positive form in the literature of the late eighteenth century, itself inspired by a long literary lineage. Psyche's lover also echoes the Renaissance tradition of the melancholic whose disease has psychological rather than physical origins:

> The wasted form, the deep-drawn, frequent sigh,
> Some slow consuming malady bespeak,
> But medicinal skill the cause in vain shall seek. (quoted in Anon.,
> *British Review* 294; *Psyche, with Other Poems* 140, ll. 349–51)

Doctors need knowledge of the lover's mind to "cure" the "consuming malady" of love; the resultant turmoil of thoughts and emotions takes an inevitable toll on the body in the form of consumption.

Despite these apparent lapses into her morbidly personal illness narrative, the critics largely relished the poignant early death of the poet, aided and abetted by William Tighe's annotation of her poetry. Mary's poem "On Receiving a Branch of Mezeron. Which Flowered at Woodstock. December, 1809" had written underneath it:

> The concluding poem of this collection was the last ever composed by the author, who expired at the place where it was written, after six years of protracted malady, on the 24th of March, 1810, in the thirty-seventh year of her age. Her fears of death were perfectly removed before she quitted this scene of trial and suffering; and her spirit departed to a better state of existence, confiding with heavenly joy in the acceptance and love of her Redeemer. (307–11)

William's claim that "her fears of death were perfectly removed" before she died was not confirmed by her writing.[7] Rather, the end of "On Receiving a Branch of Mezeron" was an agonized farewell to "ye, whose smile must greet my eye/ No more, nor voice my ear." The poet expressed this concept in sentimental terms: her friends and family "breathe for me the tender sigh/ And shed the pitying tear" (37–41). William had framed the poem in the form of a stereotypical religious consolation, cleansing the writing of its unsettling struggle with painful mortality. His statement also served as a good piece of advertising: there was nothing like early death to prove authenticity in the Romantic poet, especially if she was a beautiful young woman. The critical response to Tighe's life and work proved the point: after her death, the critics began to see her as something of a counterpart to other fast-living and fast-dying poets such as Burns, Otway, and Chatterton (Ashfield 158). In his diary entry of January 27, 1812, Sir James Mackintosh connected Tighe with familiar consumptive figures of the day: "Chaulieu, Michael Bruce, and Mrs. Tighe have written verses on the prospect of death, and hers are not the least affecting" (quoted in Tighe, *Keats and Mary Tighe* xx).

As in the case of a suffering male poet, such as Michael Bruce, critics found Tighe's poetry deeply moving and perversely pleasurable. *The British Review* reprinted "On Receiving a Branch of Mezeron," and generally praised all of Tighe's minor poems as expressing "a soft and pleasing tinge of melancholy" (Anon. 294). Her consumption gave her a (Sentimental) sense of life as a "vale of tears," to use a Keatsian phrase, in which all pleasure was vain illusion and dangerous to health, according to this review. "On Receiving a Branch of Mezeron" was particularly lauded as conveying "delicacy and exquisite pathos...which, as the last effusions of a mind conscious that it would shortly quit this world of sorrows, are perfectly irresistible" (139). *The Monthly Review* was similarly insistent on the compelling biography of the author: having given the facts of her life and death, it claimed that "this simple statement is sufficient to excite all the interest in the fate of that author we could desire" (Anon. 294). William Howitt's later Victorian reminiscences of his youthful reading of *Psyche* continued this theme: it "charmed [me] intensely," he writes, and he identifies "a tone of melancholy music in it, which seemed the regretful expression of the consciousness of a not far-off death" (282). Much of "the sad fascination thrown over both her fate and her work" was due to this biographical factor: "it was now well known that the young and beautiful poetess was dead" (282).

The *Quarterly Review* also reproduced "On Receiving a Branch of Mezeron," informing the reader that it was finished three months before the poet's death and that it was written "under pressure of an illness plainly prophetic of the worst" (Anon. 484). The reviewer

admitted that it was difficult to say how much of the emotion generated by the poem "must be ascribed to the circumstances amidst
which it was composed," but still asserted the purely poetic value of
the piece. Despite its attempt to concentrate on the poetry, rather
than the biography that informed it, the *Quarterly* was true to its
time in its persistent return to Tighe's disease and ended the article
by quoting William Tighe's editorial advert to Mary's last "melancholy and striking" poem (Anon. 485). In a dubious act of critical
judgement, the reviewer's reproduction of the poem excised the last
twelve lines as being of inferior quality, leaving the poem to end on a
bleaker and more dramatic note, with Mary's "coward heart" cling-
ing "shuddering" to dust (485, ll. 31–2). This more tragic and trun-
cated conclusion to the poem was hardly counteracted by William
Tighe's platitudes about Mary's final good death; certainly to the
modern reader there is a jarring disjunction between Mary's poetic
construction of her disease, the even more severe version printed by
the *Quarterly*, and William's final imposition. It was a feature of more
cases than that of Mary Tighe that the posterity of the consumptive poet, male or female, could be manipulated by those who were
able to gain authority over the representation of the life and work in
question. Keats was a "victim" of Shelley's rewriting of his image in
"Adonais," a complex reworking that nevertheless feminizes Keats in
order to make Shelley look more masculine—at least to Byron, as
James Heffernan has shown.

The reviewers did consider Tighe as the counterpart of other
examples of consumptive early death, but in a way that emphasized
her peculiarly feminine attributes, poetic or personal. William Howitt
transforms Tighe into a sentimental heroine who would be perfectly
at home in any novel, dying young in a haze of glamour: "she came
before the imagination in the combined witchery of brilliant genius,
and the pure loveliness of a seraph, which had but touched upon the
earth on some celestial mission, and was gone forever" (282). Female
genius is cast by Howitt in terms of the ambiguous female figure of the
witch, who seduces the young William through her feminine wiles.
"Psyche" becomes a literary lure to entrap the male critic: "the delicacy...yet intense passion of the poem, were all calculated to seize on
the kindred spirit of youth, and to make you in love with the writer."
The opposing desexualized image of the seraph uses the standard
touchstone of the angelic heroine of sentimental literature: earthly
existence is too harsh for those sent from heaven in their extreme
purity. This is usually a more passive image, but Mary has a "celestial
mission" to write enchanting poetry for the delectation of the male

critic. Howitt compares Mary to her own character, Psyche, who also yearns "for the restoration of the lost heaven and the lost heart," thus figuring Tighe in the traditional role of a woman destined to love rather than write.

Earlier critics also cast Tighe in terms of her specifically feminine consumptive genius: the British Review considered that "on the whole, there is a characteristic delicacy, a 'trew *feminitée*' about this publication, which is exceedingly attractive" and in pleasing contrast to those women writers who "prefer the din of arms" (Anon. 297). The physical "delicacy" of the suffering female transferred itself into a separate and unthreatening category of poetry labeled "feminine." Tighe knew her place in the poetic scheme of things, according to this perspective, and appropriately constrained her efforts to the female realm of love and melting melancholy rather than the male domains of war, politics, and the public sphere. The Monthly Review was similarly enamored of Tighe's moral rectitude, citing her as a good example to the nation's women: she was more angelic moral exemplar than poetic genius. It especially approved of her preface to Psyche, in which, in common with many female writers of the day, she had been careful to stress the inoffensive content of her poem—particularly regarding true and legitimate love as opposed to the lurid sort that, by implication, might be found in the more salacious romances (Anon. 138, 140).

Sir James Mackintosh, that remarkable Scottish polymath writing in his diary at roughly the same time, found this distinctly feminine quality to be almost too much for him: "For the first three cantos I felt a sort of languid elegance and luscious sweetness, as if I had been overpowered by perfumes; but the three last are of such exquisite beauty that they quite silence me. They are beyond all doubt the most faultless series of verses ever produced by a woman" (quoted in *Tighe, Keats and Mary Tighe* xx). The smitten Mackintosh exaggerates here: Tighe did have competitors for the role of greatest woman poet and was never a threat to male poets. Perhaps this was partly the point: for Mackintosh, Tighe, despite having talent, is not masculine enough, as the phrase "by a woman" and the imagery of perfume imply. He goes on to rank Tighe below Joanna Baillie and Madame de Staël, because the former has "Shakesperian genius" and the latter a "masculine understanding" (xx). Nevertheless, Tighe's verses "On the prospect of death" placed her generically in the company of another now-unknown consumptive poet, Michael Bruce, even if she was prevented from achieving true poetic greatness by her gender, according to Mackintosh's masculinist values.

The shaping of Tighe's poetic reputation was largely beyond her control: the forces of the critics and her cousin-editor were more significant determinants of the way her life and work were constructed in the imagination of a public ever-willing to read about early death and poetic genius. Clearly the pleasures of disease could be experienced by consumers as well as by sufferers.

Tighe did express a kind of pleasure in consumption in one of her final pieces, the "Sonnet Written at Woodstock, in the county of Kilkenny, the Seat of William Tighe, June 30, 1809." This poem gently hints at the use of consumption in the construction of Tighe's poetic identity (*Keats and Mary Tighe* 306). Typically, Tighe figures her relation to poetry through both her disease and the socially more legitimate poetry of her cousin William. The sonnet opens with an invocation to the Muse who has wandered among the "shades," "To their loved master breathing many a lay/ Divinely soothing" (2, 3–4). Poetry has evidently had a therapeutic function for William, as the "bright visions" sent by the Muse have disarmed "The subduing powers of mortal ill" by luring him with her "soft voice" to the idyllic country seat that in itself functions as a beautiful subject for poetry (7, 9, 10). What William's "mortal ill" has been we are not told, but Mary seeks the soothing quality of poetry for herself, asking the Muse to "be near to charm/ For me the languid hours of pain, and warm/ This heart depressed with one inspiring ray" (4–6) from the visions given to William in his time of need.

Although Mary ostensibly defers to the legitimating power of William's masculinity, symbolized both by his ownership of Woodstock and by her quotation from his poetry, the female Muse is the real power in this poem, functioning as a kind of poetic doctor and nurse, caring for the vulnerable William by "soothing" (4) him with her lays, distracting him with her "bright visions" (7), luring him to his "ivyed seat" (10), and causing him to linger "Beneath his own dear oaks" (13). The Muse is most often the subject, as the active verbs suggest, moving William around at her leisure like a mother with a child. In this way, Tighe presents an image of empowered poetic femininity that circumnavigates traditional male authority through an alternative aesthetic of healing. Tighe sees the Muse's nurturing and feminized poetic power as a means to ward off her own depression and "languid hours of pain" (5). Consumptive suffering becomes enabling and is suitable material for Tighe's writing, as it exploits a female realm of experience associated with the traditionally caring role of women in medicine. An initial tribute to her cousin and his estate becomes an assertion of both Tighe's suffering and her need to transcend that suffering in poetry. She takes on the image of the suffering poet so common to men of the Romantic age, but with a further purpose: consumption here allows the female poet to produce her poetry in a way that overcomes the influence of the male poet. The pleasure is perverse and subtle, perhaps, but still a victory.

THE DAVIDSON SISTERS AND THE PLEASURES OF CONSUMPTIVE SELF-FASHIONING

I now turn to cases in which the image of the poet was paradoxically more self-fashioned and more consciously determined, despite the extreme youth of the women and the constant interference of adults in their lives. Lucretia Maria Davidson (1808–1825) and Margaret Miller Davidson (1823–1838) were sisters who were both afflicted with consumption and were assiduously promoted by their mother (herself a frustrated poet and also named Margaret) as poetic icons of doomed youth. Puffed by luminaries such as Samuel Finley Morse, Washington Irving, and Robert Southey, these girls were evidently fascinating to male critics despite the immature quality of their poetry, a point I have discussed at length elsewhere.[8] Largely forgotten now, the Davidsons were spectacularly well-known in their own time, as Edgar Allan Poe observed: "The name of Lucretia Davidson is familiar to all readers of Poetry. Dying at the early age of seventeen, she has been rendered famous, not less, and certainly not more, by her own precocious genius than by three memorable biographies, one by President Morse, of the American Society of Arts, another by Miss Sedgwick, and a third by Robert Southey" ("Margaret Miller," *Works* 219).[9]

Poe, with his usual insight, points out the problem for the literary critic. In using Catherine Sedgwick's biography of Lucretia[10] as a stick to beat slavish Americans fawning over British literary-critical dictates in the form of Robert Southey's endorsement of the Davidsons, Poe accuses Sedgwick of being unable to distinguish between

> that which, in our heart, is love of their worth, from that which, in our intellect, is appreciation of their poetic ability. With the former, as critic[s], we have nothing to do. The distinction is one too obvious for comment; and its observation would have spared us much twaddle on the part of the commentators upon *Amir Khan* [the title of a collection of poems by Lucretia]. ("Margaret Miller," *Works* 226)

Poe himself was in step with the others in his unbounded admiration of the Davidsons' moving lives, but he was intelligent enough to realize that the poetry, although apparently an illustration of those lives, was not of the highest quality.

The biographies are also moving to a modern audience, not least because the entire family was decimated by consumption, much in the manner of the Brontës and many others of the era besides. The poignancy partly comes from the youth of the victims, but it also derives from the consciousness, especially in Margaret's case, that the disease will very likely put an end to their quest to be poets. Hence the story depicted in Washington Irving's *Biography and Poetical Remains of the Late Margaret Miller Davidson* (1841; I use the 1843 edition here) carries several elements that a Romantic-period audience would relish: the heavily domestic scene of a middle-class mother's careful attentions to her daughters and vice versa (the father, Dr. Davidson, appears little); the sentimental effects of a chronic and poetic illness; the extreme youth of the protagonists; the strong Christian beliefs and good Christian deaths of the same; poetry that illustrates clearly a consciousness of impending and actual illness and death; and, not least, doomed female poets (although the focus here was clearly on Margaret).

Despite the fact that this scenario may have been more popular with female readers, those familiar with male critics of the time will not be surprised to learn that the notion of fading young female beauty set in its proper (domestic) sphere and producing appropriately pious sentimental poetry was a compulsively alluring scenario to men on both sides of the Atlantic. The biographies—always peppered with illustrative poetry by the sisters—describe in almost excessive detail the sufferings of the family in the face of suspected or impending death from consumption, but the texts clearly brought great pleasure to a large audience, to judge from Poe's comments at least, and not merely because of some consolatory function. Poe found Margaret's bond with her mother to be a "thrilling" picture of "exquisite loveliness," and stated that "few books have interested us more profoundly" ("Margaret Miller," *Works* 220). The description of Margaret's beautiful and pious consumptive death by Mrs. Davidson in a letter to Catherine Sedgwick (quoted in full by Irving) also sent Poe into transports of pleasure: it was so "full of minute beauty, and truth and pathos, that to read it without tears would be to prove one's self less than human" ("Margaret Miller," *Works* 220). Poe had his own pathological attraction to consumptive femininity, but his culture certainly validated the fascination with dead and dying beautiful consumptive females (Bronfen 86). In a discussion of Mark Twain's satiric rendering of gloomy female poets like Lucretia in the figure of Emmeline Grangerford in *Huckleberry Finn,* Cheryl Walker characterizes the nineteenth century as one "whose interest in death sometimes bordered on the necrophiliac" (23).

What of the experience of the sufferer herself? Did she gain pleasure from consumption in the manner of Alexandre Dumas's witty description of the consumptive vogue in Paris: " 'In 1823 and 1824 it was the fashion to suffer from the lungs; everybody was consumptive, poets especially; it was good form to spit blood after each emotion that was at all sensational, and to die before reaching the age of thirty. Of course Adolphe [de Leuven] and I, being tall and very thin, considered we were entitled to indulge ourselves too' "? (quoted in Dubos 58n). The black comedy inherent in the notion of having a choice about developing an often terminal condition was not something that was afforded to the Davidsons, who were actual rather than simulated consumptives. Nonetheless, there was a large element of self-fashioning in the poetic image of the sisters. Here I will focus on Margaret, who, being younger, had the example of her sister to follow in terms of a poetic career and consumptive destiny. Irving's biography, evidently hand-in-glove with the wishes of the mother, depicted Margaret as having the same intense and inevitably consumptive hyper-sensibility as her sister. Indeed, Margaret was apparently obsessed with Lucretia and what she symbolized in terms of poetic fame:

> We cannot help thinking that these moments of intense poetical exaltation sometimes approached to delirium, for we are told by her mother that the image of her departed sister Lucretia mingled in all her aspirations; the holy elevation of Lucretia's character had taken deep hold of her imagination, and in her moments of enthusiasm she felt that she held close and intimate communion with her beatified spirit. (*Biography and Poetical Remains* 40)

One must bear in mind that Margaret was only two years old when her sister died, so Lucretia was very much an "image" to her, rather than a reality.

Clearly, however, Margaret wished to represent herself as a potential poetic genius who was fighting with, yet authenticated by, her disease—a discourse of consumptive Sensibility that her mother and biographers, both male and female, actively encouraged. This representation is evident in the following poem, written when she knew she was ill with consumption:

> The brilliant genius, which on earth
> Is struggling with disease and pain,

> Will there unfold in power and light,
> Nought its bright current to restrain. ("The Joys of Heaven,"
> *Biography and Poetical Remains* 51; ll. 43–6)

Margaret blends the sentimental Christianity appropriate to the respectable and dutiful daughter (not unlike Clarissa) with a discourse of consumptive genius that she inherits most immediately from Lucretia, who in turn took it from burning meteors of poetic Sensibility like Henry Kirke White and Keats (Lawlor, *Consumption* 112). The divine spark of the poet will naturally seek its way to heaven rather than endure the harsh environment of the sublunary world: consumption is the vehicle for that transition, as it is a disease having both religious and secular-poetic valences.

Margaret's poem "To My Sister Lucretia" (confusingly, there are two poems of this title—here I analyze the longer one discussed by Irving in the *Biography*) invokes, perhaps not without some anxiety of influence (to adapt Harold Bloom's concept), Lucretia as conscious role model. Here, consumption is the poetic and spiritualizing disease that unites, rather than separates, the two sisters:

> I cannot weep that thou art fled,—
> For ever blends my soul with thine;
> Each thought, by purer impulse led,
> Is soaring on to realms divine.
> Thou wert unfit to dwell with clay,
> For sin too pure, for earth too bright!
> And death, who call'd thee hence away,
> Placed on his brow a gem of light! (*Biography and Poetical
> Remains* 59, ll. 25–32)

This was standard fare for elegies to the consumptive dead: consumption was pleasurable in the knowledge that it brought religious consolation as the disease of the elect—or if not elect, then at least privileged. What is different about Margaret's verse is her enjoyment of the connection of poetic destiny to consumption: Lucretia's "fingers wake my youthful lyre/ And teach its softer strains to flow" (41–2). Moreover, consumption as figured in the guardian angel and sister-figure of Lucretia is idealized, unlike the often fetid breath of the real sufferers, as the bringer of the sweet breath of poetic and moral inspiration:

> I hear thee in the summer breeze,
> See thee in all that's pure or fair;
> Thy whisper in the murmuring trees,

Thy breath, thy spirit everywhere. (33–6)

This first poem continues in a veritable ecstatic trance of pleasure at the thought of the two sisters' unification in poetic destiny, albeit with the final meeting in the afterlife.

In the second and shorter poem to Lucretia (1833), there is a further pleasure in the lustre cast by Lucretia's burgeoning reputation and the reflected glory that seems increasingly likely to accrue to Margaret herself: "THOUGH thy freshness and beauty are laid in the tomb,/ Like the flow'ret, which droops in its verdure and bloom;/.... Still, still, thou art ours and America's pride." (*Biography and Poetical Remains* 143, 1–2, 6). Margaret alludes to the international reputation of her sister, and the increasing pride in American poetic and literary achievements. Consumption validated poetic authenticity, and a pointed reference to Lucretia's condition later in the poem emphasizes the divine sanction and inspiration for Lucretia, a reference that also redounds—pleasurably—to the benefit of Lucretia:

> The pure elevation which beam'd from thine eye,
> As it turn'd to its home, in yon fair azure sky,
> Told of something unearthly, it shone with the light
> Of pure inspiration and holy delight. (11–14)

The eye of the consumptive was supposed to gleam with the spark of the divine to which the soul was yearning and destined to return. Again, in fashioning the consumptive genius of her sister, Margaret constructs a pleasurable mirror-image of herself.

Margaret made further use of the poetic and cultural tropes of consumption to work this dreaded destroyer into something that could give a paradoxical form of pleasure via her self-fashioning in poetry. Even as she bemoaned the power of consumption to kill, Margaret invoked the mythology of the disease as the verification of genius and beauty:

> Consumption! child of woe, thy blighting breath
> Marks all that's fair and lovely for thine own,
> And, sweeping o'er the silver chords of life,
> Blends all their music in one death-like tone. (*Biography and Poetical Remains* 103, lines 1–4)

This fragment is quoted by her mother in the letter, reproduced by Irving, that describes the final weeks of Margaret's life in 1838. Collaborating fully with the consumptive discourse invoked by her daughter, the mother comments that "the following fragments appear to be the very breathings of her soul during the last few weeks of her life—written in pencil, in a hand so weak and tremulous that I could with difficulty decipher them" (103).

Margaret was clearly aware of the symbolic value of her status as consumptive poet in the following lines of another fragment (the genre—perhaps most appropriately, given her prematurely terminated existence—that she tended to use in her last months of life):

> It is autumn, the season of rapid decay,
> When the flow'rets of summer are hasting away
> From the breath of the wintry blast,
> And the buds which oped to the gazer's eye,
> And the glowing tints of the gorgeous sky,
> And the forests robed in their emerald dye,
> With their loveliest blossoms have past. (quoted in *Biography* 104)

Again, the mother supplies the collaborative context for this fragment, which was apparently "written on a Sabbath evening in autumn, not many weeks before her death" (*Biography* 104). All good Romantics knew full well, following a medical tradition going back to Hippocrates (Lawlor, *Consumption* 16, 19, 20), that autumn was the time for consumptives to die, a time poignant for the pleasurable juxtaposition of death and beauty that was most famously symbolized by the falling autumn leaf. This fragment ends with Margaret expressing the desire of the soul to move beyond its earthly confines and arrive at the "fountain of light and love" that is heaven.

Even if the realities of her disease were sometimes nothing less than awful, Margaret was able to fashion, or self-fashion, the pleasurable and glamorous image of doomed poetic genius in both her poetry and her actual life, an image corroborated and amplified by her mother and biographers, both male and female. Having been forgotten for about a century, Mary Tighe and the Davidsons are coming back to critical attention, thanks largely to the efforts of feminist critics, but also thanks to critics working on the effects of disease on authors and their writing, such as Diane Price Herndl and Cheryl Walker. Mary Tighe and the Davidsons provide examples of how a particular "Romantic" disease, consumption, could paradoxically provide pleasure to critics of both sexes, although sometimes for different reasons, and even to the poets themselves. The convergence of the medical and cultural discourses of Sensibility with the previous traditions of consumption as the ideal Christian disease and disease of love melancholy led to a situation in which it was possible for poets to regard themselves as authenticated in their poetic mission by that very illness. To women who regarded themselves as true poets, this was a genuine form of pleasure.

NOTES

1. According to Bourdieu (241–58), cultural capital—as opposed to social or economic capital—is an advantage in knowledge or education that boosts the status of an individual in the social system. His subcategory of embodied cultural capital comes closest to a notion of fashionable illness as conferring such a heightened social position.
2. See, for example, Klibansky et al.
3. See 'The Pleasures of the Imagination' in Fairer and Gerrard, *Eighteenth-Century Poetry: An Annotated Anthology*, 310: 109 ff. See also Wordsworth's reworking and endorsement of Cowper's famous words, "*There is a pleasure in poetic pains/ Which only Poets know;—*'t was rightly said" (*The Complete Poetical Works of William Wordsworth* 8: 70).
4. For the impact of the *Ars Moriendi* in the Victorian context, see Jalland.
5. See the footnote in John Mason Neale's "In Consumption," 21, and the discussion in Watson's *The English Hymn*, 374–5.
6. Also Almeida, 102–3.
7. Her mother's account details the painful form of consumption that Mary endured, although she and Caroline Hamilton both asserted that Mary died *compos mentis* and reconciled to her fate in the manner of the good death. See *The Collected Poems and Journals of Mary Tighe*, ed. Linkin, 243, 267.
8. For further information, see both Lawlor, "Transatlantic Consumptions," and Loeffelholz.
9. References will be given to Poe's combined review with the "Poetical remains of the late Lucretia Maria Davidson," also originally in *Graham's Magazine*, retitled "Margaret Miller and Lucretia Maria Davidson" in *The Works of the Late Edgar Allan Poe*, iii.
10. For an edition of Sedgwick's biography see Lucretia Maria Davidson, *Poetical Remains of the Late Lucretia Maria Davidson, Collected and Arranged by Her Mother (M.M. Davidson): With a Biography, by Miss [C. M.] Sedgwick.*

WORKS CITED

Akenside, Mark. "The Pleasures of Imagination." *Eighteenth-Century Poetry: An Annotated Anthology*. Ed. David Fairer and Christine Gerrard. Oxford: Blackwell, 1999. 303–21. Print.

Almeida, Hermione de. *Romantic Medicine and John Keats*. New York: Oxford UP, 1991. Print.

Anon. Review of *Psyche*. Art. III. *The Monthly Review* 66 (1811): 138–52. Print.

———. Review of *Psyche*. Art. XIV. *British Review* 2 (June 1811): 277–93. Print.

———. Review of *Psyche*. *Quarterly Review* 5 (May 1811): 471–85. Print.

Ashfield, Andrew, ed. *Romantic Women Poets 1770–1838, 1788–48*. 2 vols. Manchester: Manchester UP, 1995. Print.

Beddoes, Thomas. *Manual of Health: or, The Invalid Conducted Safely Through the Seasons*. London: J. Johnson, 1806. Print.

Bewell, Alan. *Romanticism and Colonial Disease*. Baltimore: Johns Hopkins UP, 1999. Print.

Bonaparte, Marie. *The Life and Works of Edgar Allan Poe: A Psychoanalytic Interpretation*. Trans. John Rodker. London: Imago, 1949. Print.

Bourdieu, Pierrre. "The Forms of Capital." *Handbook of Theory and Research for the Sociology of Education*. Ed. J. G. Richardson. New York: Greenwood, 1986. 241–58. Print.

Bronfen, Elizabeth. *Over Her Dead Body: Death, Femininity and the Aesthetic*. Manchester: Manchester UP, 1992. Print.

Browne, Thomas. "A Letter to a Friend, upon the occasion of the Death of his Intimate Friend." *Sir Thomas Browne: Religio Medici and Other Works*. Ed. L. C. Martin. Oxford: Clarendon P, 1964. 177–96. Print.

Bunyan, John. *The Life and Death of Mr. Badman, Presented To the World in a Familiar Dialogue Between Mr. Wiseman, And Mr. Attentive*. London: Printed by J. A. for Nath. Ponder [et al.], 1680. Print.

Cheyne, George. "A Consumption." *The Natural Method of Cureing the Diseases of the Body, and the Disorders of the Mind Depending on the Body*. London: G. Strahan, 1742. 185–7. Print.

Davidson, Lucretia Maria. *Poetical Remains of the Late Lucretia Maria Davidson, Collected and Arranged by Her Mother (M.M. Davidson): With a Biography, by Miss [C. M.] Sedgwick*. 1837. Boston: Phillips, Sampson, and Co., 1857. Print.

Davidson, Margaret Miller. *Biography and Poetical Remains of the Late Margaret Miller Davidson*. Ed. Washington Irving. 1841. Philadelphia: Lea and Blanchard, 1843. Print.

Dubos, Rene, and Jean Dubos. *The White Plague. Tuberculosis, Man and Society*. Boston: Little, Brown and Company, 1952. Print.

Fairer, David and Christine Gerrard, eds. *Eighteenth-Century Poetry: An Annotated Anthology*. Oxford: Blackwell, 1999.

Gilman, Sander L. *Difference and Pathology: Stereotypes of Sexuality, Race and Madness*. Ithaca, NY: Cornell UP, 1985. Print.

Harvey, Gideon. *Morbus Anglicus: or the Anatomy of Consumptions*. London: Nathanael Brook, 1666. Print.

Heffernan, James A. W. "*Adonais*: Shelley's Consumption of Keats." *Studies in Romanticism* 23 (1984): 295–315. Print.

Herndl, Diane Price. *Invalid Women: Figuring Feminine Illness in American Fiction and Culture, 1840–1940.* Chapel Hill: U of North Carolina P, 1993. Print.

Howitt, William. *Homes and Haunts of the Most Eminent British Poets.* 1847. London: Routledge, 1877. Print.

Jalland, Pat. *Death in the Victorian Family.* Oxford: Oxford UP, 1996. Print.

Klibansky, Raymond, Erwin Panofsky, and Fritz Saxl. *Saturn and Melancholy: Studies in the History of Natural Philosophy, Religion, and Art.* New York: Basic Books, 1964. Print.

Lawlor, Clark. *Consumption and Literature: The Making of the Romantic Disease.* Basingstoke, UK: Palgrave, 2006. Print.

———. "Poetry and Science." *Blackwell Companion to Eighteenth-Century Poetry.* Ed. Christine   Gerrard. Oxford: Blackwell, 2006. 38–52. Print.

———. "Transatlantic Consumptions: Disease, Fame and Literary Nationalisms in the Davidson Sisters, Southey and Poe." *Studies in the Literary Imagination* 36:2 (Fall 2004): 109–26. Print.

Lawlor, Clark, and Akihito Suzuki. "The Disease of the Self: Representations of Consumption 1700–1830." *Bulletin of the History of Medicine* 74 (2000): 258–94. Print.

Loeffelholz, Mary. "Who Killed Lucretia Davidson? or, Poetry in the Domestic-Tutelary Complex." *The Yale Journal of Criticism* 10:2 (Fall 1997): 271–93. Print.

Neale, John Mason. "In Consumption." *Hymns for the Sick.* Cambridge: T. Stevenson, 1843: 21-24.

Poe, Edgar Allan. "Metzengerstein." *Collected Works of Edgar Allan Poe.* Ed. Thomas Ollive Mabbott. Vol. 2. Cambridge, MA: Belknap P of Harvard UP, 1978. 15-31. Print.

———. "Margaret Miller and Lucretia Maria Davidson." *The Works of the Late Edgar Allan Poe: With Notices of His Life and Genius.* Ed. N. P. Willis, J. R. Lowell, and R. W. Griswold. 3 vols. New York: J. S. Redfield, 1850. Vol. 3. 219–28. Print.

———. Review. "Biography and Poetical Remains of the Late Margaret Miller Davidson. By Washington Irving." *Graham's Magazine* (August 1841): 90–6. Print.

———. Review. "Poetical Remains of the Late Lucretia Maria Davidson." *Graham's Magazine* (December 1841): 304-06. Print.

Rousseau, George. S. "Nerves, Spirits, and Fibres: Towards Defining the Origins of Sensibility." *Studies in the Eighteenth Century.* Ed. R. F. Brissenden and J. C. Eade. Toronto: U of Toronto P, 1976. 137–57. Print.

Shelley, Percy Bysshe. *The Letters of Percy Bysshe Shelley.* Ed. Frederick L. Jones. Oxford: Clarendon P, 1964. Print.

Tighe, Mary. *The Collected Poems and Journals of Mary Tighe.* Ed. Harriet Kramer Linkin. Lexington: UP of Kentucky, 2005. Print.

Tighe, Mary. *Keats and Mary Tighe: The Poems of Mary Tighe with Parallel Passages from the Work of John Keats.* Ed. Earle Vonard Weller. 1928. New York: Kraus, 1966. Print.

———. *The Works of Mary Tighe, Published and Unpublished.* Ed. Patrick Henchy. Dublin: Bibliographical Society of Ireland, 1957. Print.

———. *Psyche, with Other Poems. By the Late Mrs Henry Tighe.* Ed. W. Tighe. London: Longman and Co, 1811. Print.

Walker, Cheryl. *The Nightingale's Burden: Women Poets and American Culture Before 1900.* Bloomington: Indiana UP, 1982. Print.

Walton, Izaak. *The Lives of John Donne, Sir Henry Wotton, Richard Hooker, George Herbert and Robert Sanderson,* 4th ed., 1675. Intro. George Saintsbury. Oxford World's Classics. London: Oxford UP, 1927. Print.

Watson, J. R. *The English Hymn.* Oxford: Clarendon, 1997.

Wordsworth, William. *The Complete Poetical Works of William Wordsworth.* Boston and New York: Houghton, Mifflin and Company, 1919. Print.

Young, Thomas. *A Practical and Historical Treatise on Consumptive Diseases.* London: T. Underwood, 1815. Print.

CHAPTER SIX

"TAKING A TRIP INTO CHINA": THE UNEASY PLEASURES OF COLONIALIST SPACE IN *MANSFIELD PARK*

Jeffrey Cass

Edward Said, in a sparkling interview directed by Sut Jhally for the Media Education Foundation, recalls a childhood in which he gazed with wonder at Hollywood's Orientalized landscapes. He fondly recalls the swashbuckling adventures of Jon Hall and *The Arabian Nights* (1942), the sultry seductiveness of Maria Montez in *Ali Baba and the Forty Thieves* (1944), and the diffident Sabu, who graces the set of *The Thief of Bagdad* (1940) and *The Jungle Book* (1942). Though famous for his theories of Orientalism as they pertain to the serious themes of colonialism and empire, Said also emphasizes the simple pleasure of viewing these movies, even as he understands that they have no real connection either to his family or to the national cultures and histories to which the films allude and which his later political writing has vigorously explored and interrogated. The aesthetic pleasures of Orientalism do not simply disappear, for as a famous scholar of comparative literature and the author of *Orientalism*, Said displays great pleasure in Orientalist art, literature, and scholarship—the richly textured paintings of Gérome, Delacroix, and Ingres; the lush imagery of Gérard de Nerval's *Voyage en Orient*; even the academic Orientalism of Edward Lane's history, *Modern Egyptians*. Despite his ideological commitments, Said never relinquishes an aesthetics of pleasure, a distinctly humanistic strain in his work, which will not be denied simply because taking ordinary pleasure in the representations of Orientalism (within both high and low culture) seems to contradict the equally compelling commitments that a politics of pleasure may entail.

The grinding between the aesthetics and the politics of pleasure is nowhere more evident in Said's work than in his famous essay on Jane Austen and *Mansfield Park*.[1] In preparing for the "grand idea of empire," Said writes, European and American culture exhibited "tendencies—whether in narrative, political theory, or pictorial technique—that enabled, encouraged, and otherwise assured the West's readiness to assume and enjoy the experience of empire" (80). Mostly unremarked is Said's expression of enjoyment at the exercise of imperial design, which subtly underwrites Fanny's development within Austen's narrative. The "enjoyment" of empire ironically depends upon the disconnect between the aesthetic pleasure the colonizer takes in experiencing the culture(s) of the Other and in the ideological seriousness to which the colonizer subscribes in order to justify the colonization in the first place (81). Though Said energetically apologizes for reading Austen at all, when unnamed postcolonial critics have attacked her for being "white, privileged, insensitive, [and] complicit" (96), he also returns to the problem of pleasure at the end of the essay. With regard to the enigma of the Caribbean in *Mansfield Park* and its critical place in interpreting the characters of Fanny Price and Sir Thomas Bertram, Said concludes:

> From our later perspective we can interpret Sir Thomas's power to come and go in Antigua as stemming from the muted national experience of individual identity, behavior, and "ordination," enacted with such irony and taste at Mansfield Park. The task is to lose neither a true historical sense of the first, nor a *full enjoyment* or appreciation of the second, all the while seeing both together. (97; italics mine)

Said thus embeds the pleasures—our "full enjoyment"—of Mansfield (the estate, not the novel) within a seemingly omniscient perspective that can aesthetically appreciate, even as it criticizes, the construction of the narrative and its *sub rosa* imperialism. Said reminds his readers of the historical contexts and theoretical constructs of Austen's novel, but he cannot give up the aesthetic pleasure of her writing. This indulgence of humanistic feeling, in fact, forms much of the basis for attacks on Said's work.[2]

In Austen's *Mansfield Park*, the disconnect between the prerogatives of the "local" culture that reads the narrative and those of the distant colonized one that remains embedded within it principally manifests itself through a "mode" that Said labels "geographical and spatial clarification" (85). Fanny Price plays a critical role in this "clarification," for her maturation largely coincides with her increasing control over territory and space. Her resistance to change does not merely reflect unease at a situation that persistently threatens to displace her (a state of affairs illustrated by the windy perorations of Mrs. Norris); rather, such resistance derives from Fanny's instinctive dissatisfaction with the improper (and therefore unpleasant) use of space. The knowledge she derives and the pleasure she takes in controlling small spaces—as when she cordons herself and her sister Susan in a tiny bedroom within her family's cramped, chaotic household in Portsmouth, or when she retires to a small room that the rest of the family has abandoned in Mansfield Park—parallel the disintegrating social and cultural authority that Mansfield reifies; this disintegration continues even after Sir Thomas Bertram has returned from setting his Antigua estates in order. Furthermore, when others attempt unwisely to enlarge or transform space, as when the "young people" (Austen's phrase for those young adults presumably still guided by parental authority) expand their walk at Sotherton by escaping over the ha-ha, or when the "young people" attempt to produce a play by trespassing into Sir Thomas's private room when he cannot voice what would have been unambiguous opposition, Fanny is acutely uncomfortable. She remains unsettled precisely because she implicitly recognizes that such enlargement or transformation of space may incur the disapprobation of the possessor, the loss of territorial control, or both. Said argues that "the values associated with such higher things as ordination, law and propriety must be grounded firmly in actual rule over and possession of territory" (87). Moving into spaces over which one does not have "actual rule" invites dispossession of the territory one may actually have. Thus, the pleasure Fanny feels is directly proportional to the proper use of space; her uneasiness emerges primarily during its misuse.

The use, misuse, and abuse of space connects to an embedded colonialist paradigm, one that Sir Thomas fractures when he irresponsibly leaves the estate in the calculating hands of Mrs. Norris, whose parsimony merely masks her self-indulgence; her mismanagement unintentionally provides a liminal moment in which the "young people" can disrupt "the ordination, law and propriety" of Mansfield Park by trespassing into spaces over which they have no legitimate territorial control, thereby foreclosing the pleasures that Mansfield's place within the empire guarantees. Moira Ferguson has suggested that Fanny Price "helps to foreshadow and map a new colonial land-scape that upholds the moral status quo but draws the line at arbitrary judgment and excessive indulgence" (73). This kinder, gentler version of colonialism alters the original plantocratic paradigm and colonial-ist designs of Sir Thomas Bertram, permitting a tenuous apologetics that tacitly recognizes the problematic nature of colonialist hege-mony, even as it reluctantly continues to support it. When those in Fanny's circle properly take pleasure in their designated spaces, then they maintain that balance. When they break free of those designated boundaries, they upset the balance that supports a refurbished colo-nialism, which still undergirds the economic and social advantages of a tottering Mansfield Park.

Nevertheless, territorial or spatial control seldom remains constant. Fanny may preside over a changing colonialist ethic, which reveals itself through space (mis)management, but her pleasure in controlling that space is less about the perpetuation of a colonialist status quo than it is about the proper negotiation in and through contested territory. Sir Thomas's absence automatically makes Mansfield's spaces contested; in effect, Sir Thomas inadvertently deterritorializes Mansfield Park by permitting new potential landscapes and familial configurations. Consequently, he damages the very colonialist ethic that feeds into Mansfield's "local" hegemony, as well as his own standing within his social and familial hierarchies. His return by no means restores the already shaky status quo.

At the end of the novel, when Austen playfully indicates that she wishes to "restore every body . . . to tolerable comfort" (446), she may perceive that such restoration is impossible because she has endowed Fanny with a queer inertia that eventually (and ironically) leads to her safe ensconcement within and virtual control over all of Mansfield's reterritorialized spaces. After their marriage, Edmund and Fanny "feel their distance from the paternal abode an inconvenience" (457) and ultimately move back to Mansfield Park and its "patronage" (457). At the beginning of the novel, Mansfield's "grandeur" (51) frightens Fanny; at the end, it seems "thoroughly perfect" to her (457). At the beginning, Maria mocks her for being unable to "put the map of Europe together" (54). At the end, Maria and Mrs. Norris are forever banished from the confines of Mansfield Park, while Fanny's presence has "put the map of [Mansfield] together" because she has resisted the colonizing, reterritorializing efforts of others. And such control brings great pleasure. Austen writes: "With so much true merit and true love, and no want of fortune or friends, the happiness of the married cousins must appear as secure as earthly happiness can

be.—Equally formed for domestic life, and attached to country pleasures, their home was the home of affection and comfort" (456–7).
Returned from exile, no longer an outsider, and finally at the center
of Sir Thomas's chastened "patronage," Fanny has been interpellated
into Mansfield's colonialist spaces, even as she unwittingly negoti-
ates control over the spaces that bring her pleasure. She has herself
become, however unintentionally, what Jenny Sharpe has called "an
allegory of empire," the figure of the woman in the text who "sta-
bilizes the contradictions of colonialism but also threatens to expose
them" (8).

Alistair Duckworth observes that the Mansfield estate is "a met-
onym of an inherited culture endangered by forces from within
and from without" (71). It would be a mistake, however, to regard
Mansfield as the metonymic index of conservative desperation against
the forces of cultural change, for Mansfield's is not a rigid conservatism that retreats within a gentrified fortress that waits for the bit-
ter cultural and social end. Nor is Fanny Price's conservatism static.
On the one hand, Fanny's unbending virtue keeps the Bertrams and
Mansfield Park from collapsing into ruin. On the other, her virtue also
becomes the perfect cover story for a reimagined empire. Her unlikely
triumph draws attention away from empire's covert operations: nego-
tiating shifting boundary conditions, resisting tempting encroach-
ments on public and private spaces, retrenching within borders before
venturing forth once again to claim new territories—and all within
a compassionate ethic that Fanny consciously embraces. Though her
presence fleetingly threatens to expose empire's "schizophrenic habits," which Said identifies, Fanny also provides the humanitarian,
civilizing impulse that covers over the ideological contradictions of
empire with a gloss of unchallenged goodness.

Fanny's colonizing impulse still permits the pleasurable control
of space and territory, both real and imagined. Telling is the scene in
which Edmund visits Fanny in the "East Room," once the room in
which the governess Miss Lee had lived, now the abandoned space
appropriated by Fanny, an annexation that results from the "deficiency of space and accommodation in her little chamber" above the
room. (172). Although Mrs. Norris "stipulate[s] for there never being
a fire in it on Fanny's account" (173), the room and its "next of com-
forts" (174) console Fanny:

> She could go there after any thing unpleasant below, and find imme-
> diate consolation in some pursuit, or some train of thought at hand.—
> Her plants, her books—of which she had been a collector, from the

first hour of commanding a shilling—her writing desk, and her works of charity and ingenuity, were all within her reach.... Everything was a friend, or bore her thoughts to a friend. (173)

But the East Room not only provides Fanny solace from intolerable or unpleasant events at Mansfield, it also becomes her first access to spatial management. Amid the many possessions she has accumulated, Fanny retreats to the room ostensibly to consider whether or not her refusal to act is selfish and ungrateful, but more subtly to reengage the power of her own territories. Anna Despotopoulou argues that Fanny hides from "spectatorship," inasmuch as she fears riding a horse, "which would bestow extra visibility upon her body" (573), acting in a play, and "walk[ing] into the dining room where she is expected" (573). This behavior does not mean that she is timid; indeed, her own gaze on others, a moral gauge of their actions, "is self-assured, determined, and often categorical" (573). Still, Fanny enjoys watching much more than being watched because she does not want to make visible the pleasures of her colonized spaces, any more than colonizers have historically wished the public to see the close connections between pleasure and profit. Though unacknowledged, Fanny's greatest weapon against her enemies is the sheer occupation of space. When Edmund visits her there and attempts to rationalize his decision to act in the theatrical, he instinctively recognizes the problem of spectatorship and making oneself publicly visible. Since his brother Tom has decided to invite Charles Maddox, an outsider, to take part in the production, Edmund attempts to minimize possible public scrutiny and censure for their rashness and indecorousness by taking the part himself, even if acting in a play is against his better judgment. Although Fanny warns him that Sir Thomas would still be against the production, implying that his desire to minimize the damage to the Bertrams' public reputation in no way reduces his own culpability, Edmund remains determined to press forward with his decision. Interestingly, on his way out of Fanny's room, he praises her space management:

If Tom is up, I shall go to him directly and get it over; and when we meet at breakfast we shall all be in high good humour at the prospect of acting the fool with such unanimity. *You* in the meanwhile will be taking a trip into China, I suppose. How does Lord Macartney go on?...And here are Crabbe's Tales, and the Idler, at hand to relieve you, if you tire of your great book. I admire your little establishment exceedingly; and as soon as I am gone, you will empty your head of all this nonsense of acting, and sit comfortably down to your table. (177)

Fanny has managed not only to secure her "establishment," but also to impress Edmund with her seriousness, her lack of frivolity. Moreover, she can exercise her Oriental fancy by "taking a trip into China," a reference to George Lord Macartney, whose *Plates to his Embassy to China* (1796) and *Journal of the Embassy* (1807) detail his experiences in China, after King George III sends Lord Macartney there to try and negotiate a more open trading system with Britain.[3] These writings inculcate lessons about negotiation, strategy, and economic self-interest, and Fanny internalizes their most important one: the pleasure of creeping territorial acquisition. However, the play in which they are to act, *Lovers' Vows*, threatens to expose the secrets of empire by publicly enacting the hidden if altered colonialist enterprise. Moira Ferguson has written that the play "has already voiced and even accentuated the major topoi of a muzzled colonialist discourse: brutality, fractured families, and the violated bodies and psyches of innocent people" (85). The "young people" see harmless diversion in its staging, but its production and casting not only parallel their lives, but also undermine the plantation owner himself by inserting a new generation into his privileged space. Edmund's desire to minimize adverse publicity by acceding to the wishes of the group only serves its "colonizing" interests. In essence, as the inheritor of his father's estates, Tom's appropriation of his father's space for the play functions as a coup d'état, a dramatic usurpation of authority with which Edmund is complicit. Returning from the billiard room that contains what he condescendingly describes as "a horribly vile billiard table," Tom plans to transform it into the theater and turn his father's adjoining private room into "an excellent green-room" (150). At the very least, his minor alterations to his father's rooms amount to an injudicious trespass. At the most, they represent a reterritorialization of the father's space, as if the status of master of the household had already passed on to the elder son. Tom execrates his father's taste and diminishes his judgment by turning his father's study into a staging area (the green room) for actors to make their entrances and exits, a theatrical space he stage manages. When Sir Thomas unexpectedly returns during their final rehearsal, he says, "I come from your theatre....I found myself in it rather unexpectedly. Its vicinity to my own room—but in every respect indeed it took my by surprise, as I had not the smallest suspicion of your acting having assumed so serious a character" (199).

Though Sir Thomas remains composed, the "young people" have affronted him with the "seriousness" of their acting because the pleasure afforded by the appropriation and transformation of his private

space depends upon his continued absence from it. Only his unex-
pected arrival saves Fanny from being dragooned into the production
of *Lovers' Vows*, which Edmund later acknowledges would have been
a mistake in his encomium of Fanny's delicate feelings. On one level,
her feelings illustrate her propriety, a quality Sir Thomas's daughters
distinctly lack. At another level, however, Fanny's delicacy becomes
an implicit acknowledgment of Sir Thomas's lawful claims on what
becomes contested space and the pleasure it affords the colonizer. As
Joseph Litvak suggests, "Fanny is anxious about the theater precisely
because she knows that it is less a structure toward which one can
locate a safely external position than the fluctuating space in which
all positions find their tenuous footing" (479). Her reticence saves
her from being conscripted into the premature occupation of "fluctuating" territory that has not yet been abandoned or ceded by Sir
Thomas. Her refusal to act in the play reifies a cultural unwillingness
to make public the "muzzled colonialist discourse" that Elizabeth
Inchbald's comedy enacts, inasmuch as such publicity only serves
to illustrate that Sir Thomas is a plantation master attending to his
estates, and not merely the dutiful father saving his family from bankruptcy. In essence, Fanny screens the reader from the fact that stern
imperialism now masquerades as familial compassion.

The problem of territorial trespass and acquisition occurs even
earlier in the novel during the excursion to Sotherton. Approaching
Sotherton in the carriage, for example, Maria Bertram, the future
Mrs. Rushworth, views Sotherton as a valuable possession, her access
to the excesses of wealth and title:

> She could not tell Miss Crawford that "those woods belonged to
> Sotherton," she could not carelessly observe that "she believed it was
> now all Mr. Rushworth's property on each side of the road," without
> elation of heart; and it was a pleasure to increase with their approach
> to the capital freehold mansion, and ancient manorial residence of the
> family, with all its rights of Court-Leet and Court-Baron. (111)

The consequence of reducing nature to property is that Maria feels
liberated from the very boundary conditions that legitimate her tacit
authority as the future mistress of the manor; in fact, her belief in
freedom from restraint underlies the temptations of trespass, a temptation all the new generation faces. To escape the vigilant eye of their
guardians by escaping from the heavy atmosphere of the house and
chapel, "the young people, meeting with an outward door, temptingly
open on a flight of steps which led immediately to turf and shrubs,

and all the sweets of the pleasure-grounds, as by one impulse, one wish for air and liberty, all walked out" (118). Tasting the "sweets of the pleasure-grounds" mirrors the desire for spatial control, an intoxicating, dangerous, and colonialist desire for the space of the other. Moreover, occupying the "pleasure-grounds" gives the "young people" a false sense of their legitimacy over property—their own as well as someone else's. When they intrude upon the grounds beyond the ha-ha (the boundary of the cultivated areas of the estate), they imaginatively reterritorialize the "wilderness," domesticating and improving it for their own ends. In doing so, they become competitors for that space.

Of the "young people," only Fanny does not step beyond the ha-ha. Tired, she sits down on a "comfortable bench" facing the wilderness. Mary Crawford wishes to "go and look through that iron gate" (123), and she and Edmund argue about the size of the space beyond the gate. Urging Fanny to stay and rest, Edmund guides Mary into the wood in order "to determine the dimensions of the wood by walking a little more about it" (123). The next group includes Henry Crawford, Maria Bertram, and Mr. Rushworth. Henry Crawford and Rushworth "discuss the possibility of improvements with much animation" (125), clearly intent upon improving the character and desirability of Sotherton's wild spaces. Maria, too, wishes to "pass through [the gate] into the park," but "the gate [is] locked," and Mr. Rushworth has forgotten the key (125). Though Mr. Rushworth rushes off to retrieve it, Maria is impatient for his return. She says to Henry Crawford, a man with whom she has been dangerously flirting, despite her engagement to Rushworth, "Yes, certainly, the sun shines and the park looks very cheerful. But unluckily that iron gate, that ha-ha, give me a feeling of restraint and hardship. I cannot get out" (127). Fanny, of course, sees the impropriety of not waiting for Mr. Rushworth to return, but she fails to convince her cousin not to climb the gate: "You will certainly hurt yourself against those spikes—you will tear your gown—you will be in danger of slipping into the ha-ha" (127). Because the "young people" have entered the park in several groups, they wander far too long looking for each other; their desire for an independent walk has disrupted the harmony of the group, making them vie for space as well as love. Their "junction" takes place far "too late," as Austen suggests, "for re-establishing harmony" (131). By refusing to enter the park through the ha-ha, Fanny does not occupy the wrong space, she does not disrupt the harmony of the group, and she does not compete for or measure the land before her as if it were a possession and as if nature were inanimate and manipulable. Her physical weakness in this scene closely adumbrates her reticence during the production of *Lovers' Vows*. In both cases, Fanny does not attempt to enter or acquire forbidden space because to do so would be, among other problematic issues, a violation of decorum. Her unease anticipates the mad dash into uncolonized territories that occurs throughout the nineteenth century, particularly into spaces that were not as empty as the colonizers had hoped. This desire to consume previously uncharted spaces culminates in the representation of imperial rapaciousness in works such as Joseph Conrad's *Heart of Darkness* and embodies the dark, capitalist pleasures that attend British greed.

Fanny also does not violate the pleasure that the ha-ha is intended to provide. As Jillian Heydt-Stevenson remarks,

> Imperceptible from a distance, the ha-ha was a sunken fence that prevented livestock from crossing the park into the garden, but at the same time allowed the viewer to maintain the fiction that the grounds were seamlessly connected. The ha-ha was so named because viewers would react with both surprise and laughter when they realized this earthly *trompe l'oeil* had deceived them. (5)

Heydt-Stevenson rightly connects the space to spectating pleasure. The *trompe l'oeil* delightfully deceives the spectator, but the illusion is destroyed when one actually slips past the gate into the wilderness itself. The analogy to colonization could not be clearer: colonizers should not be seen enjoying their territorial acquisitions. When Fanny expresses concern about Maria Bertram "slipping" into the ha-ha, she acknowledges that taking pleasure should not become visible to spectators who might pass by, since the trespasser then becomes an object in their gaze. Heydt-Stevenson cleverly connects this moment before the ha-ha to sexual innuendo and Austen's "bawdy humor" that "ignores locked 'gates,' pushes beyond 'spike,' and threatens to 'tear' Austen's gown" by making her sexual double entendres—in this case, in both language and imagery—explicit, stark, and visible.[4] Perhaps the most interesting aspect of the scene at the ha-ha is Fanny's exhaustion, allowing her not only to rest before the *trompe l'oeil*, but to observe those who have trespassed against its illusion. She is the spectator before the gate, keenly observing the transgressiveness of others. That others occasionally try to coerce her into participating in their activities suggests that the "young people" perceive their own vulnerabilities in the face of her voyeurism, while her resistance to both entering the ha-ha and acting in the play rehearse her inclinations toward inhabiting space without necessarily being seen doing so.

The real problem for Fanny lies not in these refusals, but in those in which more dominating male figures attempt to compel compliance, either through patriarchal domination (Thomas) or masculine suaveness (Crawford). Claudia Johnson writes, "The system of female manners is supposed to eliminate the need for the nakedness of coercion, and the embarrassment this entails, by rendering women so quiescent and tractable that they sweetly serve in the designs of fathers or guardians without wishing to resist and without noting that they have no choice" (*Mansfield Park* 463–4). Fanny's refusal to marry Henry Crawford superficially violates this code of behavior; her apparent intractability forces Sir Thomas to discover ways of "coercing" her to marry Henry, the implication of which is that if Fanny makes any other choice, she betrays the very family that has nurtured her and even honored her with her own ball. Sir Thomas attempts his coercions, which he sees as being in Fanny's best interests, in the East Room. His open display of displeasure within her private space silences Fanny. His intrusion violates the peace of her retreat, draining the pleasure she has taken in controlling that space. Sir Thomas's presence effectively reterritorializes the once-abandoned room. Even his initial desire to provide her with a fire only reinforces his dominance and paternal power. As a result, Sir Thomas's actions immobilize Fanny, silencing her from stating the truth about Henry's character (which would unfortunately also indict Maria's) and clearing her from the implicit charge of ingratitude. Yet when Sir Thomas sends Fanny back to Portsmouth after she refuses to marry Henry Crawford, she still finds the necessary strength to appropriate and occupy her own space. The atmosphere of noisy male violence and female incapacity within her own family forces Fanny to alter the Prices' domestic landscape, however minutely, in order to maintain Mansfield's codes of propriety, rather like British colonists who transform the colonial landscape until it resembles the home they have left behind.

Fanny's first reaction upon returning to her childhood home is astonishment at its disorder and lack of space and the contrast it makes to Mansfield Park:

> Fanny was almost stunned. The smallness of the house, and thinness of the walls, brought everything so close to her, that, added to the fatigue of her journey, and all her recent agitation, she hardly knew how to bear it.... Yet she thought it would not have been so at Mansfield. No,

in her uncle's house there would have been a consideration of times and seasons, a regulation of subject, a propriety, an attention towards every body which there was not here. (375–6)

The lack of "regulation" and "propriety" derives primarily from the confined nature of the Portsmouth house and inability of Fanny's parents to control the activity within it. Its "smallness" and "closeness" precludes a pleasure in the occupation of space within it. When Fanny first views the room that she will share with her sister Susan, she is accordingly depressed: "There was nothing to raise her spirits in the confined and scantily furnished chamber.... The smallness of the room above and below indeed, and the narrowness of the passage and staircase, struck her beyond her imagination" (380). Moreover, she wistfully and respectfully recalls the East Room at Mansfield Park and the pleasures if affords. At Mansfield, the attic room seems pitifully small; at Portsmouth, it appears relatively spacious. She reflects, "In space, light, furniture, and prospect, there was nothing alike in the two apartments" (390). Fanny discerns that while "Mansfield Park might have some pains, Portsmouth could have no pleasures" (385).

Nevertheless, Fanny and Susan's tiny chamber forces Fanny to transform a dismal space into one that more nearly represents the cultural values and concomitant pleasures she has enjoyed at Mansfield. She persuades Susan of her own "colonial" views by intentionally segregating her from the rest of the family, altering the private space, and teaching her to imagine the landscapes beyond Portsmouth. Austen writes: "By sitting together up stairs, they avoided a great deal of the disturbance of the house; Fanny had peace, and Susan learnt to think it no misfortune to be quietly employed" (390). Gradually, they inhabit this newly configured space more and more, symbolizing their "capacity to dramatize space and to make the human drama inseparable from its physical location" (Wiltshire 66). In addition, desirous that this new space be as serviceable as the East Room at Mansfield, Fanny subscribes to a circulating library in order to amuse herself and "to give [Susan] a share in her own first pleasures, and inspire a taste for biography and poetry" (391). Fanny's advice empowers Susan, giving her access to an education that promotes the social codes embodied by Mansfield. Such an education depends on the control of contested space and, once colonized, an assertive, spatial management. Thus, there are moments in which occupation appears illegitimate, such as Fanny's reticence to act on a stage that usurps Sir Thomas's space or her hesitation in entering the ha-ha independent of the group, but there are also moments in which reterritorialization is not only legitimate, but also necessary. Fanny's refurbishing of the East Room at Mansfield and her sister's bedroom at Portsmouth illustrate this kind of legitimacy.

In her book *The Proper Lady and the Woman Writer*, Mary Poovey suggests that Fanny's heroism lies in her inertia. By outlasting all her relatives, Poovey argues, Fanny shows their "moral decay" (223). Fanny "triumphs" because "the others falter": "Tom drinks himself into illness, Mary exposes her callousness, Maria seduces Henry, and Sir Thomas, in loneliness and despair, recalls Fanny to Mansfield Park" (223). But Fanny's education of Susan within a transformed space also demonstrates self-confidence and self-assertiveness, both of which seem closely allied with the values of the "local" culture to which Said alludes in his essay "Jane Austen and Empire." As she returns to Mansfield Park from her exile in Portsmouth, Fanny's "eye" encompasses the grounds that she will once again occupy, this time at center stage since her competitors for legitimacy within the family have fled: Maria and Julia have abandoned the estate; her rival for Edmund, Mary Crawford, has revealed her cold, calculating character and has departed for London's society; and her patron, Sir Thomas, now embraces her as his only legitimate daughter:

> Her eye fell every where on lawns and plantations of the freshest green; and the trees, though not fully clothed, were in that delightful state, when farther beauty is known to be at hand, and when, while much as is actually given to the sight, more yet remains for the imagination. (434)

Mansfield Park produces a colonizing, if imaginative, mind that takes pleasure not only in the "lawns and plantations of green" that it actually sees, but also in the spaces and contested territories it imagines. In effect, imperial compulsion and its pleasures have gone underground, removing themselves from the novel's center and taking up residency beneath the complacency of Fanny's female propriety, apparently harmless and defanged. Yet the legacy of Sir Thomas's Antigua occupation of plantocratic spaces and the consequences for the slaves who live on them, a reality about which Austen is mostly silent, contribute to an emerging notion in *Mansfield Park* that links colonial pleasure and shame. George Boulukos pointedly writes:

> In any event, the point most relevant to *Mansfield Park* is that Austen has no fear of portraying a character as anxious to avoid association

with the slave trade, and showing the assumption that an association with the slave *trade* is a guilty and undesirable one. Implicitly employing the concept of a return of the repressed, Said envisions Austen herself...[as] unable to avoid mentioning the guilty secret of colonial dependence even while trying to suppress it. (370; italics in text)

But the colonialist pleasure arising from occupying space still lurks within Mansfield's now-abashed walls. The desire to reterritorialize lost properties, to reengage markets and trading partners, to reemerge into even more commodified colonialist environments and darker cultural regimes, transforms the human comedy in *Mansfield Park* into brooding, watchful waiting.

NOTES

1. Several essays have resulted from Said's controversial reading of *Mansfield Park*. See George Boulukos, "The Politics of Silence: *Mansfield Park* and the Amelioration of Slavery"; Allen Dunn, "The Ethics of *Mansfield Park*: MacIntyre, Said, and Social Context"; Diane Capitani, "Moral Neutrality in Jane Austen's *Mansfield Park*"; Susan Fraiman, "Jane Austen and Edward Said: Gender, Culture, and Imperialism."

2. See my "Interrogating Orientalism: Theories and Practices," where I outline the criticisms of Said within the postcolonial context. In particular, the work of Timothy Brennan, James Clifford, Sara Mills, Benita Parry, and Dennis Porter are important in the critique of Saidian Orientalism in general and his humanism in particular. See also Ibn Warraq's *Defending the West: A Critique of Edward Said's* Orientalism; Robert Irwin's *Dangerous Knowledge: Orientalism and Its Discontents*; Daniel Martin Varisco's *Reading Orientalism: Said and the Unsaid*; and Edmund Burke and David Prochaska's collection *Genealogies of Orientalism: History, Theory, Politics*, all of which appeared after the publication of "Interrogating Orientalism."

3. Susan Allen Ford's essay "Fanny's 'Great Book': Macartney's Embassy to China and *Mansfield Park*" speaks of the "sinomania" that erupted in England in the late 1790s, though often to contrast the "stasis" of Chinese culture with the "circulatory" motion of British imperial practices. Ford writes, "Looking more closely at Macartney's journal helps us understand how Jane Austen could depend upon—and help construct—a global perspective in her audience, how she built a similar field of vision into the character of her heroine, and how she used that perspective to help define *Mansfield Park*'s thematic texture" (7). Ford also compares the "confinement of Fanny's movements at Mansfield Park" to the "physical restrictions of Chinese women" (9) as they are portrayed in Macartney's narrative.

4. Heydt-Stevenson makes the case that "Austen's humor, her explora-tion of the body's expression of social constructions, and her presen-tation of women's histories through the everyday objects they handle all encourage a reassessment of cultural expectations" (27). For Heydt-Stevenson, Austen's surfaces reveal a comic subversiveness that helps define Austen's feminist impulses through an analysis of the woman's body in relation to the objects that surround her. Heydt-Stevenson fur-ther contends, "Austen examines the body's role in her novels, call-ing attention to the incarnations of gender inequity by finding wit in male anatomy, female sensibility, the eroticism and horror of death, the 'nothingness' of the everyday, and the inability to tolerate the motions of those who are aesthetically unappealing" (27).

WORKS CITED

Austen, Jane. *Mansfield Park*. 1966. Harmondsworth, UK: Penguin Books, 1978. Print.

———. *Mansfield Park*. Ed. Claudia L. Johnson. New York: Norton, 1998. Print.

Boulukos, George E. "The Politics of Silence: *Mansfield Park* and the Amelioration of Slavery." *Novel: A Forum on Fiction*. 39.3 (2006): 361–83. Print.

Burke III, Edmund, and David Prochaska, ed. *Genealogies of Orientalism: History, Theory, Politics*. Lincoln and London: U of Nebraska P, 2008. Print.

Capitani, Diane. "Moral Neutrality in Jane Austen's *Mansfield Park*." *Persuasions On-Line* 23.1 (2002). n. p. Web. Dec. 12, 2009.

Cass, Jeffrey. "Interrogating Orientalism: Theories and Practices." *Interrogating Orientalism: Contextual Approaches and Pedagogical Practices*. Ed. Diane Hoeveler and Jeffrey Cass. Columbus: Ohio State UP, 2006. 25–45. Print.

Despotopoulou, Anna. "Fanny's Gaze and the Construction of Feminine Space in *Mansfield Park*." *Modern Language Review* 99.3 (2004): 569–83. Print.

Duckworth, Alistair. *The Improvement of the Estate. A Study of Jane Austen's Novels*. 1971. Baltimore and London: Johns Hopkins UP, 1994. Print.

Dunn, Allen. "The Ethics of *Mansfield Park*: MacIntyre, Said, and Social Context." *Soundings* 78.3–4 (1995): 483–500. Print.

Ferguson, Moira. *Colonialism and Gender Relations from Mary Wollstonecraft to Jamaica Kincaid*. New York: Columbia UP, 1993. Print.

Ford, Susan Allen. "Fanny's 'Great Book': Macartney's Embassy to China and *Mansfield Park*." *Persuasions On-Line* 28.2 (2008). n.p. Web. Dec. 12, 2009.

Fraiman, Susan. "Jane Austen and Edward Said: Gender, Culture, and Imperialism." *Critical Inquiry* 21 (1995): 805–821. Print.

Heydt-Stevenson, Jillian. *Austen's Unbecoming Conjunctions: Subversive Laughter, Embodied History*. New York: Palgrave Macmillan, 2005. Print.

Hoeveler, Diane, and Jeffrey Cass, eds. *Interrogating Orientalism: Contextual Approaches and Pedagogical Practices.* Columbus: Ohio State UP, 2006. Print.

Irwin, Robert. *Dangerous Knowledge: Orientalism and Its Discontents.* Woodstock, NY: The Overlook Press, 2006. Print.

Jhally, Sut, Dir. *Edward Said: On Orientalism.* Media Education Foundation, 1998. VHS.

Johnson, Claudia L. "*Mansfield Park*: Confusions of Guilt and Revolutions of Mind." *Jane Austen: Women, Politics, and the Novel.* Chicago: U of Chicago P, 1988. 96–120. Rpt. in *Mansfield Park.* Ed. Claudia L. Johnson. New York: Norton, 1998. 458–76. Print.

Litvak, Joseph. "The Infection of Acting: Theatricals and Theatricality in *Mansfield Park*." *Caught in the Act: Theatricality in the Nineteenth-Century English Novel.* Berkeley and Los Angeles: U of California P, 1992. 1–26. Rpt. in *Mansfield Park.* Ed. Claudia L. Johnson. New York: Norton, 1998. 476–89. Print.

Poovey, Mary. *The Proper Lady and the Woman Writer. Ideology as Style in the Works of Mary Wollstonecraft, Mary Shelley, and Jane Austen.* Chicago and London: U of Chicago P, 1984. Print.

Said, Edward. *Culture and Imperialism.* New York: Alfred A. Knopf, 1993. Print.

Sharpe, Jenny. *Allegories of Empire. The Figure of the Woman in the Colonial Text.* Minneapolis, London: U of Minnesota P, 1993. Print.

Varisco, Daniel Martin. *Reading Orientalism: Said and the Unsaid.* Seattle: U of Washington P, 2007. Print.

Warraq, Ibn. *Defending the West: A Critique of Edward Said's* Orientalism. New York: Prometheus, 2007. Print.

Wiltshire, John. "*Mansfield Park, Emma, Persuasion.*" *The Cambridge Companion to Jane Austen.* Ed. Edward Copeland. Cambridge: Cambridge UP, 1997. 58–83. Print.

CHAPTER SEVEN

EXHAUSTED APPETITES, VITIATED TASTES: ROMANTICISM, MASS CULTURE, AND THE PLEASURES OF CONSUMPTION

Samantha Webb

Eighteenth-century literary criticism abounds with metaphors of books as food and their readers as ravenous eaters.[1] From Wordsworth's denigration of contemporary verse as "food for fickle tastes, and fickle appetites" (597), to Walter Scott's witty retrospective on novels as "bread eaten in secret" (Southam 58), to Hannah More's judgment that "an appetite for reading" among the lower classes was endangering the nation (249), critics disparaged books through a playful yet compelling language of consumption. While the image of edible books was a commonplace for centuries,[2] the frequency with which the trope is repeated in the eighteenth century locates the novel and other popular reading materials within a range of consumer discourse whose figural registers have yet to be fully investigated.[3]

The metaphor implies a critical judgment: "edible" books are disposable, unwholesome, no sooner read than discarded like cherry pits or chicken bones. Their consuming readers engage them without thought or effort. But this assessment overlooks another dimension of the metaphor of books as food: the idea that books are as necessary to life as food. If we see reading this way, it becomes an essential sustaining activity, and books become necessities rather than luxuries. This alternate vision of reading and books, with its celebration of the nourishing potential of literature, was adopted by working-class authors as they sought to articulate the aspirations of their readers. Radical authors such as Thomas Spence, Daniel Isaac Eaton, and James Parkinson rhetorically linked their books to a feeding of people who were starved for ideas at the same time that they were almost literally starved for food. While in one version of the metaphor, books are implicated in discourses of luxury, in the other, books fall into the category of necessity. I contend, in tandem with scholars such as Denise Gigante, that these gastronomic and consumption tropes should be engaged more critically and more historically. Indeed, the pejorative register of the books/food metaphor has operated as a mystification not only of literary history, especially of the Romantic novel, but also of Romanticism as a discourse that remained intensely concerned with literature as social transformation.

Critical opinion has held, since Raymond Williams's *Culture and Society* at least, that high Romanticism was a reaction against the development of the literary marketplace in which the novel and other new, supposedly subliterary, forms circulated more comfortably as commodities than did poetry.[4] More recently, Lucy Newlyn has persuasively characterized high Romanticism as "a species of reaction-formation against the new power of reading" (48). Consumption metaphors are part of this response, becoming in the eighteenth century a strategy of dismissal of the mass audience "as either mindlessly passive or voraciously appetitive" (4). This conception was applied with special urgency to novel-readers, and as James Raven has noted, the novel's status as a commodity was responsible for the abundance of images associating it with manufacture and with "irresponsible, indiscriminate consumption." These associations, according to Raven, contributed in part to the novel's "disordered literary history" (Raven, Garside, and Forster 120). Thus, when Wordsworth describes the "savage torpor" that results from the consumption of "frantic novels," he is not only obfuscating the range of novels available to the general reader, but he is also expressing fairly common anxieties about their effects on the culture at large. Like any of the mass culture products of our own time, the Romantic novel was dismissed through a language of consumption whose terms were understood both as indicators of aesthetic value and as descriptions of reception practices. But as Janice Radway argues in relation to denigrations of "trashy" modern romance novels, the insistent repetition of the metaphor of books as food prevents an interrogation of the ways in which people actually engage the books they read (9).[5] The metaphor assumes an absolute separation between producers and consumers, and consequently imagines the reader as a helpless, passive victim of the mass culture she consumes. At best, such a consuming reader possesses a degraded sense of taste; at worst, she is more susceptible to dangerous ideological manipulations. Radway's insight certainly applies to eighteenth-century uses of the books/food metaphor to describe the novel, but it applies to other literary materials as well.

Novel readers were not the only set of readers who were assumed to be passively imbibing texts. Working-class readers, those whose literacy was fostered precisely so they could read their Bibles, were also stigmatized as potential victims of seditious pamphlets, and their reading habits were subject to the same language of indiscriminate consumption. The publications of the Loyal Association and later of the Cheap Repository sought explicitly to curb the influence of radical pamphlets on supposedly suggestible readers. According to Hannah More's account of the origins of the Cheap Repository: "[A]s an appetite for reading had, from a variety of causes, been increasing among the inferior ranks in this country, it was judged expedient, at this critical period, to supply such wholesome aliment as might give a new direction to their taste, and abate their relish for those corrupt and inflammatory publications which the consequences of the French Revolution have been so fatally pouring upon us" (249). To figure readers as victims of their own "appetites" is to deny that they have acted intentionally. As Don Herzog observes, "when workers turn radical, they haven't done anything. Instead, something (awful) has happened to them" (101). More's use of the eating metaphor is thus consonant with that of critics of the novel. She expresses the same anxieties about textual proliferation and passive reading.

Although Wordsworth's and More's appropriation of consumption metaphors ultimately lead to distinctly different theories of reading and readers, this anxious rhetoric of consumption opposes the image of reading/eating to agency and transformative action. But whereas More certainly fostered political quietism in the Cheap Repository Tracts, it is difficult to maintain that Wordsworth and Coleridge's *Lyrical Ballads* sought to do so. On the contrary, their deployment of the metaphor of consuming readers registers precisely such fears of reader quietism. Economic accounts of aesthetics, especially Kurt Heinzelman's, have rightly observed that Romantic (particularly Wordsworthian) aesthetic theory guards against passive readers by deploying the figure of georgic labor. In this sense, a book's consumption is figured rather as co-production, and the reader becomes a "cooperating producer" of the text (Heinzelman 143).[6] While labor theory helps account for Wordsworth's sense of audience, it overlooks the fact that the figure of eating also offers a vehicle for imagining activity, and that it did so in the radical texts of the period. Thus, to the extent that the Romantic poetics articulated by Wordsworth, Coleridge, and other poets assumes readers' agency and transformative activity, it suggests a hostility to readerly passivity, rather than to the figure of consumption as such.

Attempts to stem the perceived tide of radical books worked in tandem, rhetorically, with critiques of the novel. As Patrick Brantlinger notes, anxieties about the novel in the eighteenth century likely had less to do with a disciplinary impulse than with the sorts of "*plaisirs de texte*" novels elicited (27). Those pleasures were imagined sexually, but they were also imagined as a kind of ravenous, undisciplined gustatory enjoyment, whose invocation registered a position toward taste, appetite, and appropriate consuming pleasures. Moreover, just as critical dismissals of consumable mass culture implicitly articulate the limits of taste and enjoyment, the dietetic and economic literature from which these food tropes derive their vehicles actually create corporeal regimes of pleasure that sought to rescue the eating reader from the "savage torpor" of their own consumption.

In the case of both edible novels and edible pamphlets, eating usually connotes a lack of agency on the part of readers: novel readers are passive because they are satiated; working-class readers are hapless imbibers of Jacobin "poison." But whereas the ravenous reader of novels does worryingly little of anything, the poisoned readers of radical pamphlets erupt into frightening violent activity. While the one set of readers undergoes a paralyzing mental stimulation, the other is led to act without thought. In both cases, a physiological response overwhelms the consuming reader's intellectual powers, "unfitting it for all voluntary exertion" (Wordsworth 599). Critics of the novel denigrated such lack of activity; critics of radical pamphlets cultivated it.

INERTIA AND STIMULATION

The anxiety about passive readers is perhaps most starkly dramatized in the reception of the Gothic novel.[7] In his review of *The Monk*, written just a few years before Wordsworth's Preface, Coleridge offers a symptomology of the typical reader of Gothic novels, while at the same time pronouncing upon the state of the public taste: "The horrible and the preternatural have usually seized on the popular taste, at the rise and decline of literature. Most powerful stimulants, they can never be required except by the torpor of an unawakened, or the languor of an exhausted, appetite.... We trust, however, that satiety will banish what good sense should have prevented" (194). Coleridge's figure of a reader who is at once idle and overstimulated seeks to distinguish taste (which can be trained) from mere appetite (which pays no attention to quality). In this case, the appetitive qualities of "the horrible and the preternatural" trump those of taste to create a reader whose ability to distinguish good from bad literature, and intellectual from bodily pleasures, has been absolutely blunted. More to the point, the lack of appetite creates "torpor" and "languor." The logic of the equation is clear: readers who are not hungry—because their appetites are either "unawakened" or "exhausted"—tend to require stronger matter to make them eat. This languor, in turn, leads to the production of novels of ever greater sensational appeal.

Crucial in this consumption model is the implied relationship between a defective appetite and inactivity. In this regard, Coleridge's key terms—taste and appetite—draw on contemporary discourses on the physiology and economics of eating. By 1797, the year of Coleridge's review, the metaphor's vehicle—the ravenous eater—had become literalized in the public imagination in the wake of a series of severe, highly publicized food scarcities that made visible the literal underpinnings of consumption metaphors. In the widespread public outcry against these scarcities, eating represented, on the one hand, a dangerously excessive luxury and on the other, a necessary life-giving activity.[8] The late eighteenth-century debate about food became a fulcrum for the expression of anxieties about the consumer revolution, and for working out the precise nature of luxury and necessity. Contributors to the debate engaged the same questions about the activity and passivity of food consumers that Coleridge's passively imbibing novel-reader reflects, and in strikingly similar terms. The well-fed rich were called upon patriotically to reduce their consumption of pies, cakes, and gravies to conserve wheat and meat, while the middle and lower classes were asked to cook and eat more frugally. Throughout the debate, the terms "hunger" and "appetite," "activity" and "idleness" are generalized not only to food economics, but also to notions of the consuming self and the pleasure that self takes in his or her consumption. One vocal commentator, George Edwards, wryly calls for "a restraint upon the appetite, which, by the rich, is not rarely indulged at the cost of the health and vigour of their constitutions" (*Effectual Means* 30). On a personal level, overeating is unhealthy because it leads to a loss of "health and vigour." On an economic level, an unrestrained appetite is dangerous for the nation as a whole because it will exhaust food supplies more rapidly, deprive the poor of their share of subsistence, and potentially lead them to riot and revolt.

Edwards uses "appetite" as a derogatory term within a general critique of luxury. In a follow-up pamphlet, he registers a difference between luxurious, idle appetites and those called up by activity:

> Even the example of rural life ought to restrain the prodigality of the tables of opulence and luxury, and the high relish of appetite procured by labour, to teach them that a simple diet is a more refined gratification than theirs. At the same time, agriculture constitutes the greatest strength of nations. The people are by it's [*sic*] means hardy and robust, and most ardently attached to the liberties of their country they are enemies to foreign habit, and artificial pleasures, but friendly to those which are native and natural, and in them experience the true happiness and the most abundant comforts. They are least susceptible of that inordinate desire of riches, which swallows up every other duty and of that fatal attachment to destructive vanities, empty pomp, and unsubstantial magnificence, which increase and multiply the wants and miseries of men, and may sacrifice not only the nation to tyranny and corruption, but even waste, in follies, luxuries, and needless profusion, those necessaries of life, that ought to support the poor and middling classes. (*Palliative and Radical Means* 16–17)

Edwards's language here travels back and forth between the literal and the synecdoche, with the prodigal tables of opulence standing in for luxury consumption of all kinds. Agricultural labor—in georgic fashion—establishes a healthy dynamic between activity, appetite, and pleasure. An appetite born out of labor leads to actual pleasure in eating; it encompasses the "high relish" that the idle well-fed lose. The pleasure of eating, then, derives more from its mediation by labor than it does from the more aesthetic dimension of the actual taste of the food, or from how much food there is. Appetite and labor are necessary for the experience of the pleasure of eating.

Edwards's highly stylized use of these terms invites consideration of the metaphor of books as food. In Edwards's account of activity and pleasure, we can glimpse what Heinzelman claims for Wordsworthian poetics: just as the pleasurable meal requires the labor of the eater, "the literary work [is] a form of labor to be exchanged for the reader's" (Heinzelman 201). While the author lays down a certain amount of labor in the writing, the reader is expected to do a little work to call up the pleasure of activity. Such an articulation lies behind not only Wordsworth's poetic project, but also those of Coleridge and other critics of popular reading material, inasmuch as they connect readerly activity with agency. In the same way that the hard-working eater experiences more pleasure than the eater who is idle, the hard-working reader resists what Coleridge terms "the languor of an exhausted appetite." As Heinzelman tellingly frames this process, "the exchanges of poetry become acts of appetite, facts of nurture" (208). But as we see from George Edwards's aestheticized economic critique, in the context of real food scarcity, the figurative literary appetite can become a literal problem of hunger.

ERUPTIONS OF HUNGER

Having an appetite is not the same thing as being hungry, and the two states give way to different forms of representation in the public debate about scarcity and food consumption. Whereas for George Edwards, in pamphlets to and about the poor, the pleasure of eating is called up only by labor, in pamphlets to and about the poor, hunger leads to the violent eruption of revolutionary activity. Conservative organizations like Reeves's Loyal Association and the creators of the Cheap Repository Tracts explicitly sought to replace radical pamphlets with "more wholesome aliment" that encouraged working-class readers to supplement their meager diets with spiritual nourishment from their Bibles (while also offering literal advice on more economical modes of cookery). In this, they drew on the biblical conceit of the Word of God as nourishment. Arthur Young, the Secretary to the Board of Agriculture, was so fearful that starvation during the scarcities would lead to a French-style revolution[9] that he abandoned his advocacy of land enclosures and proposed a land allotment system wherein poor families could sustain themselves on potatoes.[10] In Young's view, food, radical books, and revolutionary activity are intimately, even literally, connected in a distribution circuit that imagines "incessant paragraphs in the Jacobin papers,...find[ing] their way into the kitchens of so many ale and pot-houses" (*Enquiry into the State of the Public Mind* 8). Radical pamphlets, in this account, follow distribution channels of food, thus offering a kind of sustaining supplementary (and false) comfort to their hungry readers as they pave the way for revolution. As Young puts it:

> Kings and parliaments, the great and the mean, the happy and the miserable will sink in one general and indiscriminate ruin. A scene of wretchedness that will put to the test the comfort to be derived from the stores of *philosophy*, which the French Revolution has made the precursor of the French arms wherever they have carried desolation. (*Inquiry into...Wastes* 160; emphasis in original.)

Perhaps more than any other antirevolutionary writer, Young takes the metaphor of books as unwholesome food to its logical, literal conclusion. Young worries about the hungry poor's reading because their minimal understanding of politics makes them easy prey for radical authors. Their underfed bodies can be stimulated to act simply by "imbibing discontent" without the restraint that comes from intellectual judgment and taste (*Enquiry into the State of the Public Mind* 15).

While it might be easy, from our historical vantage, to dismiss such heightened rhetoric, conservative worries about the impact of food scarcity on the political actions of the poor were not wholly unmerited. Food riots, a time-honored tradition of consumer action during scarcities, were flaring up all over the country.[11] More importantly, radical texts adopt precisely this rhetorical formulation of the impact of hunger, presenting their readers as devouring radical books to ward off starvation. In contrast to the lethargic, unappetitive reader of novels, the implied reader of radical texts is the hungry reader, whose presence as a hungry, reading subject exerts revolutionary agency. In the rhetoric of radical authors, literal hunger is symbolically supplemented by radical literature and ideas. One pamphlet, ostensibly addressed to the rich and spoken by "Citizen Famine," declares: "look at the scenes of Sorrow and Starvation, of which you [the rich] are the cause, and see the victims of Famine, whom you have deprived of Bread and Cheese, feasting on the ideas of future Justice" (6). The image of the feast becomes a synecdoche not just for excess consumption but for revolutionary activity fed by reading. The pleasure of the radical text is thus not only intellectual but also corporeal, and it writes itself into the world through the revolutionary actions of its readers.

Radical pamphlets addressed to the working classes frequently announce themselves as food for a hungry people—or more precisely, for hungry swine, whose coarse literary tastes were decried by Burke. Thomas Spence's *Pigs' Meat, or Food for the Swinish Multitude* (1793–5) and Daniel Isaac Eaton's *Politics for the People; or A Salmagundy for Swine*[12] (1794–5) are just two of the most prominent examples. By rhetorically designating their books as articles of food, radical authors drew attention to the very thing that their readers presumably lacked, and offered their wares as substitutes. This was a parody of government attempts to promote substitute foods like potatoes and brown bread, but it also parodied conservative attempts to replace radical pamphlets with quietistic ones. These authors radicalize hunger and link the (imagined) emptiness of their readers' bellies to a corrupt political system. At the same time, these titles call attention to the fact that pigs will eat and grow fat on almost anything. The epigraph of the third volume of Spence's *Pigs' Meat* goes further to connect his readers' hunger with his own seven-month incarceration under Pitt's suspension of habeas corpus:

> The pigs to Starve, bad Men in pow'r,
> Their Feeder sent to doleful Goal [*sic*],
> And eager bent him to devour,
> Long time the Pigs did for him wail.
> But now the Storm is blown o'er,
> That drove him from his blest Employ;
> And to his Task return'd once more,
> He feeds them with his wonted Joy. (1–8)

There is an affectionate immediacy of relationship in this image of Spence as a gentle feeder of pigs, and as a man whose imprisonment deprived his readers of the symbolic sustenance of his books. Similarly, the first volume of Eaton's *Politics for the People* bears the subtitle "consisting of the choicest Viands, contributed by the Cooks of the present day AND Of the highest flavour'd Delicacies, composed by the Caterers of former Ages." The title page features a poem by "Old Hubert" (James Parkinson) that reads:

> Since Times are bad, and solid food is rare,
> The Swinish herd should learn to live on air:
> Acorns and Peas, alas! no more abound,
> A feast of Words, is in the *Hog Trough* found. (1–4)

Parkinson and Eaton position their books as part of a feast that replaces the ordinary food of swine. These sentiments are expanded in the letter introducing the first piece:

> SIR, As a Member of the Swinish Herd, I beg Leave to thank you for your diligence and attention, in supplying us with good wholesome Food; on which I hope we shall long continue to feast ourselves, in spite of those who would wish to ring our Noses in order to prevent us from grubbing after Truth, or to starve us to death in the "stye of taxation." But knowing that we are a very voracious species of Animals, I was fearful lest the provision should be devoured faster than even your unremitting exertions might be able to supply it; I have therefore taken the liberty to send you a few morsels from a store of "Hog's Meat" on which I lately made a repast and found very agreeable to the Swinish Palate of
>
> Yours, &c.
> A Brother Grunter (2)

The playful exaggeration of Burke's swine metaphor gives itself over almost naturally to the figure of feeding. What else have pigs to do but feed on leftover food? But these food metaphors register distinctly different concerns than the ones registered in critiques of the novel, or in the antirevolutionary texts that this pamphlet parodies. Here, the metaphor does not reflect anxieties about books as consumable objects as such; rather, it points out their necessity by identifying Eaton's and Spence's books as a regular source of urgently needed food. The terms "morsels," "feast," "repast," and "palate" connote refined pleasure, perhaps as a parody of Burkean dismissals of low plebeian tastes or as a way of insisting that "swine" are capable of experiencing the humanizing pleasures of taste. Ironically, and deliberately so, neither *Politics for the People* nor *Pigs' Meat* was made of the rude stuff that Burke or Young feared books for the poor would be; they were full of excerpts from political treatises, poetry, Constitutional history, trial transcripts, and other materials that the editors believed their readers needed to know in order to understand their rights. These contents constitute the "ideas of future Justice" with which Citizen Famine boldly taunted his readers. In the radical imaginary, writing and reading are forms of feeding and acting; censorship is a means of starving and pacifying. Accepting the opposition between agency and passivity, these radical authors suggest that neither reading nor eating is a passive, luxurious incorporation, but that both are fundamental, even humanizing aspects of life.

Clearly, these radical figurations of radical books as food disclose a different attitude toward literary consumption than the one articulated by critics and antirevolutionary commentators. They derive from classical formulations of the banquet as symposium wherein, as Michel Jeanneret describes it, "The joy of eating is accompanied by the joy of learning; the meal provides the opportunity for a practical lesson in natural philosophy" (77).[13] The radical iteration of the metaphor is just as self-consciously rooted in an aesthetic philosophy of taste as it is in a political, economic vision of access. In the passage above from "A Brother Grunter," for example, the writer suggests that his correspondence with Eaton is inspired by the need to help the editor supply the market with food. In the background of this fanciful metaphor is a sense of robust collaboration and economic exchange between literary producer and consumer. While this metaphor of exchange is reminiscent of *The Spectator*, *The Tatler*, and other dialogical publications from earlier in the century, it also becomes a heuristic for the political and economic aspirations of radical thinkers and their implied readers: people need access to food and books to be full citizens and humans. This formulation gives priority to consumption as a transformative and activating social force.

THE PLEASURES OF FRUGALITY

Modern theorists of consumption insist on the importance of the imagination in the history and process of consumption. The imagination can create a patina of status around an object that elicits desire for it, or it can access the desire for emulation.[14] Colin Campbell has argued that Romanticism endorsed a hedonistic desire to daydream about possessing something, a mental activity that is more satisfying than actually possessing the thing one wants (90). His theory is suggestive because it insists that the pleasures of consumption are as much imaginative as they are physical. While, for Campbell, the daydream helps explain the marked increase in consumption at the end of the eighteenth century, it also explains the economic figuration and imaginative economy of scarcity discourse. If, by the end of the eighteenth century, it becomes possible to imagine luxury pleasurably, it is also possible to imagine frugality as a pleasurable mode of engagement with consumer products. Indeed, this kind of counter-fantasy is offered in the literary responses to the food scarcities that I have been discussing. I use the term "frugality" in distinction from "abstention," because the latter implies absolute self-restraint rather than controlled consumption. Frugality permits consumption, and, as such, it requires a greater attention to the activity of choosing. Significantly, the frugal modes of consumption encapsulated in tracts on scarcity do not call for abstention *per se*; rather, they frame frugal consumption as a pleasurable activity. In his pamphlet *Reasons for Contentment*, which was published by the Loyal Association in 1793, William Paley argues that the poor ought to be contented—i.e. not riotous—because they are used to deprivation and hard work, and therefore they do not miss the more refined pleasures in life. Their very poverty entitles them to contentment precisely because poverty calls up the pleasures of frugality, which the rich do not experience. Describing the tedium of spending money, Paley declares, "There is no pleasure in taking out of a large unmeasured fund" (4). Paley redefines luxury from material goods to a strictly internal kind of enjoyment. In doing so, he locates luxury and plenty in the terrain of the imagination. But this

strategy of internalization becomes unsteady when he addresses the
pleasures of food:

> The rich who addict themselves to indulgence lose their relish. Their
> desires are dead. Their sensibilities are worn and tired. Hence, they
> lead a languid, satiated existence. Hardly any thing can amuse, or
> rouse, or gratify them. Whereas the poor man, if something extraor-
> dinary fall in his way, comes to the repast with appetite; is pleased and
> refreshed; derives from his usual course of moderation and temper-
> ance, a quickness of perception and delight, which the unrestrained
> voluptuary knows nothing of. . . . The luxurious receive no greater plea-
> sures from their dainties, than the peasant does from his homely fare.
> But here is the difference. The peasant, when ever he goes abroad,
> finds a feast, whereas the epicure must be sumptuously entertained to
> escape disgust. (5)

By treating food as if it were a luxury and its pleasures imaginative,
Paley not only elides the issue of literal hunger, but also articulates an
aesthetic of consumption and an economics of pleasure. The pleasure
derived from taste depends on frugal consuming behavior, not on
actual taste. Pleasure and appetite, in this account of gustatory taste,
are absolutely inseparable. The one requires the other in a delicate
balance wherein consumption never exceeds the appetite. Paley leaves
significantly unstated, of course, the fact that appetite must never slip
into hunger.

The context of Paley's intervention is economic and political, but
it also has implications for notions of literary consumption and taste.
Reeves's Loyal Association was formed precisely as a literary intervention into working-class reading, which was itself increasing because of
food shortages, war, and government censorship. Rhetorically, radical
pamphlets posit readers who are hungry, and whose reading supple-
ments that hunger by outlining the reasons they are hungry; they
point toward the future plenty that may be created through revolution. Thus, it became possible to imagine hungry readers who are
reading (in those "ale and pot-houses" that Arthur Young decries)
about their own hunger. Conservative writers like Paley, then, rede-
fine plenty as corporeal sufficiency whose pleasures are enhanced only
by the imaginative contemplation of frugality. For eating/reading to
be pleasurable, and for the matter to taste good, its consumption
requires an economy of scarcity.

Paley's "epicure" anticipates Coleridge's "exhausted" reader of
Gothic novels. Both of them engage in the same consumer behavior and suffer a similar range of physical consequences (such as the

lack of pleasure in eating, the need for increasingly stimulating fare, and being "worn and tired"). Without appetite, the activity of eating leads to a "languid" passivity and a lack of pleasure. But while Paley seeks to pacify presumably hungry readers with the imaginative pleasures of their own frugality, Coleridge's anxiety about the passive reader of Gothic novels bespeaks a more radical underlying agenda, one that implicitly seeks to draw out agency and activity on the part of satiated readers, and to define exactly what kinds of pleasurable consuming activity readers can pursue legitimately. As we have seen, in radical representations, hungry readers erupt in violent revolutionary activity; and, while Coleridge worries about this consequence, he, as an author, seeks the transformative social agency made possible by such eruptions. Thus, a metaphor grounded in a fairly conservative critique of consumption is transformed into a call for readerly agency and for the activating role of literature in the world. This view is embedded throughout his writing, but most interestingly in his expansive attack on Wordsworth's theory of meter in the *Biographia Literaria* (1817). Here, Coleridge draws on a figurative repertoire that owes much to the multivalent consumption metaphors he invokes in his review of *The Monk*. Coleridge's notion of pleasure takes it beyond the framework of imaginative frugality, and incorporates activity and agency as its central motive:

> As far as metre acts in and for itself, it tends to increase the vivacity and susceptibility both of the general feelings and of the attention. This effect it produces by the continued excitement of surprize, and by the quick reciprocations of curiosity still gratified and still re-excited, which are too slight indeed to be at any one moment objects of distinct consciousness, yet become considerable in their aggregate influence. As a medicated atmosphere, or, as wine during animated conversation, they act powerfully, though themselves unnoticed. Where, therefore, correspondent food and appropriate matter are not provided for the attention and feelings thus roused, there must needs be a disappointment felt; like that of leaping in the dark from the last step of a staircase, when we had prepared our muscles for a leap of three or four. (220)

Activity is connected intimately to Coleridge's theory of poetic pleasure, and it is important to note that such activity is a result of consumption—in this case, of drinking wine. Noting the poet's adoption of an alcohol metaphor, Anya Taylor points out that pleasure and activity are resolved here into a pleasant buzz of expectation (567); such pleasure is corporeal and active, in contrast with the "exhausted" literary gourmand. But it differs from the kind of consumption mediated by labor that William Paley, George Edwards, or even Wordsworth imagines. By yoking together images of intoxication, pleasure, and activity in his theory of meter, Coleridge appropriates consumption as a viable model not only for the pleasures of reading, but implicitly for its activating social benefits. Not rooted in an economy of scarcity, this model of reading/consuming pleasure allows that, by feeding the reader, the text provides the reader with the inspiration—or energy—to act.

The rhetoric of Romanticism actually draws on discourses of scarcity consumption, rather than rejecting consumption outright as a figure and motive for reading. While the Wordsworthian notion of "creating the taste" certainly requires readers to do a little work for their nourishment, figurations of books as food also arguably offer a model for literature as necessary aliment. The model was given a rhetorical and political urgency in the radical claim that books are necessities. If literary discourse is as necessary as food, then a space is opened for the Romantic author's fare, which is not only more wholesome, but more invigorating. As such, the Romantic attack on mass culture discloses an economic critique: make sure everyone is well fed, literally and figuratively, and stop worrying about the violent eruption of hunger or the bloated passivity of exhausted appetites. The politicized, aestheticized rhetoric of food scarcity pointed out a truth that is too frequently overlooked in a well-fed society: that food is absolutely necessary to human life. The insight of radical writers, as they attempted to appeal to their disenfranchised readers, was that literature, ideas, and an intellectual life might also be necessary to sustain a humane life. It is an insight that the Romantic poets variously appropriated for its radically democratic underpinnings, and for its celebration of the possibilities for social agency through reading.

NOTES

1. My thanks to Stephen Behrendt and the participants of the National Endowment for the Humanities Summer Seminar, "Rethinking Romantic Fiction," held at the University of Nebraska–Lincoln in 2003, for sharing their insights on early versions of this project.

2. Michel Jeanneret offers numerous examples of books/food metaphors, especially in Chapter 5, "Eating the Text." He traces the multivalence of these metaphors in classical, biblical, and Renaissance texts. The structural role played by alimentary metaphors has more recently been

established by George Lakoff and Mark Johnson in their linguistic study *Metaphors We Live By.*

3. I am drawing on a number of works on the Romantic literacy debates. R. K. Webb's *The British Working Class Reader* and Richard Altick's *The English Common Reader* remain foundational social histories of the rise of mass literacy, in addition to Jon Klancher's *The Making of English Reading Audiences* and Patrick Brantlinger's *The Reading Lesson.* More recently, William St. Clair has offered the first quantitative study of book production and dissemination, and while some of his findings complicate received ideas about actual sales of radical books (notably Paine's), they also point out the need for more attention to the Romantic-period book trade. In addition, I draw on readings of the politics of the pamphlet wars, especially on Olivia Smith's *The Politics of Language,* Ian Haywood's *The Revolution in Popular Literature,* and Don Herzog's *Poisoning the Minds of the Lower Orders.* Jacqueline Pearson's study of women's reading practices and representation also informs my discussion, as well as Reinhard Wittmann's exploration of the "reading revolution" in Europe.

4. For a more detailed discussion of the consonance of the novel with capitalist forces of production, see Terry Lovell's *Consuming Fictions.*

5. Also relevant to my discussion here is Catherine Sheldrick Ross's analysis of the consequences of food and ladder metaphors on the policies of nineteenth-century American libraries.

6. Jon Klancher also notes the hostility toward consumption models of textual reception. Theorizing consumption as a cultural practice rather than a corporeal one, he argues that Wordsworth seeks a return to the "symbolic exchange" of reception against the "commodity exchange" of consumption (143).

7. Brantlinger connects these alimentary and poison metaphors to the notion of the *pharmakon* in Chapter 1, "Gothic toxins."

8. The public debate about the food scarcity was widespread, robust, and immensely colorful. The subject was regularly featured in magazines, books, and newspaper articles, especially between 1795 and 1801. Coleridge even contributed to the debate in 1800 with his *Monopolists and Farmers,* which he wrote jointly with Thomas Poole for the *Morning Post.* For the radicalizing potential of the years of scarcity, see Thompson, *Making* and "Moral Economy." The fullest historical account of these years is contained in Roger Wells's *Wretched Faces.*

9. Spurred as it was by food shortages, the French Revolution was closely connected to ideas about food and eating in the popular British imagination, of which Marie Antoinette's "let them eat cake" became the most famous (if probably apocryphal) utterance. Images of the French revolutionaries as gluttonous eaters of rich and exotic foods, or as cannibals of their own people, were often used as descriptive shorthand for the violent excesses of the Revolution. For a literary application of the relationship between food, the French Revolution, and

British radical culture, see Penny Bradshaw's reading of the novels of Charlotte Smith alongside James Gillray's antirevolutionary cartoons. Timothy Morton also discusses the revolutionary implications of food references, especially in Chapter 1, "The Rights of Brutes."

10. Young's responses to radical reading materials are scattered throughout his works, especially in *The Question of Scarcity Plainly Stated*, *An Enquiry into the State of the Public Mind*, and *Wastes*. Young's surprising about-face on enclosure marked the end of his career with the Board of Agriculture. For his pains, he was considered to be in league with radicals and Jacobins.

11. In "The Moral Economy of the English Crowd," E.P. Thompson argues that the food riot was an accepted form of plebeian protest, designed to assert the moral duties of food producers toward consumers.

12. Also known as *Hog's Wash*.

13. Ian Haywood observes that these tropes hearken back to the " 'lanx satura' of classical satire" (28).

14. Many theories have been advanced to account for the "Consumer Revolution" of the eighteenth century, the most influential of which is Thorstein Veblen's notion of "imitative consumption." Grant McCracken argues that consumption is encouraged through the creation of a "patina" of status around an object.

WORKS CITED

Altick, Richard. *The English Common Reader: A Social History of the Mass Reading Public, 1800–1900*. Chicago: Chicago UP, 1957. Print.

Bradshaw, Penny. "The Politics of the Platter: Charlotte Smith and the 'Science of Eating.'" *Cultures of Taste/Theories of Appetite: Eating Romanticism*. Ed. Timothy Morton. New York: Palgrave Macmillan, 2004. 59–76. Print.

Brantlinger, Patrick. *The Reading Lesson: The Threat of Mass Literacy in Nineteenth-Century British Fiction*. Bloomington: Indiana UP, 1998. Print.

Campbell, Colin. *The Romantic Ethic and the Spirit of Modern Consumerism*. 3rd ed. London: Alcuin Academics, 2005. Print.

Coleridge, Samuel Taylor. *Biographia Literaria*. New York: Everyman Library, 1997. Print.

———. Review of M.G. Lewis's *The Monk*. *Critical Review* (February 1797): 194–200. Print.

Edwards, George. *Palliative and Radical Means of Counteracting the Present Scarcity, and Preventing Famine in the Future*. London: J. Johnson, 1801. Print.

———. *Effectual Means of Providing…Against the Distress Apprehended from the Scarcity and High Prices of Different Articles of Food*. London: J. Johnson, 1800. Print.

Eaton, Daniel Isaac. *Politics for the People; or A Salmagundy for Swine.* 5th ed. Vol. 1. London: D.I. Eaton, 1794. Print.

Famine, Citizen. *Le Tocsin! Or the Address of Citizen Famine!!! By A Friend to Liberty, Peace and Justice.* Hampstead, UK: W. Wellers, n.d. Print.

Gigante, Denise. *Taste: A Literary History.* New Haven: Yale UP, 2005. Print.

Haywood, Ian. *The Revolution in Popular Literature: Print, Politics and the People, 1790–1860.* New York: Cambridge UP, 2004. Print.

Heinzelman, Kurt. *The Economics of Imagination.* Boston: U of Massachusetts P, 1980. Print.

Herzog, Don. *Poisoning the Minds of the Lower Orders.* Princeton, NJ: Princeton UP, 1998. Print.

Jeanneret, Michel. *A Feast of Words: Banquets and Table Talk in the Renaissance.* Trans. Jeremy Whiteley and Emma Hughes. Chicago: Chicago UP, 1991. Print.

Klancher, Jon. *The Making of English Reading Audiences, 1790–1832.* Madison: U of Wisconsin P, 1987. Print.

Lakoff, George, and Mark Johnson. *Metaphors We Live By.* Chicago: U of Chicago P, 1980. Print.

Lovell, Terry. *Consuming Fiction.* New York: Verso, 1987. Print.

McCracken, Grant. "The Making of Modern Consumption." *Culture and Consumption.* Bloomington: Indiana UP, 1988. Print.

More, Hannah. *Works.* Vol. 1. London: H. Fisher, R. Fisher and P. Jackson, 1834. Print.

Morton, Timothy. *Shelley and the Revolution in Taste: The Body and the Natural World.* New York: Cambridge UP, 1994. Print.

Newlyn, Lucy. *Reading, Writing and Romanticism: The Anxiety of Reception.* New York: Oxford UP, 2000. Print.

Paley, William. *Reasons for Contentment.* London: R. Faulder, 1793. Print.

Pearson, Jacqueline. *Women's Reading in Britain 1750–1835: A Dangerous Recreation.* New York: Cambridge UP, 1999. Print.

Radway, Janice. "Reading Is Not Eating: Mass-Produced Literature and the Theoretical, Methodological, and Political Consequences of a Metaphor." *Book Research Quarterly* 2.3 (Fall 1986): 7–29. Print.

Raven, James, Peter Garside, and Antonia Forster. *The English Novel 1770–1829: A Bibliographical Survey of Prose Fiction Published in the British Isles. Volume 1: 1770–1799.* New York: Oxford UP, 2000. Print.

Ross, Catherine Sheldrick. "Metaphors of Reading." *The Journal of Library History* 22 (Spring 1987): 147–63. Print.

St. Clair, William. *The Reading Nation in the Romantic Period.* New York: Cambridge UP, 2004. Print.

Smith, Olivia. *The Politics of Language.* New York: Oxford UP, 1984. Print.

Southam, B.C., ed. *Jane Austen: The Critical Heritage.* New York: Routledge and Kegan Paul, 1968. Print.

Spence, Thomas. *Pigs' Meat; or Lessons for the People Alias (According to Burke) The Swinish Multitude.* Vol. 3. London: T. Spence, 1795. Print.

Taylor, Anya. "Coleridge and the Pleasures of Verse." *Studies in Romanticism* 40.4 (Winter 2001): 547–69. Print.

Thompson, E. P. "The Moral Economy of the English Crowd." *Customs in Common: Studies in Traditional Popular Culture*. New York: The New Press, 1993. Print.

———. *The Making of the English Working Class*. New York: Penguin Books, 1968. Print.

Webb, R. K. *The British Working Class Reader 1790–1848. Literacy and Social Tension*. London: George Allen & Unwin, 1955. Print.

Wells, Roger. *Wretched Faces: Famine in Wartime England, 1793–1801*. New York: St. Martin's, 1987. Print.

Wittman, Reinhard. "Was There a Reading Revolution at the End of the Eighteenth Century?" *A History of Reading in the West*. Ed. Guglielmo Cavallo and Roger Chartier. Trans. Lydia G. Cochrane. Amherst: U of Massachusetts P, 1999: 284–312. Print.

Williams, Raymond. *Culture and Society: Coleridge to Orwell*. 1958. London: The Hogarth Press, 1990. Print.

Wordsworth, William. Preface to *Lyrical Ballads. William Wordsworth*. Ed. Stephen Gill. The Oxford Authors. New York: Oxford UP, 1990. Print.

Young, Arthur. *An Inquiry into the Propriety of Applying Wastes to the Better Maintenance and Support of the Poor*. Bury, UK: J. Rackham, 1801. Print.

———. *The Question of Scarcity Plainly Stated and Remedies Considered*. London: B. McMillan, 1800. Print.

———. *An Enquiry into the State of the Public Mind Amongst the Lower Classes*. London: W.J. and J. Richardson, 1798. Print.

Chapter Eight

"Diminished Impressibility": Addiction, Neuroadaptation, and Pleasure in Coleridge

Thomas H. Schmid

> *O dear God! give me strength of Soul to make one thorough Trial–if I land at Malta/ spite of all horrors to go through one month of unstimulated Nature–yielding to nothing but manifest Danger of Life!–O Great God! Grant me grace truly to look into myself, & to begin the serious work of Self-amendment.*

> —Samuel Taylor Coleridge, *Notebooks* 2: 2091

Samuel Taylor Coleridge's thought and work provide particularly rich material for analyzing the links between neuroscience, addiction, and aesthetics in the Romantic period, not least because of Coleridge's sustained interest in the subject of pleasure and its role in human behavior and in literary composition and reception. As Anya Taylor emphasizes, " 'pleasure' is a frequent term in Coleridge's lexicon" (*Bacchus* 104), entering into his thinking on poetic creation and response, transcendence, and the conditions for moral action.[1] But "pleasure" also preoccupies Coleridge during dysphoric moments of reflection on his opium use and the particular kinds of pleasure and pain it has occasioned. A frequently cited entry in the Malta notebook of 1804, for instance, in which Coleridge prays for "one month of unstimulated Nature" and a release from addiction, actually begins with a suggestion for "An Ode to Pleasure—not sought for herself, but as the conditio sine qua non of virtuous activity," before turning quickly to an elaboration of the intestinal and other pains—"Weight, Languor, & the soul-sickening Necessity of attending to barren bodily sensations"—opium has produced (*Notebooks* 2: 2091). What is striking in the tortured mix of prayer and suffering in this well-known journal entry is the seeming unavailability of a certain kind of pleasure for Coleridge, as well as the absence of a certain kind of pain: mere inertia ("weight") and barrenness take the place of feelings, both pleasurable and painful, that could lead to something, such as "virtuous activity" or a poem. That Coleridge never writes the proposed "Ode to Pleasure" is not surprising: for all his interest in it, pleasure can be a painful subject for him.

One reason for Coleridge's ambivalent feelings about pleasure, this essay will propose, lies in the specialized adaptations of the brain's pleasure centers that occur under the influence of addictive substances and behaviors, the subject of vigorous current neuroscientific research by specialists such as George Koob, Eric Nestler, and Robert Malenka. The consensus of that research suggests that, as the brain's neuropathways adapt to the stimulus of the substance, the experience of pleasure becomes compromised to the point that "ordinary" pleasures no longer excite a hedonic response. While Coleridge lacked today's medical knowledge, his thoughts on his own physical and emotional state, as expressed in various notebook entries, letters, and poems such as "Dejection: An Ode," aptly describe the effects of such neuronal adaptation on pleasurable perception and sensation. Particularly, Coleridge recognizes in the Dejection Ode his own inability to respond in a non-addictive way to nature, to take the kind of pleasure in the contemplation of nature that typified his own pre-addicted responses, as well as those of non-addicts such as Wordsworth. The poem can be seen, then, as both the record and consequence of inner, biochemical transformations and adaptations; and while the Ode resists reduction to a mere function of biological impulses, the neuroscientific evidence provides fresh insights for reevaluating its twin poles of "dejection" and "joy."

Numerous scholars, including M. H. Abrams, Alethea Hayter, Elisabeth Schneider, Molly Lefebure, and Neil Vickers, have focused productive critical lenses on Coleridge's relationship with opium, exploring issues ranging from the influence of opium on creativity and imaginative vision (Abrams, Hayter, and Schneider), to the relationship between Coleridge's psychological background and his addiction (Lefebure), to, more recently, the question of Coleridge's medical understanding of his drug use (Vickers). Lefebure, moreover, touches on the dysphoric aspects of drug dependence as they pertain to Coleridge, the subject of the present essay as well. Yet none of these studies has examined the specific effects of neuroadaptation on the experience of pleasure as a way to read Coleridge's various representations of "dejection." Such an examination has the advantage of updating and qualifying a number of the conclusions of the older studies, which, Vickers excepted, were necessarily shaped without the benefit of the most recent neuroscientific research.

A more strategic concern that any argument on opium and Coleridge must address involves the historical and cultural contingency of addiction discourses themselves, the focus of several important studies that question the usefulness of addiction as a conceptual category for analyzing Romantic-period literary works. Harry G. Levine's groundbreaking essay "The Discovery of Addiction," in its careful mapping of the emergence of addiction as a disease concept in nineteenth-century America, sounds an important theoretical caution against applying the term uncritically to past historical ages, a caution many have since repeated. Thus, Berridge and Edwards have influentially argued that "Addiction, in fact, was not the point at issue for" nineteenth-century users of opium, including Coleridge and De Quincey (60–1), while both Vickers (92–3) and Youngquist have agreed that, in Youngquist's words, "however tempting it may be to describe Coleridge as an opium addict historical accuracy requires other terms.... *Addiction* as a physio-cultural concept emerged later in the nineteenth century, the effect of a multiplicity of [cultural] forces" (n. 4; italics in text).[2] Such historical caveats are well taken and are abetted by poststructuralist critiques of "addiction" as an unusually open-ended cultural signifier that can mean almost anything to anybody.[3] Still, even those scholars who point to the lack of a codified addiction concept in the early nineteenth century agree that it is precisely with Romantic writers such as Coleridge that the seeds of its development are sown: "In fact, Coleridge becomes one of the early architects of the concept," Youngquist summarizes (n. 4). A neurobiological reading of Coleridge can ably attend to both the discursive parameters of the historical moment in which Coleridge wrote and the interpretive insights that recent research on the cerebral experience of pleasure can bring. Coleridge's own discourse is what matters most to the following reading, both in its historical specificity and in its description of a radically compromised ability to feel pleasure. Recent research helps to describe the specific ways in which opium quite likely contributed to that loss of pleasurable affect and serves usefully to bracket the question of "addiction" as a culturally relative term in favor of an approach centered on specific drug–brain interactions.

THE NEUROSCIENCE OF ADDICTED PLEASURE

While addiction remains difficult to define, recent advances in neuroscientific research have shown great promise in helping specialists understand how addiction affects the brain's processing and experience of pleasurable sensation. Under normal circumstances, the brain's limbic system or reward circuitry serves to reinforce advantageous survival behaviors such as eating, drinking, and sex through the release of chemicals that induce a pleasurable, and therefore rewarding, response. Addictive substances and behaviors tend to "commandeer," to use Eric Nestler and Robert Malenka's term for it, the normal functioning of that system, creating new set points for the experience of pleasure and reward, and creating strong motivation to continue seeking the object of addiction (par. 8). As David Friedman and Sue Rusche summarize, "*Drugs change the way the limbic system works. Just as your brain stem signal[s] hunger and induce[s] your limbic system to create commands to get you to seek food, drugs essentially make the limbic system create commands to get people to seek drugs*" (28; italics in text). While the precise mechanisms for how different addictive drugs accomplish this cerebral rewiring vary from substance to substance and are intricately complex, in general all addictive substances and behaviors work by accelerating the release of dopamine from the neurons in the ventral tegmental area (VTA) of the brain into the nucleus accumbens in the basal forebrain, the normal route for the stimulation of pleasure and reward. Again, in Friedman and Rusche's words, "When something activates the VTA neurons, they release dopamine into your nucleus accumbens. When this happens, you feel pleasure. A variety of natural events, such as eating when you are hungry or drinking when you are thirsty, turns on the brain reward system. But nothing turns it on with as much force as cocaine, heroin, and other addictive drugs" (29). That difference in intensity ultimately triggers the neuronal adaptations in addiction.

The explanation for such adaptation is that while "natural" pleasures turn on the limbic system slowly and subtly, addictive drugs and behaviors do it with what Friedman and Rusche call a "jolt": "If natural reinforcers turn on a light," they comment, "drugs set off fireworks" (103). Neuroscientist George Koob describes it this way: "we have so much money in the bank in terms of pleasure in our lives, and we can expend that money over the course of a single weekend's binge on cocaine or we can expend it over a two-week period in the normal pleasures of everyday life" (Moyers interview). To illustrate the contrast, Koob uses the personal example of his interest in gardening, especially growing peaches: the investment in the pleasurable goal of ripe peaches for eating is a long-term one and is itself associated with small satisfactions in the regular tasks of watering and fertilizing the trees, pruning, et cetera; significant amounts of time and work, in other words, are required in order to achieve the reward. On the other hand, drugs such as cocaine and opium flood the system with dopamine, immediately providing huge rewards with almost no work. As Eric Nestler and Robert Malenka describe it, they "goose" the system with unusual intensity and effectiveness (par. 21). In addition, all addictive drugs interfere with the reward pathway's natural mechanisms for *limiting* the intensity and duration of pleasure (by eventually shutting down the release of dopamine and "repackaging" it for later use). For instance,

> Cocaine and other stimulants temporarily disable the transporter protein that returns the neurotransmitter [dopamine] to the VTA neuron terminals, thereby leaving excess dopamine to act on the nucleus accumbens. Heroin and other opiates, on the other hand, bind to neurons in the VTA that normally shut down the dopamine-producing VTA neurons. The opiates release this cellular clamp, thus freeing the dopamine-secreting cells to pour extra dopamine into the nucleus accumbens. Opiates can also generate a strong "reward" message by acting directly on the nucleus accumbens. (par. 15)

These neurochemical signals and interruptions of signals, then, create a double whammy of pleasure, both "goosing" the system and then keeping it goosed for far longer than a natural reward does.

But addictive substances not only stimulate the reward circuit that results in pleasurable sensation; they can also, paradoxically, suppress pleasurable sensation. Such suppression lies behind the well-known effects of tolerance (the continual need to increase the amount of substance to achieve results) and dependence (characterized by withdrawal and craving during periods of abstinence) that can develop with chronic drug use. The biochemical mechanisms underlying the development of tolerance and dependence are too complex to treat with any thoroughness here, but they represent remarkable adaptations in the brain's normal pleasure circuitry. In Koob's banking terms, with the advent of tolerance and dependence, "you have bankrupted the system. There's no more pleasure in your account"

(Moyers interview). The reason, as Nestler and Malenka explain, is that the heightened concentrations of dopamine lead to the increased rate of release of other chemicals, such as dynorphin, which acts to inhibit the neurons in the VTA. In Nestler and Malenka's summary, "induction of dynorphin...thereby stifles the brain's reward circuitry, inducing tolerance by making the same-old dose of drug less rewarding. The increase in dynorphin also contributes to dependence, as its inhibition of the reward pathway leaves the individual, in the drug's absence, depressed and unable to take pleasure in previously enjoyable activities" (par. 19). Ordinary pleasures such as George Koob's peach-growing or eating a good meal do not normally lead to these effects, since the amount of dopamine released is much less and takes place over a longer period—a trickle rather than a flood. When the reward pathway is flooded, it adapts to such excessive "goosing" by developing the reactive neurochemical responses characterized in tolerance and dependence. Moreover, Nestler and Malenka stress, these adaptations comprise long-term "changes in the structure and function of the system's neurons that last for weeks, months or years after the last fix" (par. 4). The addicted brain becomes (perhaps in some cases permanently) hard-wired for fireworks, not sunsets. The result is that addiction changes the addict's experience of pleasure, both of the firework and the sunset kind. For Koob, this is the very essence of addiction, which he defines as a state in which "Your pleasure centers have been usurped" and "you no longer seek out natural pleasures because the drug is driving the system" (Moyers interview).

Coleridge would appear to gesture toward an analogous recognition of his own system's usurpation when he prays for a return to a state of "unstimulated Nature" in 1804. The phrase is something of a tautology: natural bodily and mental states do not require the introduction of opium for their normal functioning or self-regulation, and "natural pleasures"—like gardening or watching the sun set—do not unduly stimulate or stress the body's hedonic system. "Unstimulated nature" is really just *nature*, a physical and mental state in which the bank account of pleasure is perpetually balanced and comparatively free of sharp dips and spikes. But Coleridge appears to recognize that his own bodily nature needs correction, that it needs *un*-stimulation in order to experience *natural* stimulation again. Though he could not have understood the exact mechanisms of neuroadaptation involved in his body's gradual tolerance to the pleasures of opium and in his concurrent deadening to less intense stimulation, he could feel the loss. It is a loss he had already written about in "Dejection: An

Ode" two years before praying for a release from opium in the Malta journal.

Coleridge and "Diminished Impressibility"

From the standpoint of the neuroscience of addiction, the Dejection Ode can be seen to express a painful loss of hedonic affect. Few scholars deny that some definition of addiction fits the facts of Coleridge's life, though critics do disagree as to his awareness of addiction or its effect, if any, on his thought and work. But assuming Coleridge had developed a full-blown opium addiction by the time he wrote the "Ode" in 1802 (scholars generally assume addiction by 1800),[4] it is reasonable also to assume that his experience of pleasure would have been compromised in the ways the current neuroscientific research describes—whether Coleridge was aware of it or not—and that such a radically diminished ability to feel pleasure might contribute something to the persistent imagery of loss, lack of feeling, and emotional paralysis in the Dejection Ode.

The Ode begins, for instance, with a prayer for relief from a "dull pain" that, as the poem continues, seems to represent not so much painful feeling as painful *lack* of feeling, one that resists stimulation and movement:

> … O! that even now the gust were swelling,
> And the slant night-shower driving loud and fast!
> Those sounds which oft have rais'd me, while they aw'd,
> And sent my soul abroad,
> Might now perhaps their wonted impulse give,
> Might startle this dull pain and make it move and live! (15–20)[5]

Coleridge here uses the language of nervous stimulation common to the medical thought of his day and with which he was quite familiar. As Neil Vickers points out, for medical writers such as Erasmus Darwin, Thomas Beddoes, John Brown, and Samuel Crumpe, bodily stimulation, whether from drugs such as opium or from physical causes, tended to be a matter of pure "physics": "For them, the purpose of taking stimulants was to jump-start the body by getting the muscle tissue to contract" (31).[6] For Coleridge in the Dejection Ode, depression, lack of spirits, is also constructed in terms of physics, its amelioration depending, at least in the poem's beginning, on "impulses," something to shake or "startle" the system and make it "move." Indeed, such impulses, the speaker of the poem makes clear, could in the past "raise" his living being, his "soul," as well as the pain that threatened to deaden the soul. The problem the speaker identifies in the present is a chronic inability to *be* moved or stimulated, a state aptly described in the oxymoron "dull pain." In this state the "wonted impulses" are met with an *un*wonted lack of inner response; they fail to move, to send the soul abroad, or so it would seem from the subjunctive verbal mood of prayer in the sentence. As in the Malta journal entry on "unstimulated Nature," the Ode here uses prayer to express a wish for a return to a former state of responsiveness that now proves elusive. In further parallel with the journal entry, the Ode also constructs the speaker's inability to be moved as implicitly unnatural, since his wish that a rough wind might stir him is contrasted with the natural atmospheric effects of strong weather cells themselves, which never fail to "rouse" the night, as suggested in line 4, and to "ply a busier trade" than the "dull sobbing draft" of milder breezes (4; 6). If the "dull pain" from which the speaker suffers recalls the "dull" air, it is also something that, unlike the air, seems incapable of being whipped up into something "busier": where an incoming storm will predictably agitate the air, the same stimulus cannot be counted on to move the speaker, who can only pray that it *might* give its customary impulse and *might* help startle his dull pain. Such provisional constructions suggest that there is little hope of a natural response for the speaker. Even given a "wonted impulse" the speaker implicitly recognizes he might just as easily remain "unrous'd," to use the word he embeds in a negative construction to describe the night's contrasting responsiveness to the potential storm in lines 3–4: "This night, so tranquil now, will *not* go hence/ Unrous'd by winds" (italics mine). The speaker's subsequent prayer, then, is a response to nature's own kinetic capabilities, expressing a desire *not* to remain, as nature does not remain, "unroused" by things. To remain "unroused" is to be, in fact, dejected—to experience "dull pain."

Coleridge had recently described himself in similar terms in a letter of late January 1802, when he complained to William Godwin of "a diminished Impressibility from *Things*," an apt description for the mood of the Ode as well (*Collected Letters* 2: 782; italics in text). The "dejection" of the title likely stems from a number of contributing factors in Coleridge's life, including a perceived loss of poetic power, the unhappiness of Coleridge's marriage with Sara Fricker, his unrequited love for Sara Hutchinson, as well as the physical effects of poor health and chronic opium use—but I would suggest that no phrase better glosses the emotional state described in the beginning of the poem than "diminished Impressibility." The phrase is a crucial one, given Coleridge's ambivalent and continually evolving philosophical commitments to various contemporary theories of stimulus, disease, and cognition. Jennifer Ford, among others, has convincingly documented Coleridge's extensive familiarity with the prominent medical theories of stimulation in his day, arguing that "These life-science debates were topics to which Coleridge frequently returned throughout his life" and asserting, "Not only was Coleridge aware of these debates, he consciously participated in them" (29; 31). Particularly, Coleridge was well versed in Brunonian principles, the theories of nervous stimulation and "excitability" made famous in his day by the Scottish physician John Brown and enthusiastically supported by Coleridge's close friend Thomas Beddoes, though ultimately rejected by Coleridge himself: as Ford notes, "if [Coleridge] was temporarily swayed by Brown's theories in the 1790s...he later spoke of the Brunonian system as a 'false theory,' and by 1817 had repudiated its 'tyranny of the mechanic system in physiology'" (29).[7] What Coleridge primarily questioned was the idea that the mind and emotions, as well as the body, must be dependent solely on external stimuli, a question that also lay behind his rejection of Hartley's associationism after a similar initial enthusiasm in the 1790s, and his turn toward German idealist philosophy. However, Alan Richardson stresses that, despite Coleridge's periodic rejections of Brunonian and other "mechanic" explanations of the workings of mind and body, "Materialist, naturalistic, and embodied notions of the psyche would continue to play an ambiguous role in Coleridge's thinking throughout his career, particularly in regard to his speculation on the emotions and on the unconscious" (41). For Richardson, one example of this is Coleridge's interest, derived from his reading of Erasmus Darwin's *Zoönomia*, "in phenomena that...eluded the boundary between psychology and physiology," including such things as blushing, contagious yawning, and feverish hallucination. In writing on such phenomena (in an 1821 fragment on "Zoomagnetism")[8] Coleridge makes "his nearest approach to physiological accounts of mind," Richardson concludes, adding that "It should come as no surprise that Coleridge coined the term 'neuropathology'" (43), even when he ultimately longed for a more transcendent concept of mind than the physiological model of his contemporaries.

The notion of a "diminished Impressibility from *Things*" even more emphatically suggests Coleridge's belief in the relationship between stimuli, receptivity, and, most importantly, movement of thought and feeling. In the letter to Godwin, the phrase is listed as one of several related causes for what Coleridge sees as his dysfunctional indolence and neglect of duties to friends:

> Partly from ill-health, & partly from an unhealthy & reverie-like vividness of *Thoughts*, & (pardon the pedantry of the phrase) a diminished Impressibility from *Things*, my ideas, wishes, & feelings are to a diseased degree disconnected from *motion* and *action*. In plain & natural English, I am a dreaming & therefore an indolent man—. I am a Starling self-incaged, & always in the Moult, & my whole Note is, Tomorrow, & tomorrow, & tomorrow. (*Collected Letters* 2: 782; italics in text)

As in the Dejection Ode, diminished receptivity here contributes to mental and emotional paralysis, an inability to be impelled in some productive direction, or to feel and act. Coleridge distinguishes three different mental modes: thinking ("ideas"), wishing, and feeling. Though all three are impaired in Coleridge at this time, they represent separate capabilities; and though all three seem to be affected equally by all the causes listed, "diminished Impressibility" seems logically to be associated more with "feeling." Both terms occur at the end of their respective series of words or phrases, making them potentially apposite. More importantly, the second cause for Coleridge's indolence and psychic immobility (a "reverie-like vividness of *Thoughts*") not only refers to thinking, or ideas, but is also, by virtue of its vividness, an apparent opposite of "diminished Impressibility." The distinction is an important one: Coleridge can still think, though in what he calls a "diseased" way, and his thoughts at this time are even more vivid than usual, more impressive; their very vividness, in fact, leads paradoxically to mental paralysis. But feelings seem contrastingly deadened by a lack of impressibility, a malfunction in the ability to be impressed by external stimuli. The result is Coleridge's sense of being trapped within his own emotional and mental torpor, a "Starling self-incaged, & always in the Moult," who is fully cognizant of the world around him, his responsibilities, and the demands of relationships, but who somehow cannot feel properly or act on those feelings. The phrase "in the moult" is a perfect analogue for this lack of feeling, literally referring to a bird's change of plumage but figuratively used in Coleridge's time to denote "a melancholy or sorry state" (*OED*). To be "in the moult" is to be missing one's full plumage, an organic, systemic part of one's being that normally can be counted on to enable one's spirit to soar—or, in the construction of the Dejection Ode, to send the "soul abroad."

Coleridge partly misses, in his mental and emotional experience, the impressions of everyday life that make up human existence. A remarkable aspect of the limbic system of the brain is that it rewards human beings simply for living, by making little things pleasurable: exercise, eating and drinking, the thoughts that come and go throughout the day, the small thrill of accomplishing a difficult task, and so on. In response to the chronic flooding of the limbic circuits with opium-induced pleasure, the ability to experience those little rewards gradually lessens. In the Ode and assorted comments in the letters and journals, Coleridge gives readers an early, uncertain, yet moving account of what such an addicted altered state feels like: empty, numb, and bereft of affective capacities once possessed.

This loss of affective capability is particularly emphasized in section II of the poem, where images of absence, lack, and anaesthetic numbing are piled one upon the other in apposition to the "dull pain" of section I:

A grief without a pang, void, dark, and drear,
A stifled, drowsy, unimpassion'd grief,
Which finds no nat'ral outlet, no relief,
In word, or sigh, or tear—. (21–4)

Though Coleridge uses the word "grief" twice here, he also qualifies it as an unnatural grief that cannot be solaced by the conventional grieving processes of speech (talking about one's sorrow) or weeping. Neuronal hijacking takes Coleridge out of the ordinary realm of both pleasure and sorrow, closing off "natural" inlets and outlets to both. He cannot simply take a walk, or be roused by winds, or enjoy a full moon, or have a good cry and then feel better. In the Cornell manuscript of the "Letter" to Sara Hutchinson, Coleridge inserted three additional lines here, which he later removed from both the *Morning Post* and *Sybilline Leaves* versions of "Dejection": "This, Sara! well thou know'st,/ Is that sore Evil which I dread the most/ And oft'nest suffer" (25–7). The added lines reveal that the "drowsy unimpassioned grief" is chronic rather than singular. This state is not something that simply goes away, even, presumably, with a dose of opium; it is a form of grief without a specific object and lacking a specific "pang" that could be identified and removed; it is, in extension of the earlier oxymoron of "dull pain," fundamentally "unimpassioned."

The grief from which the speaker claims "oft'nest [to] suffer" is, in fact, identical with an absence of passion. Being "void," it lacks a definite or exclusive signified, remaining open-ended and therefore leaving the speaker inconsolable. This grief derives not from a particular feeling of bereavement but from a general state that is bereft of feeling, like that described by the analogous phrases "dull pain" and "diminished impressibility." In an 1828 fragment "On the Passions," Coleridge rather poetically defines "passion" itself as, simply, "a state of undergoing" (*Shorter Works* 2: 1422). A couple of paragraphs later he expands the definition to "a state of emotion which whatever its outward object or occasion may be, in ourselves or out of ourselves, has its proper and immediate cause not in this, but in our Thoughts respecting it" (2: 1423; strikeout in text). Passion in both definitions is described as a "state," a condition marked by some kind of mental processing of experience. In talking about being "unimpassioned" in the Ode, then, Coleridge literally describes an altered state, one in which the intellectual processes by which objects or events are converted into emotions have been disabled. To be "unimpassioned" is no longer to "undergo" life's events in a normal way. The fault, however, lies not in the events or stimuli themselves but in a person's subsequent failure to process them appropriately. Scientists now know that the brain's limbic pathway is one structure governing human affective experience, and Coleridge's idea of "undergoing" experiences aptly describes the way in which the limbic system normally functions. In contrast, the excessive "goosing" of the limbic pathway in addiction can be considered as so *over*writing the experience of pleasure that eventually "*under*going" it becomes nearly impossible. The "unimpassioned grief" in the Ode can be interpreted as just such an inability to feel pleasure—even the small and mixed pleasure of grieving, which provides some solace to emotional pain. Interestingly, Coleridge links pleasure and pain in the fragment "On the Passions," suggesting that both are subjectively experienced and, somewhat obscurely, that "Pain [is] not a pure antithesis to pleasure." His further statement that "Pleasure...may have a *real* existence" (2: 1428; italics in text) suggests, too, that Coleridge could admit the possibility of an organic, material component to pleasure, one that could therefore be materially altered as well. As Jennifer Ford notes, also with reference to the fragment "On the Passions," emotions in general for Coleridge, including those associated with pleasure, "were not to be seen in strictly psychological terms: Coleridge believed that they should also be discussed in relation to physiology, physics and anatomy" (175). In speculating that pleasure "may have a *real* existence," or physiological basis, Coleridge opens up the inverse possibility as well: that loss of pleasure may also be attributable to material causes.

In whatever terms Coleridge may have understood the cerebral processing of pleasurable experience, the Dejection Ode records a chronic and profound dysphoria that strikingly resembles the current neuropathological model. Significantly in the poem, even the customary solaces of nature make no impact on the speaker's unimpassioned grief, his diminished impressibility. He looks on the beauties of nature as he had been accustomed to do in the past, but now observes them with what he calls a "blank...eye" (30). Speaking of the fine cloudscapes, the stars, the "crescent Moon" (35), the speaker comments, "I see them all, so excellently fair," "I *see*, not *feel*, how beautiful they are!" (38–9; italics in text). The distinction between seeing and feeling registers a failure in the same chain of internal processing that Coleridge sketches or implies in both the letter to Godwin and the fragment on passion. In this case, pleasurable impressions impact the optic nerves, but they fail to be *felt* as pleasure. The stimuli have been duly recorded by a mind thoroughly trained in the aesthetic appreciation of nature, and yet the "state of undergoing" an aesthetic experience is never achieved. Such a failure constitutes the very essence of limbic suppression in opium dependence: too used to being goosed with opium, the pleasure pathway fails to be activated by so ordinary a stimulus as the sight of a crescent moon, just as in the beginning of the poem, the speaker fails to be roused by winds.

Needless to say, such insensitivity to nature represents a dire state of affairs for a Romantic poet. In some of the most frequently analyzed lines of the Ode, Coleridge writes, "I may not hope from outward forms to win/ The passion and the life, whose fountains are within" (46–7) and "we receive but what we give,/ And in *our* life alone does Nature live" (47–8; italics in text), which have been interpreted to mean that Coleridge here rejects Wordsworth's model of nature as healer (as expressed in the "Immortality" Ode) and embraces instead a subjectivist approach. Regardless (and I do not think that the neurochemical view of things is at all inconsistent with the philosophical reading), the lines again point to some kind of inner experience—at the very least an internal processing of natural stimuli that in part determines a "passion" for nature. Though Coleridge might not have fully realized the dysphoric effects of opium dependence at this stage of his life, he explicitly states in this part of the poem that the speaker no longer gets a "kick" from viewing the beauties of nature. Given what is known about the neurochemistry of addiction, the lack of feeling makes sense. In addition to whatever else he was dealing with emotionally and creatively at the time, Coleridge's pleasure centers were likely bankrupt, to recall Koob's illustration, by 1802. The poem carries over that sense of hedonic bankruptcy, in fact, from the speaker's initial prayer that the winds "ply a busier trade" than the "dull sobbing draft" and his "dull pain" can transact. Throughout the Ode, the speaker finds himself unable to deal in the accustomed currency of aesthetic pleasure in nature; Coleridge's own fund of such pleasure had, in all probability, been largely depleted.

JOY

That the Dejection Ode is fundamentally concerned with the sensory mechanisms of pleasure is revealed finally in its delineation of the contrast between the "dull pain" and "blank" eye of the opening three sections and the adumbration of "joy" in sections IV, V, and IX. If the dejection of the poem's title results from or even equates with "diminished impressibility," then the joy that eludes the speaker comprises a contrary state of "unstimulated nature." In section IV, joy is associated explicitly with both nature and purity: it is reserved only for the "pure . . . in their purest hour" (66) and represents the "spirit and the pow'r,/ Which wedding Nature to us gives in dow'r/ A new earth and new Heaven" (67–9). Joy is thus precisely the power to *feel* rather than merely to *see* the beauties of nature to which the speaker is deadened. It is a connecting power that actively imbues sensory input with pleasure and makes it full of what Coleridge calls "mirth" in section V (84). The speaker claims to have possessed this pure power of joy in the past, but he now laments its absence. Without "mirth" or joy he can neither connect with nature nor feel "natural" pleasure in its contemplation. Joy in this poem signifies a number of related principles for Coleridge, including the imagination, connection with others and, in J. Robert Barth's persuasive reading, "love of every kind" (94), but consistent with and underlying all of these is the power to take pleasure in ordinary things. By 1802, Coleridge had lost a good deal of that power and he knew it. The Ode records Coleridge's grief at the loss.

The sections on joy also comprise, as Paul Magnuson and others have energetically discussed, Coleridge's most direct response to Wordsworth (the "Edmund" of the *Morning Post* version), whose own poem on personal loss of vision, the "Immortality" Ode, Coleridge had heard before setting down to compose "Dejection." Joy, described as so irrevocably impaired in "Dejection," is positively associated with Wordsworth, whose power to "undergo" pleasure is vital and strong, in Coleridge's estimation. Having enumerated the "pow'r" of joy in section IV, Coleridge turns in section V to a concomitant expression of its disappearance from his own life:

> But now afflictions bow me down to earth:
> Nor care I, that they rob me of my mirth,
> But O! each visitation
> Suspends what nature gave me at my birth,
> My shaping spirit of imagination. (83–7)

As Magnuson observes, the "afflictions" cited here clearly reflect a number of biographical issues, most particularly Coleridge's failed marriage, while his location of a naturally bestowed imaginative power in childhood actually predates Wordsworth's later inclusion of a similar idea in the "Immortality" Ode (301). But the series of "visitations" also can connote the repeated doses of opium that were acting to diminish Coleridge's ability to feel joy. These would have been working to "suspend" the brain's natural reward system, which too is given "at birth." In a set of lines from the "Letter" to Sara Hutchinson, not included in the later versions, Coleridge is even more explicit about the deleterious effects of his "afflictions" on the experience of joy, calling them "Poison in the Wine" that "Eats out the Pith of Joy, makes all Joy hollow!/ All Pleasure a dim dream of Pain to follow!" (160–2). Coleridge might very well be thinking here only of his failed marriage—what he later in the "Letter" calls the "habitual Ills,/ That wear out Life, when two unequal minds/ Meet in one House" (242–4)—but the references to habit and the poisoning of pleasure evoke a systemic, physiological sense as well.

Wordsworth, "Dejection" makes clear, is spared this kind of pleasure-poisoning; he is one of the "pure" referred to in line 66 who continues to experience joy in nature without impediment; he retains that state of "unstimulated Nature" to which Coleridge himself later prays for a return. The Ode concludes, in fact, in praise of Wordsworth's powers of joy, along with a prayer for their continuance:

> O EDMUND, friend of my devoutest choice,
> O rais'd from anxious dread and busy care,
> By the immenseness of the good and fair,
> Which thou see'st ev'ry where
> Joy lifts thy spirit, joy attunes thy voice,
> To thee do all things live from pole to pole,
> Their life the eddying of thy living soul! (129–35)

Wordsworth exemplifies the healthy mind and body for Coleridge here, the un-poisoned consciousness that not only perceives the world but can also process those visual stimuli in a joyful state of "impressibility." In this sense, Wordsworth also represents what Andrew Weil calls "straight thinking," the kind of naïve discourse of the non-addict who can never seem to understand the entrenched dysphoria of the addict (116). While Coleridge clearly lauds and perhaps envies Wordsworth's undiminished impressibility at the end of the Ode, its contrast with his own altered hedonic state seems poignantly absolute.

Coleridge could not have understood the neurochemical mechanisms of his addiction, but he could feel their effects and write of them vividly and poetically. Analyzing Coleridge's "illness career" between 1801 and 1803, Neil Vickers maintains that "Only in the autumn of 1802 did Coleridge openly voice the suspicion that opium might be responsible for at least some of his ills" (97), but the covert references appear throughout the Ode and letters. The later letters to John Morgan in 1814, in which Coleridge refers to "this dirty business of Laudanum," show an explicit awareness of the effects of the drug on his physical and emotional health (*Collected Letters* 3: 490). Many of the period's medical writers, including George Young, Erasmus Darwin, Thomas Trotter, and Samuel Crumpe, wrote about the effects of addiction, including the phenomenon of gradual tolerance leading to a suppression of pleasure, about which they understood a great deal. In *Zoönomia*, for instance, Erasmus Darwin proposed a model of actual physiological adaptation in chronic drug use of all kinds: "When a stimulus is repeated more frequently than the expenditure of sensorial power can be renewed in the acting organ, the effect of the stimulus becomes gradually diminished .... Hence all medicines, repeated too frequently, gradually lose their effect, as opium and wine" (XII. iii. 1); and, writing of alcohol dependency, Thomas Trotter noted in 1804 that

> The drunken paroxysm, as far as can be observed in those who are addicted to the habit, has some variation from the history now given of the phenomena. The chearfulness of mind, and lively countenance, with all the agreeable and pleasurable feelings, are by no means exhibited in the same degree. In short, like all human enjoyments, the exhilarating powers of wine lose their fine zest and high relish, by being too frequently indulged. (28–9)

With such statements about the dysphoric effects of chronic alcohol and opium use current in the literature of Coleridge's day, it would be surprising if Coleridge did not at least wonder about the effects of opium on his own affective experiences.

Coleridge's writing on his compromised ability to experience everyday pleasures both fits within this larger discourse of addictive adaptation in his period and corroborates the findings of modern neuroscientific research on addiction. To read Coleridge's sense of dejection through this lens is to agree with Molly Lefebure's early perception that his "body's chemistry was radically altered by his drug," but also to qualify her conclusion that "His world was now the junkie's exclusive world of irrational, irrelevant delusion" and that "The exterior world was no longer viable for S.T.C.; it had become one aching, eternal weariness peopled by the dead; his chief desire was to have as little contact with it as possible" (447). There was nothing irrational or delusional about Coleridge's quite accurate perception that he could *see* but not *feel* the beauties of the external world. Even in his most dejected state, Coleridge recognized that he had the capacity for taking pleasure in external nature, but that the capacity had somehow been impaired. In a notebook entry from October of 1803 he wrote: "I write melancholy, always melancholy: You will suspect that is the fault of my natural Temper. Alas! No.—This is the great Occasion—that my Nature is made for Joy—impelling me to Joyance—& I never, never can yield to it.—I am a genuine *Tantalus*" (*Notebooks* 1: 1609; italics in text). Similarly, in a letter from early in that same year Coleridge claimed that he did not "think it possible that any bodily pains could eat out the love & joy, that is so substantially part of me, towards hills, & rocks, & steep waters! And I have had some trial" (*Collected Letters* 2: 916). The neurochemical research on the limbic suppression of addiction suggests that while bodily pains perhaps could not erode Coleridge's sense of joy in nature, artificial pleasures paradoxically could.

NOTES

1. In her excellent article on "Coleridge and the Pleasures of Verse," Anya Taylor likewise notes that "Coleridge luxuriates in the word *pleasure*. Where his eighteenth-century predecessors had used the word in the plural, he uses the singular form to interrogate the quality of that pleasure itself"; Taylor adds that "Coleridge's notion of pleasure is more exclusively physical than Wordsworth's. Although Coleridge knows that 'the term, pleasure, is unfortunately so comprehensive, as frequently to become equivocal' (SWF 1.362), he calls pleasure the immediate aim of poetry" (558–9; italics in text).

2. Milligan, Parsinnen, Peters, and Siskin provide related discussions of historical contingency in addiction studies of the nineteenth century.

3. Derrida's well-known interrogation of Plato's *pharmakon* in *Dissemination* (63–171) has sponsored provocative deconstructions of "drugs" as both "remedy" and "poison," which have obvious implications for the psychopathology and cultural rhetoric of addiction; in "The Rhetoric of Drugs: An Interview," Derrida speculates on several aspects of the cultural logic of addiction, including such issues as writing as addiction, addiction and supplementarity, and the role of drugs in the legislation of "normalcy." Eve Kosofsky Sedgwick influentially questions the truth value of "addiction" in a modern world of proliferating "addictions" (such as to exercise) in "Epidemics of the Will." Finally, Avital Ronell perhaps best summarizes the deconstructionist approach in *Crack Wars*, maintaining that "drugs resist conceptual arrest" (51) and that "The contagious spread of the entity described as drugs is discursively manifest. Drugs cannot be placed securely within the frontiers of traditional disciplines.... While everywhere dealt with, drugs act as a radically nomadic parasite let loose from the will of language" (52).

4. On the beginnings of Coleridge's addiction, J. Robert Barth comments: "Coleridge had suffered a prolonged illness during the winter of 1800–1801, during which he experienced considerable physical pain; he took refuge from his pain not only in opium (this seems to have been the real beginning of his addiction) but also in 'abstruse research'" (94).

5. The complex manuscript and publication history of the Ode is well known. Generally, citations to the poem within this essay refer to the text first published in the *Morning Post* in 1802, which may be considered the default edition. Occasional comparisons are made with the verse "Letter" to Sara Hutchinson (Cornell ms.) and are so noted throughout. All citations refer to the reading texts edited by Stephen Parrish in *Coleridge's* Dejection: *The Earliest Manuscripts and the Earliest Printings.*

6. The heated debates and confusion over whether opium itself constituted a stimulant or a narcotic are notorious. Dr. John Brown and his followers tended to see opium as a stimulant, while William Cullen tended more toward the narcotic view, which, according to Molly Lefebure, was apparently shared by Coleridge himself (185). Still, in speaking of a release from opium addiction as a return to "unstimulated Nature," Coleridge would appear, at least in that one instance, to embrace a notion of the drug as a stimulant. Regardless, opium has now long been classified as a narcotic, and the focus of the present essay is more on the limbic adaptations of addiction rather than the historical question of opium's classification. For more information on

the historical debate, see the general discussions in Lefebure, Berridge and Edwards, Milligan, and Vickers.

7. Ford's reference is to a long note of Coleridge's in the chapter on Schelling (Ch. 9) in *Biographia Literaria* 1: 163.

8. Coleridge, *Shorter Works and Fragments* 2: 913.

Works Cited

Abrams, M. H. *The Milk of Paradise:The Effect of Opium Visions on the Works of De Quincey, Crabbe, Francis Thompson, and Coleridge.* Cambridge: Harvard UP, 1934. Print.

Barth, J. Robert. *Coleridge and the Power of Love.* Columbia: U of Missouri P, 1988. Print.

Berridge, Virginia, and Griffith Edwards. *Opium and the People: Opiate Use in Nineteenth- Century England.* London: Allen Lane, 1981. Print.

Coleridge, Samuel Taylor. *Shorter Works and Fragments.* Ed. H. J. Jackson and J. R. de J. Jackson. 2 vols. Princeton, NJ: Bollingen Press of Princeton UP, 1995. Vol. 2. Print.

———. *Coleridge's* Dejection: *The Earliest Manuscripts and the Earliest Printings.* Ed. Stephen Maxfield Parrish. Ithaca: Cornell UP, 1988. Print.

———. *Notebooks of Samuel Taylor Coleridge.* Ed. Kathleen Coburn. 5 vols. New York: Pantheon/Princeton UP, 1957–2002. Vols. 1–2. Print.

———. *Collected Letters of Samuel Taylor Coleridge.* Ed. Earl Leslie Griggs. 6 vols. Oxford: Clarendon Press, 1956–1971. Vols. 2–3. Print.

Crumpe, Samuel. *An Inquiry into the Nature and Properties of Opium.* London: G.G. and J. Robinson, 1793. Print.

Darwin, Erasmus. "Of Drunkenness." *Zoönomia.* 4 vols. London: Joseph Johnson, 1801. Vol. I, 357–68. Print.

Derrida, Jacques. "The Rhetoric of Drugs: An Interview." *Differences* 5.1 (Spring 1993): 1–25. Print.

———. *Dissemination.* Trans. Barbara Johnson. Chicago: U of Chicago P, 1981. Print.

Ford, Jennifer. *Coleridge on Dreaming.* Cambridge: Cambridge UP, 1998. Print.

Friedman, David P., and Sue Rusche. *False Messengers: How Addictive Drugs Change the Brain.* Amsterdam: Harwood Academic Publishers, 1999. Print.

Hayter, Alethea. *Opium and the Romantic Imagination.* Berkeley: U of California P, 1968. Print.

Lefebure, Molly. *Samuel Taylor Coleridge: A Bondage of Opium.* New York: Stein and Day, 1974. Print.

Levine, Harry G. "The Discovery of Addiction: Changing Concepts of Habitual Drunkenness in America." *Journal of Studies on Alcohol* 15 (1978): 493–506. Print.

Magnuson, Paul. *Coleridge and Wordsworth: A Lyrical Dialogue*. Princeton, NJ: Princeton UP, 1988. Print.

Milligan, Barry. *Pleasures and Pains: Opium and the Orient in Nineteenth-Century British Culture*. Charlottesville: U of Virginia P, 1995. Print.

"Moult/Molt." *Oxford English Dictionary Online*. 2nd ed. 2008. Web. Dec. 16, 2008.

Moyers, Bill. "An Interview with George Koob, M.D." *Close to Home: Moyers on Addiction*. PBS. Web. Dec. 20, 2008.

Nestler, Eric J., and Robert C. Malenka. "The Addicted Brain." *Scientific American* 290.3 (March 2004): 78–85. Web. Dec. 17, 2008.

Parsinnen, Terry M. *Secret Passions, Secret Remedies: Narcotic Drugs in British Society, 1820–1930*. Philadelphia: ISHI, 1983. Print.

Peters, Dolores. "The British Medical Response to Opiate Addiction in the Nineteenth Century." *Journal of the History of Medicine* 36.4 (October 1981): 455–88. Print.

Richardson, Alan. *British Romanticism and the Science of the Mind*. Cambridge: Cambridge UP, 2001. Print.

Ronell, Avital. *Crack Wars: Literature, Addiction, Mania*. Lincoln: U of Nebraska P, 1992. Print.

Schneider, Elisabeth. *Coleridge, Opium, and Kubla Khan*. Chicago: U of Chicago P, 1953. Print.

Sedgwick, Eve Kosofsky. "Epidemics of the Will." *Tendencies*. Durham, NC: Duke UP, 1993. 130–42. Print.

Siskin, Clifford. *The Historicity of Romantic Discourse*. New York and Oxford: Oxford UP, 1988. Print.

Taylor, Anya. "Coleridge and the Pleasures of Verse." *Studies in Romanticism* 40 (2001): 547–69. Print.

———.*Bacchus in Romantic England: Writers and Drink, 1780–1830*. Basingstoke and New York: Palgrave, 1999. Print.

Trotter, Thomas. *An Essay, Medical, Philosophical, and Chemical, on Drunkenness, and Its Effects on the Human Body*. 1804. Rpt., with an introduction by Roy Porter. London: Routledge, 1988. Print.

Vickers, Neil. *Coleridge and the Doctors, 1795–1806*. Oxford: Oxford UP, 2004. Print.

Weil, Andrew. *The Natural Mind: A New Way of Looking at Drugs and the Higher Consciousness*. Boston: Houghton Mifflin, 1972. Print.

Young, George. *A Treatise on Opium*. London: A. Millar, 1753. Print.

Youngquist, Paul. "Rehabilitating Coleridge: Poetry, Philosophy, Excess." *English Literary History* 66.4 (1999): 885–909. Web. Dec. 10, 2008.

CHAPTER NINE

NATURE, IDEOLOGY, AND THE PROHIBITION OF PLEASURE IN BLAKE'S "GARDEN OF LOVE"

Kevin Hutchings

What is it men in women do require
The lineaments of Gratified Desire
What is it women do in men require
The lineaments of Gratified Desire
　　—William Blake E474–75[1]
[T]he body is always simultaneously (if conflictually) inscribed in both the economy of pleasure and desire and the economy of discourse, domination and power.
—Homi K. Bhabha 67

PRELUDIUM: BLAKE'S PHILOSOPHY OF NATURE REVISITED

With a few notable exceptions, modern-day scholars have agreed that William Blake was an anti-empiricist who rejected the material world of nature in favor of spiritualized abstractions like "imagination" and "eternity." But this implicitly dualistic reading of the Blakean universe is difficult to reconcile with the poet's celebrated tendency to denounce oppositional models of the relationship between body and soul. Moreover, it does not adequately account for Blake's exuberant celebration of the naked human form in its pursuit of sensual pleasure and "The lineaments of Gratified Desire." The very idea that Blake regarded the physical world of nature as "no more than the Mundane Shell or Vegetative Universe that was the vesture of Satan" (Ackroyd 328) raises some serious questions. How could Blake celebrate human sensual experience while at the same time denouncing the material contexts in which sensuality is expressed and explored? If the body is indeed a "portion of Soul," as Blake claims in *The Marriage of Heaven and Hell* (4; E34), then its pleasure-seeking physical impulses presumably have a spiritual basis. When in *The Four Zoas* Blake asks "where are human feet for Lo our eyes are in the heavens" (*FZ* Night 9, 122.25; E391), his question gestures toward the potential perils of a dualistic distinction between spirit and materiality, which threatens to devalue and even lose sight of the body and its environment, the physical Earth upon which the body stands. Either the critics are not telling the full story when they claim that Blake "despised" the material world (Ackroyd 257, 328) and "rejected nature utterly" (Riede, *Swinburne* 7), or Blake's own philosophy is a tissue of contradictions difficult or impossible to reconcile.

To be sure, Blake's perceived hostility to material nature is evident in some of his own writings, which can seem unequivocal in their privileging of a transcendent human imagination and an unearthly eternity. Scattered throughout Blake's work—not only in the illuminated poetry but also in his annotations, letters, and notebook entries—are remarks indicating suspicion of, or even contempt for, the physical world: "Where man is not nature is barren" (*MHH* 10; E38); "a Fig for all Corporeal" (E716); "Natural Objects always did & now do Weaken deaden & obliterate Imagination in Me" (E665). Taking such utterances as Blakean gospel in his highly influential *Fearful Symmetry* (1947), Northrop Frye argued that Blake understood nature as "miserably cruel, wasteful, purposeless, chaotic, and half dead"—and thus as something "there for us to transform," if not, indeed, something that it is "all very well to abuse" (39–40). No matter that a less selective reading of Blake's discourse on nature turns up numerous statements that contradict or complicate such assertions;[2] no matter, indeed, that so many undergraduate students, exhibiting a critical "innocence" deriving from their lack of immersion in modern critical scholarship, often see Blake as a veritable champion of the green world (and so must receive careful "corrective" tutoring in the antinatural school of Blake studies if they are ultimately to toe the line of critical consensus): the notion that Blake ultimately negated nature by coming down firmly on the side of transcendent imagination and spirit still informs and influences much Blake scholarship (Lussier 397).

Such a view has not always held sway among Blake's readers. For example, Blake's very first typescript editor and one of his earliest critical commentators, J. J. Garth Wilkinson, went so far as to compare Blake's prophetic poetry to the writings of a reviled (because atheistical) Percy Bysshe Shelley, accusing Blake of courting a mode of "Pantheism, or natural spiritualism" (xviii) that attributed *too much* positive moral or ethical value to nature. How far removed from such a position is Frye's antinatural Blake! And yet, to my mind, neither Wilkinson's nor Frye's argument ultimately does justice to the poet's thought, for each pays insufficient attention to the various nuances informing Blake's poetics of nature as a whole, nuances that can contribute to a better understanding of Blake's poetical response to ascetic practices that denied the body's pleasure-seeking impulses and actions. For this reason, critical studies that explore the various *tensions* between Blake's pro- and antinatural positions often provide the most satisfying and convincing critical insights. Among the most important of such studies was Mark Schorer's *William Blake: The Politics of Vision* (1946). Published only a year before Frye's *Fearful Symmetry* burst upon the critical scene, Schorer's book persuasively demonstrated that Blake's attitude toward nature was marked not simply by denunciation, nor by admiration, but by a profound ambivalence indicating "the most enduring and the most extensive conflict in his personality and poetry" (6). Schorer thus anticipated Mark Lussier's more recent eco-critical reframing of Blake's philosophy of nature, which questions the "persistent attitude" in literary criticism "that Blake's hostility to nature extends throughout the canon." For Lussier, this critical perspective "needs to be reexamined simply because Blake's stance to nature did not crystallize into such a single vision" (398). In this essay, I expand upon Schorer's and Lussier's insights by exploring the material and ecological implications of Blake's famous celebration of sensual or bodily pleasure. To quote from Timothy Morton's recent eco-critical manifesto *Ecology without Nature*, "'the body' (as it is so often called in contemporary art and theory) *is* the environment" (43; italics in text); thus, to be logically coherent and sustainable, an affirmation of bodily pleasure must imply at least some measure of respect for the material and biological contexts that make the expression of such pleasure possible. This claim rings especially true when we consider the writings of a poet such as Blake, who often overtly connects bodily and environmental contexts by depicting "bodies which dissolve into landscapes" (Connolly viii).

Caught up in the politics of religion and gender, however, there is (as in Blake's discourse on materiality *per se*) nothing straightforward about Blake's philosophy of human embodiment and the pursuit of sensual pleasure. Before proceeding to the ecological-materialist gist of my analysis, therefore, a few more preliminary remarks are in order. Although the apprehension of spiritual truths will, in Blake's view, "come to pass by an improvement of sensual enjoyment" (*MHH* 14; E39), this affirmation of the sensual realm does not always fully account for "the civil situation of women" in the patriarchal society of the Romantic period (Worrall 48). In literary criticism, the nature of Blake's discourse on women's roles in society is at least as conflicted as his discourse on nature—largely, of course, because he tends to represent nature itself as female or feminine. At one extreme end of the critical spectrum of feminist responses to Blake's writings, the poet has been roundly indicted as "sexist to the core" (Mellor, quoted in Clark 34); while at the other, he is said to offer his readers a "visionary utopia of gender equality" that "eliminates or, rather, transcends, *all* corrupt forms of sexuality" (Ankarsjö 39, 37). In contradistinction to such polarized views, critics such as Tristanne J. Connolly and Alicia Ostriker have articulated nuanced perspectives that investigate contradictions and tensions existing between the sexist and egalitarian positions informing Blake's sexual politics (just as scholars such as Schorer and Lussier have shed new light on Blake's philosophy of nature by accounting for similar contradictions and tensions in his references to the material world). I have considered the environmental and ethical implications of Blake's gendering of nature elsewhere,[3] so I will not repeat myself here. But since it is through education and other forms of social conditioning that human attitudes toward nature, sexual difference, and the pursuit of sensual pleasure are acquired, I focus here on the role that religion plays in Blake's understanding of this social pedagogy, particularly in key poems from *Songs of Innocence and of Experience* (1794).

NATURE AND ASCETICISM

In the *Songs*, the poem that most clearly portrays the social mechanisms by which people come to internalize orthodox views of nature and the experience of sensual pleasure is "The Garden of Love." In only twelve brief lines, Blake encapsulates his iconoclastic critique of the dualistic theology that functions to negate both the material world and the pleasures of the flesh by advocating, in the name of piety and chastity, an ascetic renunciation of both. One of the poem's particular concerns is to expose the ways in which ascetic attitudes and practices function to support the interests of an authoritative Priesthood. I highlight this essentially political critique because I am convinced that Blake's apparent suspicion of nature is based not on an outright rejection of the material world of embodied existence—the world in which the delights of sensual pleasure are experienced—but upon an awareness of the ways in which contemporary institutions deployed dualistic *concepts* of nature to police human bodily acts. In its basic outline, "The Garden of Love" is a poem about a fall marking the end of prelapsarian innocence. Blake's poem attributes this fall not to any personal sin of disobedience to divine dictate (as in Milton's *Paradise Lost*) but to the intervention in a child's paradise of an institutionalized religious order, an order functioning to constrain the speaker's childish exuberance by transforming the "green" spaces in which he or she had formerly come to indulge in the joys of innocent "play":

> I went to the Garden of Love
> And saw what I never had seen.
> A chapel was built in the midst,
> Where I used to play on the green. (1–4; E26)

In these opening lines, Blake establishes a temporal economy similar to the one that Wordsworth would portray four years later in "Lines composed a few miles above Tintern Abbey" (1798). Like the speaker in Wordsworth's poem, Blake's speaker returns, after a period of absence, to a favorite childhood spot, only to find that the joys he had experienced during his previous visit are no longer available to him. And like Wordsworth's speaker, he reflects on and attempts to come to terms with a sense of profound loss associated with this change in circumstances. But in Wordsworth's poem the speaker attributes his sense of loss not to any change in the external environment, but to a transformation that has occurred in his own character since he last visited the scene: Nature's "beauteous forms" (22) remain the same, but, due to the maturation of his mind, the speaker can no longer indulge in the "glad animal movements" (74) that had characterized his former, non-self-reflexive mode of being, "when like a roe" he had "bounded o'er the mountains, by the sides/ Of the deep rivers, and the lonely streams,/ Wherever nature led" (67–70).

For the speaker in Blake's poem, however, the inability to access pleasures previously experienced in the "Garden of Love" derives not only from a change in his own mindset (caused by his entry into the self-reflexive state of Experience), but also from the intrusion into paradise of an ideology and practice associated with the newly built chapel, whose unprecedented construction in the garden's "midst" has resulted in a wholesale transformation of the immediate environment. Whereas formerly the garden had been a space of Edenic innocence, a locus of the free "play" (4; E26) and uninhibited *jouissance* of childhood, it is now the site of institutionalized religious worship, its formerly open green spaces having been enclosed by impenetrable gates and doors, prophylactic symbols of Priesthood's dualistic separation of inner from outer, sacred from profane, spirit from body, the austere pursuit of religious piety from the pleasurable pursuit of earthly delights. As the transformed garden's new motto— "Thou shalt not" (6)—indicates, the newly erected chapel functions in the poem as a figure for the ideological repression of human sensual desire. Involving an orthodox privileging of spirit over body, the implicit dualism here has grave implications not only for the speaker's well-being but also for that of the formerly "green" environment, substituting "tomb-stones where flowers should be" (10; E26). For Blake, in short, the repression of human sensual experience and its attendant pleasures entails, by extension, not only the devaluation but the outright negation of the material contexts that enable the playful expression of human joy.

In the poem's second quatrain, Blake depicts the speaker's immediate response to the transformation of his former playground:

> And the gates of this Chapel were shut,
> And Thou shalt not, writ over the door;
> So I turn'd to the Garden of Love,
> That so many sweet flowers bore. (5–8; E26)

In these lines, the causal phrase "*So I turn'd* to the Garden of Love" suggests that the speaker's about-face is a direct and deliberate response to the chapel's shut gates[4] and to the strangely intransitive prohibition inscribed above its doorway, a prohibition whose lack of a specific object indicates a generalized negation of desire and the pursuit of pleasure. Blake's suggestion is that the negative commandment "Thou shalt not" has functioned dialectically to generate its own transgression. The speaker comes to the garden, in short, to seek the pleasure of free play and love, discovers that such joys have been prohibited, and so immediately "turns" to seek them elsewhere, thereby demonstrating not so much "his own cooperation" with the newly imposed social order, as Brian Wilkie has suggested (128), but an implicit desire to resist it. The speaker's immediate response to this institutionalized prohibition brings to mind Jean-Jacques Rousseau's insight, in his *Discourse on the Origin of Inequality* (1755), regarding the workings of imposed law. Although Blake would surely have challenged the French philosopher's all-too-reasonable observation that "the more violent the passions are, the more are laws necessary to keep them under restraint," he would probably have appreciated the caveat Rousseau subsequently articulates in qualifying this claim. Speaking of the "evils" associated with violent human passions and "the inadequacy of laws" designed to restrain them, Rousseau remarks: "we should do well to inquire if these evils did not spring up with the laws themselves; for in this case, even if the laws were capable of repressing such evils, it is the least that could be expected from them, that they should check a mischief which would not have arisen without them" (Rousseau 345). *Quae negata grata*—that which is denied is desired.

THE RETURN OF THE REPRESSED

When Blake's speaker deliberately turns away from the chapel and the stern moral legalism articulated in the negative commandment "Thou shalt not," he brings the ontological status of the garden itself into question. For although he tells us at the outset of the poem that he "went to the Garden of Love," and that it was in this garden that he discovered the newly built chapel, he nevertheless "*turn[s]* to the Garden of Love" in order to escape the chapel's imposing institutional order. The poem evokes *two* gardens: the present garden whose space is fully circumscribed by the dictates of a recently imposed moral law, and a remembered or imagined garden whose joyous, unrestricted spaces might offer an ideological antithesis to such control. Of course, when he turns away from the chapel, the speaker finds that his *desired* garden, the delightful playground of his youth, no longer exists; appropriated by the religious order, its life-affirming green space has been filled with gravesites and tombstones, grim symbols of death and decay. If the remembered, unfallen garden is a figure for the green world of nature as it existed prior to its appropriation or inscription by religious orthodoxy, then arguably its transformation into a graveyard figuratively portrays what happens to nature when it is incorporated into a dualistic system of thought.

Moreover, if the speaker seeks to experience "joys & desires" (12; E26) when he enters the "Garden of Love" at the poem's outset, the dualistic religion that prohibits the pursuit of such pleasures in the name of an ostensibly higher form of love may be understood to function as a potent mechanism of social repression. The song's accompanying illustration (see Figure 9.1) depicts the process of social conditioning whereby this repression of desire and negation of pleasure is brought about.

Doctrinal text in hand, a priestly representative of institutionalized religion leads two young children in an apparently pious act of prayer; but the tombstone and open grave toward which the three kneeling figures bend in a seeming attitude of obeisance suggest that this

Figure 9.1 Plate 44, "The Garden of Love"

Songs of Innocence and of Experience, Copy Z
Lessing J. Rosenwald Collection, Library of Congress.
© 2009 the William Blake Archive. Used with permission.

pious act, far from being life-affirming, might be seen as a tribute to decay and death.

Erecting "tomb-stones where flowers should be" (10), an ascetic religious orthodoxy replaces the child's pleasing world of carefree "play" (4) with a chastened world of sorrow and subjugation, thereby "binding with briars" the "joys & desires" of embodied existence (12). By defining the speaker's joys and desires as evil passions in need of restraint or obliteration, the church encourages a life-negating attitude of *contemptus mundi*; for according to the logic of religious dualism, one of the best ways to prove one's love for God is to renounce or turn one's back on the things of this world. Arguably, if there are two distinct gardens in the poem—a remembered prelapsarian space associated with the "green" world, free "play," and the unbridled pursuit of "joys & desires," and a present postlapsarian space associated with an unseen heaven, its stern moral laws, and a priestly cult of death— then there are also two kinds of love referred to in the poem and its title: one associated with a life-affirming and pleasurable sensuality, and another with an ascetic distrust or denial of embodied existence and its sensual enjoyments. One form of love affirms life in the material and temporal here-and-now; the other implicitly negates it by locating all true value—indeed life itself—outside the world in the realm of spirit, or what Blake elsewhere calls "an allegorical abode where existence hath never come" (*Europe* 5.7; E62). One cannot help but be reminded of Friedrich Nietzsche's aphoristic assertion that "Life…comes to an end where the 'kingdom of God' begins" (490)—an assertion with which Blake would surely have agreed, as suggested by his injunction: "Seek not thy heavenly father…beyond the skies" (*M* 20.31–2; E114).

The political implications of this Blakean imperative may be clarified by a brief discussion of the body's status in Western theological and philosophical traditions. As the son of a Moravian mother who believed that sensual experience was grounded in "the dignity and worth of men and women in their bodily existence" (Atwood),[5] Blake was well aware that mainstream forms of Christian belief tended to represent the physical body not as something to be celebrated, but as a corrupt earthly prison-house in which the transcendent soul is temporarily forced to reside during its earthly incarnation. This dualistic understanding of embodied existence is implicit, for example, in some modern-day interpretations of Blake's poem "The Sick Rose," where the beautiful flower's destruction by a parasitical worm is understood to represent "the spirit destroyed by the flesh" (see Wilkie 130). As I have noted elsewhere,[6] one of the most extreme examples of this concept of embodied existence is epitomized in the ancient Greek formula "*Soma–sema*, the body–a tomb"—which conceives of the living human form (and by extension the physical world in which it is manifest) not only as a prison but as a veritable sepulcher (Jonas 13), a seemingly paradoxical death-in-life. In the Christian biblical canon, a similar idea of material existence informs what David Riede refers to as "the Pauline sense of entrapment within the body" as figured by St. Paul's reference to the "body of this death" ("Blake's *Milton*" 266; Rom. 7.24) from which we need to escape if we are to arrive at our proper, heavenly home or *telos*. Admittedly, Blake himself is not immune to the use of such orthodox rhetoric, as demonstrated, for example, by his reference in *Milton* to a "false Body: an Incrustation over [the] Immortal/ Spirit" (40: 35–6; E142). Obviously, where the physical body itself is associated with death, imprisonment, and falsehood, the pleasurable pursuit of "joys & desires" is brought into question in the most fundamental way. Yet Blake by no means consistently supports such dualistic logic. At times he undertakes a thorough critique of Christian dualism, a critique that in some ways anticipates Michel Foucault's poststructuralist model of Christian "pastoral technology." According to Foucault, confessional modes of Christianity encourage their adherents to internalize the soul in the form of a conscience—understood as the soul's voice residing in our physical being—that functions constantly to police and regulate bodily acts. As the internalized representative of a dualistic and ascetic concept of the soul, the conscience admonishes believers to eschew the pleasures of the flesh (or at least to engage in sensual acts like sexual congress only in the sanctioned context of heterosexual marriage). Foucault thus inverts the classical formula, arguing not that the body is the soul's prison but that "the soul"—understood as an ideological principle of social surveillance—"is the prison of the body" (30). In "The Garden of Love," Blake's critique of priestly prohibitions against the pursuit of earthly "joys & desires" suggests a similar dynamic, according to which the conventional privileging of spirit over body functions to control the body's pleasure-seeking impulses by demonizing sensual expression and the physical world in which such expression occurs.

Blake's critique of dualism and its social and environmental consequences in "The Garden of Love" can be further illuminated by the examination of another poem from the *Songs*, "Ah! Sun-Flower," which succinctly explores the *contemptus mundi* trope and its relationship to an ascetic practice that denies the moral value of earthly pleasures.

Ah Sun-flower! weary of time.
Who countest the steps of the Sun:
Seeking after that sweet golden clime
Where the travellers journey is done. (1–4; E25)

In these lines, the sunflower's "wear[iness] of time" indicates a conventional longing to be freed from the world of mundane temporality
(the sort of longing associated with the pious attitude of *contemptus mundi*). Such world-weariness is predicated upon a binary logic
privileging the spiritualized abstraction of timeless eternity over a
debased conception of earthly time. Admittedly, the stanza's poetical
figures raise some questions of detail. As it "countest the steps of the
Sun," is the flower mathematically demonstrating its enslavement to
the temporal order of Newtonian physical law, or is its act of enumer-
ation part of an aspiration to escape that temporal order—as it would
be, for example, if "Sun" were understood to provide a punning reference to "Son of God," whose "steps," when dutifully traced, would
lead the world-weary traveler from this earthly vale of tears to the
"sweet golden clime" of Heaven? In either case, of course, the logic
is the same: while the temporal world is degenerate and thus worth
escaping, eternity—that which transcends time—is good and thus
worth "Seeking."

Perhaps the most interesting aspect of "Ah! Sun-Flower" is the
way its second quatrain yokes the sunflower's meditation on time and
eternity to the realm of human sexual desire:

Where the Youth pined away with desire,
And the pale Virgin shrouded in snow:
Arise from their graves and aspire,
Where my Sun-flower wishes to go. (5–8)

The pining "Youth" and the "pale Virgin" in her deathly shroud
depict the unfortunate consequences of an ascetic doctrine that, to
borrow an apt phrase from "The Garden of Love," "bind[s] with
briars" the "joys & desires" associated with the pursuit of sensual
or sexual pleasure. As they "Arise from their graves," however, it is
not entirely clear whether the resurrected Youth and the pale Virgin
are reaping a spiritual reward for having ascetically renounced the
pursuit of pleasure during their lifetimes, or whether their resurrection marks an earthly return of repressed sexual energy. But given
the unhealthiness associated with the Virgin's pallor and the Youth's
pining away, it seems most logical to read the passage as a poetical

critique of institutionalized sexual repression and a condemnation of the erroneous antimaterialist philosophy that informs such a doctrine. Moreover, the association of the ascetic and sexually repressed "Youth" and "pale Virgin"—both of whom in Blake's view are "creation[s] of the Christian world" (Matthews 95)—with the sunflower is significant, because, following naturalists like Linnaeus and Erasmus Darwin, eighteenth-century society commonly associated flowers with sexual fecundity (see Bewell *passim*). The implication here seems to be that, upon their resurrection from the "grave" of ascetic doctrine, the youth and the virgin will shed their socially conditioned repression and strive uninhibitedly to embrace the pleasures of a life-affirming sexuality.

The return of the sexually repressed "youth" and "pale virgin" in "Ah! Sun-Flower" recalls "The Garden of Love," in which Blake also explores the repression of sensual pleasure in subtle but significant ways. This aspect of the poem may be brought into focus by first considering Blake's engagement with similar concerns articulated by one of his most influential literary precursors, John Milton. In a recent essay, Eugenie R. Freed draws attention to important parallels informing Blake's and Milton's indictments of the Church's role in the negation of the human physical form. Quoting a "strongly anticlerical" passage from Milton's *The Reason of Church Government* (1642), Freed notes that "Milton accused the 'Prelat Bishops' of his time of '[proclaiming] the best of creatures, mankind...unpurified and contagious...[making] profane that nature which God not only cleans'd, but Christ also hath assumed'" (58).[7] As an exuberant celebrant of the "human form divine" ("The Divine Image" 11; E13), Blake would certainly have sympathized with Milton's anticlerical outburst. But what incensed Blake even more was his own conviction that members of the clerical class did not actually practice the pious austerity they preached, that their sexual asceticism was in fact a form of "hypocrite modesty" (*VDA* 6.16; E49) of the sort evinced by Theotormon in *Visions of the Daughters of Albion*.[8] One wonders, then, what Blake would have made of another key passage from *The Reason of Church Government*, wherein Milton, engaging in his own critique of institutional religious hypocrisy, exclaims: "consider well from what a masse of slime and mud, the sloathful, the covetous and ambitious hopes of Church-promotions and fat Bishopricks, [Prelaty] is bred up and nuzzl'd in" (quoted in Freed 58). Would Blake, who occasionally reveals an irreverently carnivalesque sense of humor, have laughed at Milton's reference to "fat Bisho*pricks*," seeing there a punning reference to the "nuzzl'd," swollen phalluses or "pricks" thrusting forth behind the guise of a hypocritical sexual modesty?[9]

Such a reading is reinforced by the images in the illuminated plate to "The Garden of Love" (Figure 9.1), in which the tombstone vaguely resembles an erect phallus in its outline and forward-thrusting tilt, and in which the young penitents appear to be praying to the tombstone while the priest seemingly strokes it with his outstretched hand. In this reading of the plate, religion's enforced repression of sensual pleasure—the paradoxically obsessive *desire* to *rid oneself of desire*—unwittingly makes an idol of that which is denied. To quote Francis Bacon's essay entitled "Of Nature in Men," "Nature is often hidden, sometimes overcome, [but] seldom extinguished. Force maketh nature more violent in the return" (177). Alluding to efforts to control the body's various appetites and pleasure-seeking impulses, Bacon thus warns: "let not a man trust his victory over his nature too far, for nature will lay buried a great time, and yet revive upon the occasion or temptation" (177–8). But whereas Bacon, despite this sober warning, ultimately advocates moderation of physical passions and pleasures, Blake would have readers choose the "road of excess" rather than "nurse unacted desires" (*MHH 7*; E35, 10; E38).

When Blake opens a conversation between the prophetic Bard and the Earth itself in the first two poems of *Songs of Experience*, he addresses the theme of nature's banishment or repression and the promise of its potential return in significant ways. After invoking the "Holy Word" and the "ancient trees" of the lost Garden of Eden in the opening stanza of the "Introduction," the Bard exclaims:

> O Earth O Earth return!
> Arise from out the dewy grass;
> Night is worn,
> And the morn
> Rises from the slumberous mass. (11–15: E18)

It is certainly tempting here to read, with Northrop Frye, the speaker's reference to "the slumberous mass" as a subtle indictment of a material world understood as inert, asleep, or "half dead" (*Fearful Symmetry* 39). Elsewhere, Frye observes of this passage: "The ordinary world that we see is a mindless chaos held together by automatic order: an impressive ruin, but a 'slumberous mass,' and not the world man wants to live in" ("Blake's Introduction" 61). From the standpoint of an environmental ethic, Frye's comment raises an important question: given the often equivocal and polysemous character of

Blakean words and figures, might Blake's reference to "the slumber-ous mass" signify more than merely "sleeping matter"? Might it also signify the orthodox church service or uninspired "mass" that itself deadens creation not only by condemning pleasurable sensual expe-rience, but more fundamentally by locating life outside the material world in a hyper-hygienic spiritual realm prophylactically separated from the world of materiality? Perhaps when the Bard calls for the Earth's "return," he is speaking of the need for humans to cleanse the doors of perception so that they will be equipped to recognize the ways in which faulty percepts, conditioned by a questionable antima-terial dogma, have themselves obscured a veritable world of vision, a world in which we might otherwise be free to embrace and celebrate our own corporeality, a world in which the "improvement of sensual enjoyment" might be realized without guilt or shame.

Responding to the Bard's call in "Earth's Answer," a sentient, per-sonified Earth seems very much to recognize the role that ideology has played in the process of her own abjection. Directly addressing the Bard, who acts as humanity's prophetic representative, Earth issues a forceful imperative:

> Break this heavy chain,
> That does freeze my bones around
> Selfish! Vain!
> Eternal bane!
> That free Love with bondage bound. (21–5; E19)

Here, the "heavy chain" is a version of Blake's famous "mind-forg'd manacles" ("London" 8; E27), a figure for the internalization of social prohibitions or "thou shalt not[s]" that function to regulate our actions at the subjective level, without the external application of coercive force. As Lussier has argued, the Earth's response to the Bard's address "makes clear that her 'Prison'd' state is the result of the 'selfish father of men' attaching chains of jealousy to control 'free Love with bondage bound'" (402–3). Or, more precisely, the Earth's imprisonment stems from human *concepts* of such a paternal God, concepts that the black-gowned priests who colonize the "Garden of Love" disseminate in order to prohibit members of their flock from indulging in free "play" and the pleasurable pursuit of "joys & desires."

Blake makes this life- and pleasure-negating concept of deity par-ticularly apparent in *Visions of the Daughters of Albion*, where his protagonist, Oothoon, forcefully indicts the Urizenic "Father of

Jealousy" for having taught her beloved Theotormon an "accursed" ascetic doctrine (7.12–13; E50) that disables him from freely embracing earthly, physical joys. Shunning "the horrible darkness" resulting from Theotormon's dualistic degradation of the material world, Oothoon affirms a bright vision of life whose motto is not a dismal "Thou shalt not" but an exuberant "Take thy bliss O Man!/ And sweet shall be thy taste & sweet thy infant joys renew!" (6.2–3; E49). This openly permissive (rather than prohibitive) approach to pleasurable indulgence would, Oothoon asserts, signify the restoration of paradise, a garden of love in which innocence is not subject to the biophobic and psychologically repressive constraints of ascetic moral law:

> Infancy, fearless, lustful, happy! nestling for delight
> In laps of pleasure; Innocence! honest, open, seeking
> The vigorous joys of morning light, open to virgin bliss.
>   (6.4–6; E49)

The vocabulary of pleasure here is delightfully excessive. Aside from the direct reference to "pleasure" itself, Blake loads this brief encomium to innocence with a plenitude of related terms, including "lustful[ness]," "delight," "joys," and "bliss"—all of which are directly associated with a "vigorous" or life-affirming openness to the world. Needless to say, such a vision contrasts sharply with that of Theotormon's grimly austere mindset, which brands "virgin joy" with "the name of whore" and turns embodied existence into "a sickly charnel house" (6.11–12, E49; 2.36, E47).

QUALIFICATIONS AND CONCLUSIONS

In *The Marriage of Heaven and Hell*, Blake offers a succinct alternative to the sexually repressive, antimaterialist vision I have been outlining in this chapter, prophesying that "an improvement of sensual enjoyment" will make "the whole creation"—including all environments and physical bodies—"appear infinite" and "holy." This revelatory outcome is predicated upon a prior work of deconstructive insight and activism: before we can envision creation's infinitude and holiness, "the notion that man has a body distinct from his soul, is to be expunged" (14; E39). Affirming the body's spiritual aspect by dismantling the oppositional limit conventionally severing body from soul, Blake renders physical impulses and desires holy; thus, when he proclaims that "The road of excess leads to the palace of wisdom" (7.3; E35), he affirms the unregulated pursuit of bodily enjoyments.

Or does he? With regard to the pursuit of pleasure, how far does Blake's philosophy of excess go? Does the road of excess *always* lead to wisdom's palace, or are there ethical limits that the pleasure-seeking traveler must heed when following this route? Blake provides implicit answers to such questions in both *The Marriage of Heaven and Hell* and *Visions of the Daughters of Albion*, each of which was engraved, like the *Songs of Experience*, in the early 1790s. When he declares in *The Marriage* that "You never know what is enough unless you know what is more than enough" (9.46; E37), Blake implies, among other things, that the pursuit of excessive pleasures ("what is more than enough") provides, as an ultimate consequence, an understanding of pleasure's limits ("what is enough"). Simply stated, these implicit limits pertain to the ethical imperative to treat other desiring subjects with respect and, thus, to do them no harm. Hence Blake's rhetorical question: "is he honest who resists his genius or conscience, only for the sake of present ease or gratification?" (13; E39). Qualifying this question by referring explicitly to "*present* . . . gratification," Blake suggests that there are other kinds of gratification that should take precedence, for example, over such immediate pleasures as "the joys of riches and ease" (*VDA* 4.21; E48). Indeed, when in *Visions* he asks such questions as "How can one joy absorb another?" (5.5; E48), or "Can that be Love, that drinks another as a sponge drinks water?" (7.17; E50), he implies that joys that are merely products of self-centered desires are not true joys at all. And when, in *The Marriage*, he states that "The most sublime act is to put another before you" (7.17; E36), he makes it clear that we need to take other people into account when considering our own gratification. Indeed, by not specifying who or what he is referring to here in his reference to "another," he implies the need to act in accordance with an expansive ethic that respects otherness in all its manifestations, whether human or otherwise. For a poet who believed that "ev'ry Bird that cuts the airy way,/ Is an immense world of delight" (*MHH* 7; E35), the experience of pleasure, it seems, is not merely a human prerogative.[10]

I do not mean to suggest that Frye's antinatural Blake should ultimately be replaced by the notion of Blake as a poet who loved the natural world unconditionally. Indeed, perhaps the greatest difficulty that arises for an ecological-materialist analysis of Blake's philosophy of sensual pleasure involves his frequent use of figures derived *from nature* to criticize *institutionalized* modes of social control that devalue the body and its material contexts. If Blake wrote "Ah!

Sun-flower" to denounce the antimaterialist contempt implicit in an attitude pretending to be "weary of time," for example, he nevertheless attributes such weariness to a representative of the realm of Flora. And if in "The Garden of Love" he is criticizing a moral law based on negative commandments or "Thou shalt not[s]," he nevertheless chooses the "natural" figure of the briar (rather than, say, the industrial figure of "mind-forg'd manacles") to represent that which binds the speaker's "joys & desires" (where, reminiscent of Christ's crown of thorns, the briar also suggests that humans themselves are sacrificed to moral orthodoxy).[11] And if, for instance, in "The Voice of the Ancient Bard" Blake is referring to members of a corrupt Priesthood when he indicts those who "wish to lead others when *they* should be led," he represents their "Folly" as an "endless maze" not of chartered streets but of "Tangled roots" (E31–2; italics added). In *The Marriage of Heaven and Hell*, furthermore, Blake sometimes couches his criticism of religious dualism and ascetic doctrine in a metaphorical language that, far from celebrating nature, suggests nature's culpability: "As the catterpiller chooses the fairest leaves to lay her eggs on, so the priest lays his curse on the fairest joys" (9; E37). It is as if the ascetic priest, like the egg-laying caterpillar, is fulfilling a natural and indeed life-sustaining impulse when he "lays his curse" on the joys of bodily pleasure. Clearly, Blake's celebration of the pursuit of joys and desires—despite its basis in a critique of antimaterialist dualism–does not necessarily amount to a celebration of material nature *per se*. As his reference to the destructive caterpillar suggests, there are biological processes like parasitism and violent predation that ultimately prevent Blake from invoking nature as an unproblematic model for human ethics, an ethics that "puts another before you." Surely, such suspicion is ultimately warranted and need not provide cause for eco-critical alarm, for, as Timothy Morton has noted, that which we refer to as nature is patently *not* always "full of love and light" (198).

Nevertheless, readers would do well to bear in mind that, unlike such self-proclaimed contemporary nature worshippers as Wordsworth and Coleridge, Blake did not generally exclude from his purview of nature the bugs, slugs, gnats, earwigs, maggots, fleas, lice, tapeworms, and other conventionally objectionable creatures that inhabit our ecosystems and often incite our repulsion.[12] Idealized views of nature are themselves products of a dualistic mode of thought that effaces and thus negates *realities* deemed less than pleasant. By refusing unequivocally to idealize the realm of material and biological nature, Blake arguably avoids simply inverting, and thus subtly perpetuating, the violent hierarchical structures and modes of thought that in his era so commonly privileged soul over body, mind over matter, spiritualized Heaven over material Earth—dualisms that constantly threaten to foreclose the "improvement of sensual enjoyment" (*MHH* 14; E39) so necessary to human fulfillment and enlightenment as Blake understood it.

Notes

1. All references to Blake's work are to David V. Erdman's edition of *The Complete Poetry and Prose of William Blake*, as cited in the bibliography. In my parenthetical citations I refer first to plate and line numbers (where appropriate), and second to the page number where the citation occurs (for example, E134, where "E" refers to Erdman's edition). In my citations I also make use of the following abbreviations, where necessary, to signify individual works: *FZ* for *The Four Zoas*; *M* for *Milton*; *MHH* for *The Marriage of Heaven and Hell*; and *VDA* for *Visions of the Daughters of Albion*. Research for this essay was undertaken, in part, thanks to funding received from the Canada Research Chairs Program and the Social Sciences and Humanities Research Council of Canada. I am also grateful to the University of Northern British Columbia for ongoing support. I would like to thank Charity Matthews for providing helpful research assistance.

2. For an analysis of the nuances informing Blake's discourse on nature, see Hutchings, *Imagining Nature*, especially 37–75.

3. See, for example, Hutchings, *Imagining Nature* (172–88); and Hutchings, *Romantic Ecologies and Colonial Cultures* (70–91).

4. Citing Stanley Gardner's 1986 monograph entitled *Blake's Innocence and Experience Retraced* in her discussion of "The Garden of Love" and "I saw a chapel all of gold," Eugenie R. Freed notes that in late-eighteenth-century Britain "the doors of many chapels were literally 'shut' to those who could not afford to pay rent for a pew" (56). Freed makes this comment in the context of posing a challenge to readers who would see the chapel in Blake's poems as merely metaphorical, noting that such a reading risks eliding contemporary concerns regarding the socio-material circumstances Blake addresses in his work.

5. For a discussion of Blake's recently discovered Moravian connections, see Davies and Schuchard.

6. See Hutchings, *Imagining Nature* (62–3).

7. Freed quotes Milton's *The Reason of Church Government* from *Complete Prose Works of John Milton*. Vol. 1. 1624–1642. New Haven: Yale UP, 1953, 845. Freed quotes her ensuing reference to "fat Bishopricks," which I cite subsequently in my own discussion, from page 858 of *The Reason of Church Government*.

8. For a discussion of Theotormon's asceticism and its social and environmental implications, see Hutchings, *Romantic Ecologies and Colonial Cultures* (76–9). See also Hutchings, "Pastoral, Ideology, and Nature" (9–13).

9. Among its definitions of "prick," the *OED* lists as a "coarse slang" usage "[t]he penis." The first example the *OED* cites of such usage occurs in 1555, and there are numerous nineteenth-century examples provided.

10. Ashton Nichols quotes this passage in the opening paragraph to his online essay "The Loves of Plants and Animals: Romantic Science and the Pleasures of Nature," suggesting that Blake, like other Romantic poets and scientists, believed that "all living things (and perhaps even 'nonliving' things) were connected by a force that could be described, at least partly, in terms of the natural ability to please or to be pleased" (paragraph 1).

11. I am grateful to Michelle Faubert for suggesting this reading in her comments to an early draft of this chapter.

12. See, for example, *Milton* (27.11–24; E124).

WORKS CITED

Ackroyd, Peter. *Blake*. London: Sinclair-Stevenson, 1995. Print.

Ankarsjö, Magnus. *William Blake and Gender*. Jefferson, NC, and London: McFarland, 2006. Print.

Atwood, Craig D. "The Moravian Roots of Blake's Sex-Positive Spirituality." *Blake at 250 Conference*. University of York. York, UK. 31 July 2007. Conference Paper.

Bacon, Sir Francis. "Of Nature in Men." *The Essays*. 1597/1625. Ed. John Pitcher. London: Penguin, 1985. 177–8. Print.

Bewell, Alan. "'Jacobin Plants': Botany as Social Theory in the 1790s." *The Wordsworth Circle* 20.3 (1989): 132–9. Print.

Bhabha, Homi K. *The Location of Culture*. London and New York: Routledge, 1994. Print.

Blake, William. *The Complete Poetry and Prose of William Blake*. Newly Revised Edition. Ed. David V. Erdman. New York and London: Doubleday, 1988. Print.

Clark, David L. Rev. of *Creating States: Studies in the Performative Language of John Milton and William Blake*, by Angela Esterhammer. *Blake: An Illustrated Quarterly* 31.1 (1997): 29–34. Print.

Connolly, Tristanne J. *William Blake and the Body*. New York: Palgrave Macmillan, 2002. Print.

Davies, Keri, and Marsha Keith Schuchard. "Recovering the Lost Moravian History of William Blake's Family." *Blake: An Illustrated Quarterly* 38.1 (2004): 36–42. Print.

Foucault, Michel. *Discipline and Punish: The Birth of the Prison*. 2nd ed. Trans. Alan Sheridan. New York: Vintage, 1995. Print.

Freed, Eugenie R. "Blake's Golden Chapel: The Serpent Within and Those Who Stood Without." *Women Reading William Blake.* Ed. Helen P. Bruder. New York: Palgrave Macmillan, 2007. 53–61. Print.

Frye, Northrop. "Blake's Introduction to Experience." *Twentieth-Century Interpretations of 'Songs of Innocence and of Experience': A Collection of Critical Essays.* Ed. Morton D. Paley. Englewood Cliffs, NJ: Prentice-Hall, 1969. 58–67. Print.

———. *Fearful Symmetry: A Study of William Blake.* 1947. Reprint. Princeton, NJ: Princeton UP, 1970. Print.

Hutchings, Kevin. *Imagining Nature: Blake's Environmental Poetics.* Montreal and Kingston: McGill-Queen's UP, 2002. Print.

———. "Pastoral, Ideology, and Nature in William Blake's *Visions of the Daughters of Albion.*" *Interdisciplinary Studies in Literature and Environment* 9.1 (2002): 1–24. Print.

———. *Romantic Ecologies and Colonial Cultures in the British Atlantic World, 1770–1850.* Montreal and Kingston: McGill-Queen's UP, 2009. Print.

Jonas, Hans. *The Phenomenon of Life.* 1966. Rpt. New York: Dell, 1968. Print.

Lussier, Mark. "Blake's Deep Ecology." *Studies in Romanticism* 35.3 (1996): 393–408. Print.

Matthews, Susan. "Blake, Hayley and the History of Sexuality." *Blake, Nation and Empire.* Ed. Steve Clark and David Worrall. New York: Palgrave Macmillan, 2006. 83–101. Print.

Morton, Timothy. *Ecology without Nature: Rethinking Environmental Aesthetics.* Cambridge, MA, and London: Harvard UP, 2007. Print.

Nichols, Ashton. "The Loves of Plants and Animals: Romantic Science and the Pleasures of Nature." *Romanticism & Ecology.* Ed. and intro. James McCusick. 2001. 27 pars. *Romantic Circles Praxis Series.* College Park: U of Maryland P, 2001. Web. Jan. 27, 2009.

Nietzsche, Friedrich. *The Portable Nietzsche.* Trans. Walter Kaufmann. Reprint. New York: Penguin, 1982. Print.

Ostriker, Alicia. "Re-Deeming Scripture: My William Blake Revisited." *Women Reading William Blake.* Ed. Helen P. Bruder. New York: Palgrave Macmillan, 2007. 189–99. Print.

"Prick." Def. 12b. *The Oxford English Dictionary Online.* 2nd ed. 2009. Web. Jan. 28, 2009.

Riede, David. "Blake's *Milton*: On Membership in the Church Paul." *Re-membering Milton: Essays on the Texts and Traditions.* Ed. Mary Nyquist and Margaret W. Ferguson. New York and London: Methuen, 1987. 257–77. Print.

———. *Swinburne: A Study of Romantic Mythmaking.* Charlottesville: UP of Virginia, 1978. Print.

Rousseau, Jean-Jacques. "A Discourse on a Subject Proposed by the Academy of Dijon: What Is the Origin of the Inequality among Men, and Is It

Authorised by Natural Law." 1755. *Great Books of the Western World: Montesquieu, Rousseau.* Ed. Robert Maynard Hutchins. Trans. G. D. H. Cole. Chicago and London: William Benton, 1952. 323–66. Print.

Schorer, Mark. *William Blake: The Politics of Vision.* 1946. Reprint. New York: Vintage, 1959. Print.

Wilkie, Brian. "Blake's *Innocence and Experience*: An Approach." *Blake Studies* 6.2 (1975): 119–37. Print.

Wilkinson, J. J. Garth. Preface. *Songs of Innocence and of Experience,* by William Blake. London: J. J. Garth Wilkinson, 1839. Print.

Wordsworth, William. "Lines Composed a Few Miles above Tintern Abbey." *William Wordsworth.* Reprint. Ed. Stephen Gill. Oxford: Oxford UP, 1990. 131–5. Print.

Worrall, David. "Thel in Africa: William Blake and the Post-Colonial, Post-Swedenborgian Female Subject." *Blake, Nation and Empire.* Ed. Steve Clark and David Worrall. New York: Palgrave Macmillan, 2006. 40–62. Print.

CONTRIBUTORS

Jeffrey Cass is dean of the College of Arts and Sciences at the University of Louisiana at Monroe. He co-edited *Romantic Border Crossings* (Ashgate Press, 2008) and *Interrogating Orientalism* (Ohio State University Press, 2006). He has also recently published essays on Felicia Hemans, Maria Edgeworth, and Elizabeth Hamilton.

Joel Faflak is associate professor in the Department of English and the Centre for the Study of Theory and Criticism at the University of Western Ontario. He is the author of *Romantic Psychoanalysis: The Mystery of the Burden* (2008) and has edited and co-edited several collections of essays: *Cultural Subjects: A Popular Culture Reader* (2005), *Nervous Reactions: Victorian Recollections of Romanticism* (2004), *Sanity, Madness, Transformation: The Psyche of Romanticism* (2005), and *Romantic Psyche and Psychoanalysis* (2008). He is also editor of two issues: *European Romantic Review* (2003, 2006) and a special issue of *English Studies in Canada* on "Guilt" (2007). In 2001 he won the John Charles Polanyi Prize for Literature.

Michelle Faubert is associate professor of English at the University of Manitoba and visiting fellow at Northumbria University. She is the author of *Rhyming Reason: The Poetry of Romantic-Era Psychologists* (Pickering & Chatto, 2009) and, with Allan Ingram, co-author of *Cultural Constructions of Madness in Eighteenth-Century Writing: Representing the Insane* (Palgrave, 2005). She is currently working on an edition of Mary Wollstonecraft's *Mary* and *The Wrongs of Woman* for Broadview Press (2011) and, with Allan Ingram, co-editing a volume of medical texts on depression for the four-volume set, *Depression and Melancholy, 1660–1800* (Pickering & Chatto, 2012). Her current monograph project is on Romantic suicide.

Denise Gigante is professor of English at Stanford University. She is the author of *Taste: A Literary History* (Yale University Press, 2005) and *Life: Organic Form and Romanticism* (Yale University

Press, 2009). She has edited *Gusto: Essential Writings in Nineteenth-Century Gastronomy* (Routledge, 2005), a collection of essays about the pleasures of food (literal taste) from England and France.

Kevin Hutchings is associate professor of English and Canada research chair in literature, culture, and environmental studies at the University of Northern British Columbia. He is the author of *Romantic Ecologies and Colonial Cultures in the British Atlantic World 1770–1850* (McGill-Queen's University Press, 2009) and *Imagining Nature: Blake's Environmental Poetics* (McGill-Queen's University Press, 2002). He is also co-editor, with Tim Fulford, of *Native Americans and Anglo-American Culture 1750–1850: The Indian Atlantic* (Cambridge University Press, 2009).

Clark Lawlor is reader in English literature at Northumbria University, and has published many works on Romantic literature—particularly literature and medicine—including *Consumption and Literature: The Making of the Romantic Disease* (2006), which was short-listed for the ESSE book prize 2006–8. At present he is writing *Depression: The Biography* (Oxford University Press, forthcoming 2011).

Thomas H. Schmid is associate professor of English at the University of Texas at El Paso. He is the author of *Humor and Transgression in Peacock, Shelley, and Byron: A Cold Carnival* (1992), which won the Rocky Mountain Modern Language Association Book Award, and numerous scholarly papers and articles. He is currently writing a book on Romanticism and the neuroscience of addiction.

Richard C. Sha is professor of literature at American University in Washington, D.C. He is the author of *Perverse Romanticism: Aesthetics and Sexuality in Britain, 1750–1832* (Johns Hopkins University Press, 2009) and *The Visual and Verbal Sketch in British Romanticism, 1750–1832* (University of Pennsylvania Press, 1998). His current book project examines how scientists and poets understood the imagination in the British Romantic period. Essays from this project will appear in *Configurations*, the *Blackwell's Handbook to Romanticism*, and *ERR*. The writing of this essay made him nostalgic for the felicific calculus.

Betsy Winakur Tontiplaphol is assistant professor of English at Trinity University in San Antonio, Texas, where she teaches courses in nineteenth-century British literature. In addition to her work on

Keats, she has written and spoken about Jane Austen, Elizabeth Barrett Browning, Alfred Tennyson, and Gerard Manley Hopkins. Her book *Poetics of Luxury in the Nineteenth Century* is forthcoming from Ashgate.

Samantha Webb is associate professor of English at the University of Montevallo. She has published articles on Samuel Taylor Coleridge and Hannah More, and is currently working on a book-length project on the aesthetics of scarcity in Romantic literature.

INDEX